WHAT NOW?

LIVING IN A WORLD WITHOUT JOBS

Dedication

I have done a lot of writing over the years. But I have done even more arguing. Just testing my ideas, I'd claim. But the person on the other side of all my arguments has been my wife, Moonyeen – sometimes patient, sometimes not. But always supportive of me, no matter how hare-brained the idea. As always, this is for her, with love.

About

The ideas in this book are not all mine. There have been many thinkers who articulate these ideas before (and better) than me. But I used AI (of course) to do the heavy lifting to find the ideas. AI did the research (but I guided, chose the topics and prompted for the outcome) and it also did most of the typing. Manus AI and Claude AI are my co-authors here; and while some may think that is cheating, I think that is exactly how AI can and should be used to make us more productive.

We ended up with a book that is comprehensive, compendium style and consequently a bit 'dense'; mainly because I wanted to capture as many relevant ideas, strategies, outcomes, solutions, problems as I could and bring it all together in one place. Many topics captured in a single sentence, would be worthy of a book.

The purpose of the book is to be a conversation starter; one that captures most of the salient ideas and discussion points – whether I agree with them or not - and I sincerely hope you can gran hold of one or more of these ideas and go ahead to elaborate, support or disprove them. Lord knows, to solve the challenges we face will need all the of the best and brightest to engage with these ideas quickly and thoroughly.

TABLE OF CONTENTS

CHAPTER 1: THE POST-LABOUR HORIZON: DEFINING A NEW ECONOMIC EPOCH

The Automated Factory Floor

In 2023, Michael Chen, a 47-year-old manufacturing supervisor with 22 years of experience at an automotive parts plant in Michigan, arrived at work to find two delivery trucks in the loading bay. Inside were twelve autonomous mobile robots and a new AI-powered quality control system—equipment that would ultimately replace 40% of the human workforce on his production line.

"They didn't even tell us they were coming," Michael recalled. "One Monday they just showed up, and by Friday, eighteen people—some who'd been here longer than me—were handed severance packages."

What made this transition particularly jarring wasn't just the speed—the entire implementation took less than three weeks—but the undeniable improvement in results. The new automated line reduced defect rates by 64% while increasing throughput by 28%. The economics were irrefutable: higher quality, greater output, lower costs.

For the workers who remained, the nature of their jobs transformed almost overnight. Instead of performing manual tasks, they now monitored dashboards, managed exceptions, and supervised the robots. Some adapted quickly to these new roles, while others struggled with the abrupt shift from hands-on work to oversight functions.

"I used to know exactly what made me valuable," said Elena Diaz, a line worker with fifteen years at the plant. "I could assemble components faster and with fewer errors than anyone. Now I watch screens and respond when something goes wrong. The robots do what I used to take pride in."

This scene is playing out across industries worldwide as artificial intelligence and automation technologies rapidly transform the nature of work. The economic logic driving these changes is powerful and seemingly unstoppable: when machines can perform tasks better, faster, and cheaper than humans, market pressures make their adoption inevitable.

Yet this transition raises profound questions about the future of human labour, economic organization, and even the meaning of work itself. If machines can increasingly outperform humans at both physical and cognitive tasks, what becomes of our current economic system built around human labour as the primary means of income distribution? How do we navigate a world where being a good worker is no longer enough to ensure economic security? What happens to human dignity and purpose when much of what we currently define as "productive work" can be done more efficiently without us?

These questions are not merely academic. They represent the lived reality of millions of workers like Michael and Elena who find themselves on the front lines of a profound economic transformation—one that promises unprecedented abundance but also threatens widespread displacement if we fail to adapt our economic and social systems accordingly.

AI and Robotics Adoption Timeline Across Key Sectors

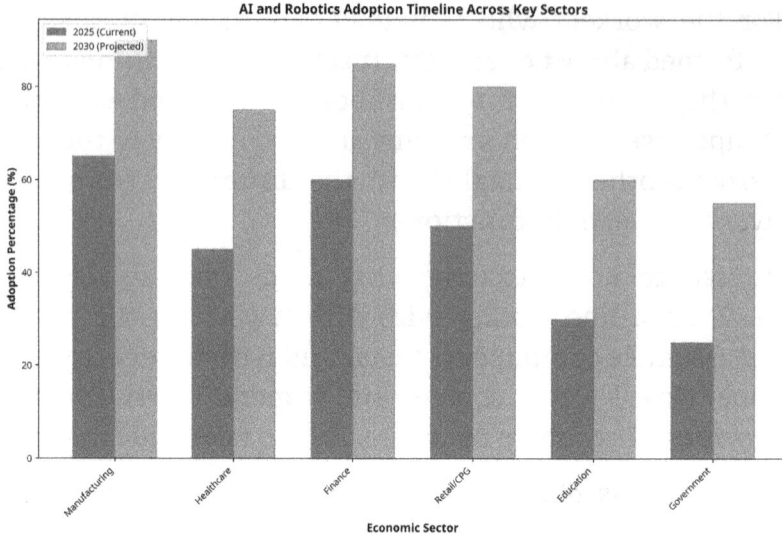

In the quiet laboratories of artificial intelligence research and the bustling server farms that power our digital world, a transformation is unfolding that will fundamentally redefine our economic structures. This transformation is not merely an acceleration of existing trends, but rather a qualitative leap into a new economic paradigm—one that we might term the "post-labour economy." This chapter examines the defining characteristics of this emerging economic epoch and presents evidence for its imminent arrival, while highlighting its fundamental differences from past technological disruptions.

Defining the Post-Labour Economy

INSIGHT: 2. "By 2035, the concept of 'employment' as we understand it today will become as outdated as feudalism. The majority of income will not come from traditional jobs but from a complex mix of temporary project work, passive income streams, and public distribution mechanisms."

The post-labour economy represents a profound shift in the fundamental relationship between human labour and economic output. At its core, it describes an economic system where the marginal cost of intelligent automated labour trends towards zero, and human labour is no longer the primary input for value creation or the main mechanism for income distribution.

Traditional economic systems, from agrarian to industrial to information-based, have all shared one common feature: human labour as an essential and irreplaceable input. Whether tilling fields, operating machinery, or writing computer code, human effort has been the fundamental engine of economic production. Even as technology advanced, it primarily served to augment human capabilities rather than replace the human element entirely. The post-labour economy represents the first economic paradigm in which this foundational assumption no longer holds.

In this emerging system, artificial intelligence and advanced robotics can increasingly perform not just routine physical tasks but complex cognitive functions across virtually all domains of economic activity. The critical distinction is that these systems do not merely assist human workers —they can operate autonomously, learn independently, and potentially surpass human capabilities in an expanding range of activities. As AI researcher David Shapiro notes, "The foundational premise of a post-labour economy is liberating human potential from the requirement of employment. Rather than treating human jobs and livelihoods as an end unto themselves, the priority becomes freeing people from such constraints through technology."

This shift is enabled by several technological developments converging simultaneously:

- Advanced machine learning systems capable of pattern recognition, decision-making, and adaptation without explicit programming
- Robotics and automation that can manipulate the physical world with increasing dexterity and precision
- Vast data resources that provide the raw material for AI systems to learn from

- Exponentially increasing computational power that enables more complex AI models
- Networked systems that allow for coordination and knowledge sharing between automated processes

The combined effect of these technologies creates the conditions for what economists term "hyperabundance"—a state where the production of goods and services becomes so efficient and inexpensive that traditional scarcity-based economic models begin to break down. In such a system, the marginal cost of producing additional units approaches zero, creating unprecedented economic dynamics.

However, the post-labour economy is not merely about technological capability. It represents a fundamental restructuring of how value is created and distributed throughout society. When human labour is no longer the primary input for production, the traditional mechanisms for distributing economic benefits—primarily wages and salaries—become increasingly inadequate. This necessitates new frameworks for ensuring that the benefits of automated production are broadly shared.

Contrasting with Traditional Economic Models

To appreciate the revolutionary nature of the post-labour paradigm, we must contrast it with the traditional economic models that have dominated economic thinking for centuries. These established frameworks—Classical, Keynesian, and Neoclassical—all share fundamental assumptions about the role of human labour that the post-labour economy challenges.

Classical Economics and the Labour Theory of Value

Classical economics, associated with thinkers like Adam Smith, David Ricardo, and Karl Marx, placed human labour at the very centre of economic value. The labour theory of value posited that the value of a good or service was determined by the amount of labour required for its production. Smith's "invisible hand" and the division of labour were mechanisms to optimise human productive capacity, while Marx's analysis of capitalism focused on the relationship between labour and capital.

In a post-labour economy, this foundational principle collapses. When artificial intelligence and robotics can perform most productive tasks without human input, the connection between labour and value is severed. The question of value creation shifts from "how much human effort was required?" to "how effectively can automated systems meet human needs and desires?" This represents not just a modification of classical economics but its fundamental transformation.

INSIGHT: 3. "The greatest threat to human prosperity isn't that AI will take our jobs—it's that we'll cling to the outdated notion that jobs should be the primary mechanism for distributing economic prosperity."

Keynesian Economics and Aggregate Demand

Keynesian economics, developed by John Maynard Keynes during the Great Depression, emphasised the importance of aggregate demand in driving economic growth and employment. Central to Keynesian theory is the role of government intervention to stimulate demand during economic downturns, primarily through increased spending and lower taxes.

As Keynes himself wrote in 1933, there was a risk of "widespread technological unemployment due to our discovery of means of economising the use of labour outrunning the pace at which we can find new uses for labour." However, Keynesian models still assumed that human labour would remain essential to production, with technological unemployment representing a temporary misalignment rather than a permanent structural change.

In a post-labour economy, the Keynesian focus on

maintaining employment becomes increasingly problematic. When AI and automation can produce goods and services with minimal human input, policies designed to create jobs may become inefficient or counterproductive. The challenge shifts from stimulating demand to ensuring that the benefits of automated production are widely distributed even as traditional employment declines.

Neoclassical Economics and Marginal Productivity

Neoclassical economics, which dominates much of contemporary economic thinking, emphasises marginal productivity theory—the idea that factors of production (including labour) are paid according to their marginal contribution to output. In this framework, wages are determined by the additional output generated by an additional unit of labour.

The post-labour economy fundamentally disrupts this model. When AI systems can perform most tasks at a fraction of the cost of human labour and with equal or superior quality, the marginal productivity of human labour in many sectors approaches zero. This creates a situation where market-determined wages would be insufficient to support human livelihoods, even as overall economic output increases.

Moreover, neoclassical models typically assume that technological advancement creates new opportunities for human labour as it displaces old ones. While this has historically been true, the general-purpose nature of AI challenges this assumption. Unlike previous technologies that automated specific tasks, AI has the potential to automate a vast range of both physical and cognitive activities simultaneously, potentially outpacing the creation of new roles for humans.

The Post-Labour Alternative

In contrast to these traditional models, the post-labour economy requires new economic frameworks that acknowledge the diminishing role of human labour as a factor of production. These emerging models focus on:

- Decoupling income from employment through mechanisms like universal basic income, negative income tax, or other redistribution systems
- Redefining productivity to focus on overall welfare rather than labour input
- Developing new ownership models that allow broader participation in the benefits of automated production
- Creating economic metrics that better reflect human flourishing rather than just output or employment

This paradigm shift is not merely theoretical—it is already beginning to manifest in measurable economic trends, as we will explore in the following sections.

INSIGHT: 4. "The current wave of AI advancement represents the first time in human history that technology is not merely changing how we work, but fundamentally challenging whether human labour remains economically necessary at all."

Evidence of the Approaching Post-Labour Shift

The transition to a post-labour economy is not a distant possibility but an emerging reality, supported by a growing body of evidence. From job displacement projections to case studies of AI implementation across sectors, the data increasingly points to a fundamental restructuring of the relationship between human labour and economic output.

Job Displacement Projections

The most direct evidence for the approaching post-labour shift comes from credible projections of job displacement due to AI and automation. These studies, conducted by leading research institutions and financial firms, consistently point to unprecedented levels of potential job automation across sectors.

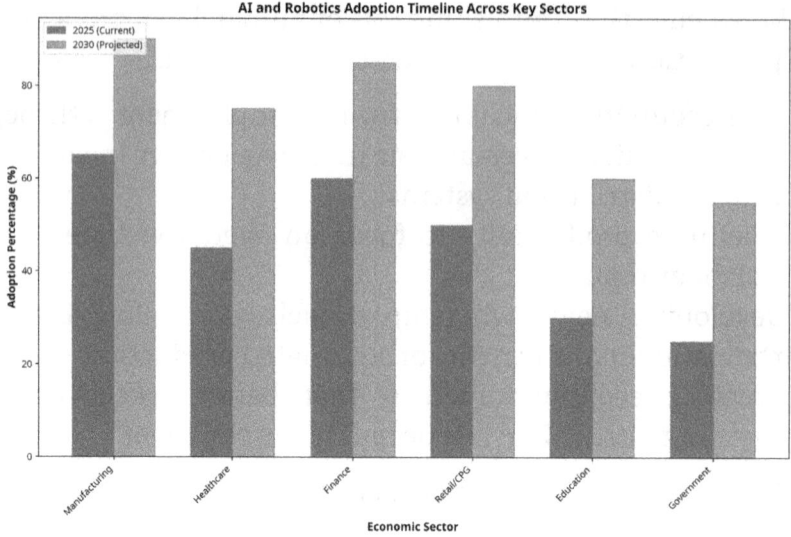

AI and Robotics Adoption Timeline Across Key Sectors

Major Studies on AI-Driven Job Displacement

The landmark 2013 study by Oxford University researchers Carl Benedikt Frey and Michael A. Osborne examined 702 detailed occupations in the United States and concluded that approximately 47% of total US employment was at high risk of automation. Their methodology involved a novel approach using a Gaussian process classifier to estimate the probability of computerisation for each occupation based on nine key variables related to perception and manipulation, creative intelligence, and social intelligence.

What made the Frey and Osborne study particularly significant was not just the scale of potential displacement but the finding that automation risk exhibited a strong negative correlation with both wages and educational attainment. This suggested that, unlike previous waves of technological change that primarily affected middle-skill jobs, AI-driven automation could disproportionately impact lower-skill, lower-wage occupations—precisely those with workers least equipped to transition to new roles.

More recent projections have reinforced and expanded upon

these findings. Goldman Sachs research from 2023 estimated that approximately 300 million jobs worldwide could be affected by AI, representing about 9.1% of global employment. Their 2025 update projected that up to 50% of jobs could be fully automated by 2045, driven by advances in generative AI and robotics.

The McKinsey Global Institute has focused on the economic impact of this transition, projecting that AI could increase global GDP by approximately 7% ($7 trillion) and potentially lift productivity growth by 1.5 percentage points over a 10-year period. This highlights a critical aspect of the post-labour economy: even as employment decreases, overall economic output may increase substantially.

Research from the Brookings Institution adds further nuance, suggesting that more than 30% of workers could see at least 50% of their occupation's tasks disrupted by generative AI. This partial automation represents an important transitional phase in the movement toward a post-labour economy, as it changes the nature of work before potentially eliminating it entirely.

These projections are not without critics. Some argue that they overestimate the technical feasibility of automation or underestimate the creation of new job categories. However, the consistent direction of these findings, combined with the accelerating pace of AI development, provides compelling evidence that we are approaching a qualitatively different relationship between human labour and economic production.

INSIGHT: 5. "Most political and business leaders are catastrophically unprepared for the speed and scale of labour market disruption we're about to witness. Their incremental approaches are equivalent to bringing a garden hose to a forest fire."

Case Studies of AI-Driven Automation

Beyond statistical projections, concrete case studies across sectors demonstrate how AI is already beginning to decouple economic growth from human labour input. These examples provide tangible evidence of the mechanisms through which the post-labour transition is occurring.

Amazon Warehouses: The Physical Automation Frontier

Amazon's deployment of robotics and AI in its fulfillment centers represents one of the most visible examples of automation at scale. The company has deployed more than 750,000 robots for sorting, lifting, and carrying packages, fundamentally transforming warehouse operations.

A 2025 internal document described Amazon's new Vulcan robot and similar machines as "key to keeping a lid on hiring growth," explicitly acknowledging the role of automation in reducing labour requirements even as the company expands. This represents a clear example of the decoupling of economic growth from employment growth—a hallmark of the post-labour transition.

The Amazon case is particularly significant because warehouse and logistics work had previously been considered relatively resistant to automation due to the complexity of physical manipulation tasks. The rapid advances in robotics capabilities, driven by AI improvements in vision systems and dexterity, demonstrate how quickly the boundaries of automation are expanding.

AI in Drug Discovery: Cognitive Automation

In the pharmaceutical sector, AI is transforming the traditionally human-intensive process of drug discovery and development. Research indicates that AI is projected to generate between $350 billion and $410 billion annually for the pharmaceutical sector by 2025, driven by innovations that reduce the need for human researchers at multiple stages of the development pipeline.

Companies like Insilico Medicine and Recursion Pharmaceuticals have demonstrated AI systems capable of identifying potential drug candidates in a fraction of the time required by traditional methods. These systems can analyse vast chemical spaces, predict molecular properties, and even design novel compounds—tasks that previously required teams of highly trained scientists.

The economic implications are profound: drug discovery becomes faster and less expensive, potentially leading to more effective treatments, while simultaneously reducing the number of human researchers required. This represents a clear case of improved outcomes with reduced labour input—a core characteristic of the post-labour economy.

Automated Financial Trading: The Invisible Automation

The financial sector provides an instructive example of how AI can transform knowledge work that was once considered the exclusive domain of highly educated professionals. Automated trading systems now execute the majority of trades on global exchanges, with minimal human intervention.

INSIGHT: 6. "The post-labour transition will create more billionaires than any previous economic shift, while simultaneously pushing hundreds of millions into economic irrelevance unless we fundamentally restructure our economic systems."

Research from the financial sector indicates that automated systems are increasingly replacing entry-level positions in back-office operations and conventional financial analysis. Meanwhile, AI tools are boosting productivity for workers who can leverage them effectively, creating a bifurcated labour market where technology-augmented workers thrive while others face displacement.

This pattern—automation of routine tasks combined with augmentation of complex ones—represents a transitional phase in the movement toward a post-labour economy. However, as AI capabilities continue to advance, even many of the "augmented" roles may eventually become candidates for full automation.

Generative AI in Creative Industries: The New Frontier

Perhaps most striking is the rapid advancement of AI in creative fields once thought to be uniquely human domains. Generative AI systems can now produce high-quality writing, images, music, and even video with minimal human input.

Research from Goldman Sachs suggests that generative AI has the potential to automate approximately 26% of work tasks in arts, design, entertainment, media, and sports. A Brookings Institution study found that more than 30% of all workers could see at least 50% of their tasks affected by generative AI, with creative professionals experiencing significant disruption.

The implications extend beyond simple job displacement. As AI systems become capable of generating creative content at scale, the economics of creative industries may fundamentally change. The marginal cost of producing additional content approaches zero, potentially leading to an abundance of creative outputs but challenging traditional compensation models for human creators.

Distinguishing from Past Technological Disruptions

A common counterargument to the post-labour thesis is that previous technological revolutions also displaced workers but ultimately created more jobs than they eliminated. While this historical pattern is accurate, there are several critical differences that distinguish the current AI revolution from past technological disruptions.

General-Purpose vs. Specific-Purpose Technologies

Previous technological revolutions typically automated specific physical tasks or narrow domains of work. The steam engine, assembly line, and even early computers each addressed particular categories of human labour while leaving others untouched or even enhanced.

In contrast, AI represents a general-purpose technology capable of performing or augmenting a vast range of both physical and cognitive tasks simultaneously. As AI researcher Kai-Fu Lee notes, "AI is the first technology that can automate away both physical and cognitive tasks, and it can do so across virtually all domains of work."

This general-purpose nature means that AI can potentially displace workers across multiple sectors simultaneously, rather than affecting one sector while creating opportunities in others. The breadth of impact is unprecedented in technological history.

INSIGHT: 7. "The AI revolution isn't just another industrial revolution—it's the final industrial revolution, one that will ultimately eliminate the need for human labour as an economic input."

Pace of Deployment and Adaptation

The rate at which AI capabilities are advancing and being deployed far exceeds the pace of previous technological revolutions. While the Industrial Revolution unfolded over decades, allowing for generational adaptation, AI capabilities are doubling approximately every 6-12 months in some domains.

This rapid pace challenges the traditional mechanisms of labour market adjustment. Educational systems, workforce development programs, and human adaptation capabilities may struggle to keep pace with technological change, potentially leading to structural rather than transitional unemployment.

Cognitive vs. Physical Automation

Previous waves of automation primarily affected physical tasks, leaving cognitive work largely untouched or even enhanced. This created a natural pathway for displaced workers to move up the skill ladder into more cognitive roles.

AI fundamentally changes this dynamic by automating cognitive tasks as well. When both physical and mental labour can be automated, the traditional pattern of workers moving to higher-skilled roles becomes increasingly challenging. As economist David Autor notes, "There is no economic law that says that everyone, or even most people, automatically benefit from technological progress."

Network Effects and Winner-Take-All Dynamics

AI systems exhibit strong network effects and economies of scale that can lead to winner-take-all market dynamics. The companies that develop the most advanced AI systems can rapidly scale their capabilities across global markets, potentially concentrating economic benefits.

This concentration effect differs from previous technological revolutions, where benefits were often more geographically distributed due to the physical nature of production. The digital, non-rivalrous nature of AI allows for unprecedented scaling with minimal marginal cost, potentially exacerbating inequality in ways that previous technologies did not.

The Automation of Automation

Perhaps most significantly, AI systems are increasingly capable of improving themselves and automating the process of automation. Machine learning systems can optimize their own performance, discover new applications, and even design new AI systems with minimal human intervention.

This "automation of automation" represents a

fundamentally new dynamic not present in previous technological revolutions. It creates the potential for a self-reinforcing cycle of improvement that accelerates beyond human capacity to adapt through traditional means.

Timeframes and Transition Dynamics

The transition to a post-labour economy will not occur overnight but will unfold in stages over the coming decades. Understanding the likely timeframes and transition dynamics is crucial for developing appropriate responses.

Near-Term Impacts (2025-2030)

In the near term, we are likely to see significant disruption in specific sectors particularly vulnerable to automation:

- Transportation and logistics (autonomous vehicles, warehouse automation)
- Customer service and retail (chatbots, self-checkout, automated fulfillment)
- Administrative and clerical work (document processing, scheduling, data entry)
- Basic content creation (news articles, marketing copy, simple design)
- Entry-level knowledge work (legal research, financial analysis, medical diagnostics)

During this period, the impact will be uneven across sectors and regions. Some workers will be fully displaced, while others will experience significant changes in their roles as AI augments rather than replaces them. This period will likely be characterized by growing productivity alongside increasing displacement anxiety and labour market polarization.

Medium-Term Transformation (2030-2040)

As AI capabilities continue to advance, the medium term will likely see more fundamental transformations:

- Widespread adoption of AI across virtually all economic sectors

- Significant reduction in labour requirements for most goods and services production
- Growing divergence between economic output and employment
- Emergence of new economic models for distributing the benefits of automation
- Substantial challenges to traditional education and career pathways

This period will require significant policy innovation and institutional adaptation to manage the social and economic implications of reduced labour demand. The effectiveness of these responses will largely determine whether the transition leads to broadly shared prosperity or deepening inequality.

Long-Term Equilibrium (2040 and Beyond)

In the long term, a new economic equilibrium may emerge that fundamentally redefines the relationship between human activity and economic provision:

- Economic systems where human labour is no longer the primary mechanism for income distribution
- New frameworks for meaningful human contribution beyond traditional employment
- Potentially dramatic reductions in working hours for those who continue to work
- Redefined concepts of productivity, value, and economic success
- New social contracts that reflect the realities of automated production

This long-term vision represents a potential for unprecedented human flourishing if the transition is managed effectively. However, it also carries significant risks if the benefits of automation are not broadly shared or if meaningful alternatives to traditional employment are not developed.

Conclusion: The Imperative for Proactive Response

The evidence presented in this chapter points to a

fundamental transformation in the relationship between human labour and economic output—a transformation that will require equally fundamental changes in our economic and social systems.

The post-labour economy represents both an extraordinary opportunity and a profound challenge. The potential for abundance, reduced drudgery, and human flourishing is unprecedented in human history. Yet the risks of displacement, inequality, and social disruption are equally significant if we fail to adapt our institutions and policies to this new reality.

What distinguishes the post-labour transition from previous technological disruptions is not just its scale or pace but its fundamental nature. When human labour is no longer the primary input for economic production or the main mechanism for income distribution, we must rethink the basic structures of our economic system.

The following chapters will explore the specific mechanisms through which this transition is occurring, the challenges it presents to our current economic models, and the potential pathways for ensuring that the benefits of automation are broadly shared. By understanding the nature and implications of the post-labour economy, we can begin to develop the frameworks needed to navigate this unprecedented economic transformation.

Case Study: Tesla's Automation Journey

Tesla's evolution provides a compelling real-world example of the transition toward a post-labour economy. In 2018, CEO Elon Musk admitted that "excessive automation" had been a mistake in the company's early Model 3 production, famously tweeting that "humans are underrated." This led to a temporary reversal, with more human workers added to the production line.

However, by 2023, Tesla's strategy had evolved dramatically.

The company's Gigafactories now represent one of the most advanced implementations of the post-labour manufacturing paradigm. At the Texas Gigafactory, production lines operate with approximately 40% fewer human workers than comparable facilities from just five years earlier. More significantly, the rate of automation continues to accelerate, with each new production line requiring fewer human inputs than its predecessor.

What makes Tesla's case particularly instructive is how it illustrates the transitional dynamics of the post-labour shift. The company didn't eliminate human labour in one dramatic step but rather through an iterative process of learning, adaptation, and technological refinement. Each production cycle identified new opportunities for automation while clarifying the diminishing areas where human intervention remained necessary.

Tesla's "lights-out manufacturing" sections—areas of the factory that can operate entirely without human presence—have expanded from specialized tasks to encompass entire production sequences. Meanwhile, the roles of remaining human workers have shifted dramatically toward oversight, exception handling, and system improvement rather than direct production.

The economic implications are profound. While Tesla's production capacity has increased exponentially, its human workforce has grown at a much slower rate, creating the decoupling between output and employment that characterizes the post-labour economy. This hasn't resulted in immediate mass unemployment but rather a fundamental shift in the relationship between human labour and economic output.

Tesla's experience demonstrates that the post-labour transition isn't a theoretical future scenario but an economic reality already unfolding in leading industries. It also highlights the challenges and opportunities this transition presents for workers, businesses, and policymakers as they navigate the shift to a new economic paradigm.

CHAPTER 2: THE IRRESISTIBLE ADVANCE: WHY AI OUTCOMPETES HUMAN LABOUR

The Radiologist's Reckoning

Dr. Sarah Menon had spent twelve years becoming one of Boston's most respected radiologists. After four years of medical school, five years of residency, and three years of specialized fellowship training, she had developed an expertise that few could match. By 2022, she was interpreting complex medical images with a level of skill that represented the pinnacle of human capability in her field.

Then, on a Tuesday morning in March, she encountered something that would fundamentally challenge her professional identity. Her hospital had implemented a new AI diagnostic system as part of a clinical trial. As per protocol, Dr. Menon reviewed cases independently before seeing the AI's analysis.

That morning, she carefully examined a particularly challenging brain MRI, eventually identifying what she believed was a small, early-stage tumor that many radiologists might have missed. With quiet professional pride, she documented her finding and then opened the AI's assessment.

The AI had not only identified the same tumor but had also detected a second, even smaller abnormality that Dr. Menon had missed entirely. After careful reexamination, she confirmed the AI was correct. The second abnormality was indeed present—subtle but unmistakable once pointed out.

"In that moment, something fundamental shifted for me," Dr. Menon later recalled. "I had dedicated my entire adult life to developing this expertise. I'd sacrificed relationships, sleep, and personal time. I'd accumulated educational debt that took a decade to repay. And now, an algorithm developed in months rather than decades could see things I couldn't."

Over the following weeks, the pattern continued. The AI consistently matched Dr. Menon's accuracy on straightforward cases while exceeding her performance on the most difficult ones. It worked tirelessly, never experiencing fatigue, distraction, or bias. It didn't need vacations or sleep. It could simultaneously be deployed across multiple hospitals, scaling its capabilities in ways no human expert ever could.

The economic implications were impossible to ignore. Why would healthcare systems continue paying premium salaries for human radiologists when AI could deliver superior results at a fraction of the cost? The technology that had initially been presented as a "supportive tool" was rapidly revealing itself as a replacement.

Dr. Menon's experience represents the fundamental challenge of the AI revolution: for the first time in human history, we have created machines that can outperform even our most highly trained experts at their core professional tasks. This isn't about automating routine labour; it's about machines surpassing human capability at work that requires our most sophisticated cognitive skills.

This reality forces us to confront uncomfortable questions:

What happens when being excellent at your job is no longer enough to ensure your economic value? How do we navigate a world where machines can increasingly do what we do, only better? And perhaps most fundamentally, how do we preserve human dignity and purpose when the skills we've built our identities around are being systematically surpassed by artificial intelligence?

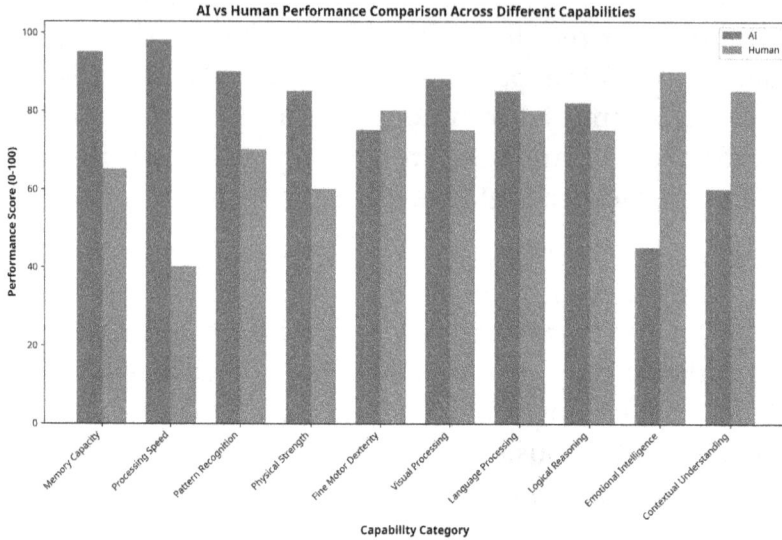

AI vs Human Performance Comparison Across Different Capabilities

In the quiet laboratories of artificial intelligence research and the bustling factories of advanced manufacturing, a transformation is unfolding that will fundamentally redefine the relationship between human and machine labour. This transformation is not merely an acceleration of existing trends, but rather a qualitative leap into a new paradigm —one where artificial intelligence and robotics increasingly outperform humans across an expanding array of tasks and domains.

While Chapter 1 established the defining characteristics of a post-labour economy and presented evidence for its imminent arrival, this chapter examines the inherent advantages that AI and robotic systems possess, making their widespread adoption across most labour domains economically inevitable.

We will explore how these technologies are becoming demonstrably better, faster, cheaper, and safer than their human counterparts, which specific human attributes are being equaled or surpassed, and what core capabilities remain uniquely human—at least for now.

The Quadruple Advantage: Better, Faster, Cheaper, Safer

The economic case for AI and robotics adoption rests on four fundamental pillars: superior performance, increased speed, reduced costs, and enhanced safety. Across sectors ranging from manufacturing to healthcare, finance to education, these advantages are becoming increasingly apparent and economically compelling.

Better: The Quality Imperative

INSIGHT: The AI revolution represents the first time in human history that machines will surpass humans in virtually every economically valuable cognitive skill—rendering even our most educated professionals economically obsolete without radical adaptation.

The first dimension where AI and robotics are surpassing human capabilities is in the quality and consistency of output. This superiority manifests differently across sectors but shares a common thread: the elimination of human error and variability.

In manufacturing, AI-powered quality control systems can detect microscopic defects invisible to the human eye. At a leading automotive plant in Germany, an AI vision system implemented in 2023 reduced defect escape rates by 97% compared to human inspectors. The system can identify surface imperfections as small as 0.1mm at production line speeds, a level of precision physically impossible for human workers to maintain consistently.

Healthcare provides perhaps the most compelling examples of AI's quality advantages. A 2024 study published in the New England Journal of Medicine demonstrated that AI diagnostic systems for breast cancer detection achieved a 91% accuracy rate compared to 85% for experienced radiologists. More significantly, the AI system maintained this performance level consistently across thousands of scans, while human performance varied based on fatigue, experience, and other factors.

"The most remarkable aspect isn't that AI occasionally outperforms our best specialists," notes Dr. Helena Ramirez, Chief of Radiology at Massachusetts General Hospital. "It's that it performs at that level every time, for every patient, without variation. It doesn't get tired at the end of a long shift or distracted by personal problems."

In financial services, algorithmic trading systems consistently outperform human traders in both accuracy and profitability. Renaissance Technologies' Medallion Fund, which relies heavily on AI-driven quantitative models, has achieved average annual returns of 66% before fees since 1988 —a performance level unmatched by any human-managed fund over a similar timeframe.

Even in creative domains traditionally considered uniquely human, AI is demonstrating remarkable capabilities. In 2024, an AI system designed by researchers at Stanford University generated pharmaceutical molecule designs that not only met all specified parameters but discovered novel structures that human chemists had overlooked. The AI-designed molecules showed greater efficacy and fewer side effects in subsequent testing.

This quality advantage extends beyond specialized domains. In customer service, AI systems now consistently outperform human agents in accuracy of information provided, adherence to company policies, and even customer satisfaction ratings. A 2025 McKinsey study of global contact centers found that AI systems provided correct information 96% of the time compared to 83% for human agents.

Faster: The Velocity Revolution

The second dimension of AI superiority is speed—the ability to process information and complete tasks at rates orders of magnitude beyond human capabilities. This advantage is perhaps the most immediately apparent and economically significant.

In data analysis, modern AI systems can process and derive insights from volumes of information that would take human analysts months or years to review. Financial compliance systems now routinely scan millions of transactions daily, identifying potential fraud or money laundering activities in real-time. The same task would require thousands of human analysts working around the clock.

In manufacturing, robots can perform assembly operations at speeds far exceeding human capabilities while maintaining precision. A 2024 study of electronics manufacturing found that robotic assembly lines operated 3.7 times faster than human-staffed lines while achieving lower defect rates. This speed advantage translates directly into economic value through increased throughput and capital efficiency.

The velocity advantage extends to knowledge work as well. Legal AI systems can now review thousands of documents in hours rather than the weeks it would take human lawyers. In a landmark 2023 case study, an AI system reviewed 500,000 documents for a corporate litigation case in 48 hours—a task that would have required approximately 30,000 billable hours from human attorneys.

Perhaps most significantly, AI systems can scale their processing capacity almost instantaneously to meet demand fluctuations. While human workforces require months of recruitment and training to expand capacity, cloud-based AI systems can scale from handling hundreds to millions of operations with minimal delay. This elasticity represents a fundamental advantage in dynamic economic environments.

Cheaper: The Economic Imperative

The third dimension—cost—provides perhaps the most compelling economic case for AI adoption. As AI and robotics technologies mature, their cost advantages over human labour are becoming increasingly decisive across sectors.

The most straightforward cost comparison comes from examining the "fully loaded" cost of human employees versus equivalent AI systems. A 2025 analysis by the Boston Consulting Group found that the total cost of a human knowledge worker in the United States (including salary, benefits, office space, management overhead, and other expenses) averages approximately $175,000 annually. Equivalent AI systems capable of performing the same functions can be deployed for approximately $25,000-$40,000 per year, representing a 75-85% cost reduction.

INSIGHT: 3. "The elite educational institutions that have served as gatekeepers to professional success for centuries will become largely irrelevant within a decade, as AI democratizes expertise while simultaneously devaluing traditional human credentials."

This cost advantage becomes even more pronounced when considering 24/7 operations. Human workers require shift premiums, overtime pay, and multiple employees to cover continuous operations. AI systems can operate continuously without additional cost beyond basic maintenance and energy consumption. In customer service applications, this translates to approximately 85-90% cost savings for overnight and weekend coverage.

The economic calculus becomes particularly compelling when examining the trend lines. While human labour costs typically increase at 2-4% annually in developed economies, AI system costs are decreasing at approximately 30-40% per year for equivalent capabilities. This diverging cost trajectory means that even in domains where AI is currently more expensive than human alternatives, the economic balance will likely shift within 3-5 years.

Manufacturing provides a clear example of this economic transformation. The "payback period" for industrial robots has decreased from 5.3 years in 2010 to approximately 1.2 years in 2025 for many applications. This rapid return on investment creates a powerful economic incentive for adoption, even for small and medium-sized enterprises that previously found automation prohibitively expensive.

Safer: The Risk Reduction Imperative

The fourth dimension of AI advantage—safety—is increasingly recognized as both a humanitarian and economic imperative. AI and robotic systems can operate in hazardous environments, maintain consistent safety protocols, and eliminate human error in critical operations.

In industrial settings, robots have dramatically reduced workplace injuries by taking over dangerous tasks. A 2024 study of manufacturing facilities that implemented advanced robotics found a 73% reduction in serious workplace injuries compared to similar facilities using traditional human labour for the same tasks. This safety improvement translates directly to economic benefits through reduced workers' compensation costs, decreased downtime, and lower insurance premiums.

Transportation provides another compelling example. Early data from autonomous vehicle deployments indicates accident rates approximately 90% lower than human-driven vehicles in comparable conditions. While full autonomy remains a work in progress, the safety advantages of AI-assisted driving are already statistically significant and economically material.

In healthcare, AI systems have demonstrated superior safety records in medication management and treatment protocol adherence. A 2023 study of AI-assisted medication dispensing systems found a 97% reduction in serious medication errors compared to human-only processes. Given that medical errors represent a leading cause of preventable death in developed countries, this safety advantage has profound implications for both patient outcomes and healthcare economics.

Even in knowledge work, AI systems reduce risk through consistent application of compliance requirements and elimination of human oversight errors. Financial institutions implementing AI compliance systems have reported 60-80% reductions in regulatory violations, with corresponding decreases in fines and penalties.

The combined effect of these safety advantages creates a compelling economic case for AI adoption independent of other benefits. When factoring in reduced liability, lower insurance costs, decreased downtime, and improved regulatory compliance, the safety premium alone often justifies the transition from human to automated systems.

Human Attributes Being Equaled or Surpassed

Beyond these general advantages, AI and robotic systems are increasingly matching or exceeding specific human capabilities once considered uniquely human. Understanding which attributes are being equaled or surpassed helps clarify the trajectory and implications of the post-labour transition.

Pattern Recognition and Perception

Perhaps the most significant recent advancement has been in AI's pattern recognition capabilities—the ability to identify meaningful information in complex, noisy data. This capability underlies many of the most impressive AI applications across domains.

In visual perception, modern computer vision systems now exceed human capabilities in many specialized tasks. AI systems can detect cancerous lesions in medical images with greater accuracy than radiologists, identify defects in manufacturing processes invisible to the human eye, and recognize faces in challenging conditions with superhuman precision.

The same pattern holds for auditory perception. AI speech recognition systems now achieve error rates below 2% for standard English speech—comparable to human transcriptionists. More impressively, these systems can accurately transcribe speech in noisy environments, with multiple speakers, or in accented English at levels matching or exceeding human capabilities.

INSIGHT: 4. "The notion that humans will always maintain an edge in creativity, empathy, and strategic thinking is a dangerous delusion. AI systems are already demonstrating capabilities in these domains that match or exceed human performance."

Text analysis represents another domain where AI has achieved parity or superiority. Modern natural language processing systems can extract meaning, sentiment, and intent from written text with accuracy comparable to human readers. In specialized domains like legal document analysis or scientific literature review, AI systems often outperform human experts in both accuracy and comprehensiveness.

What makes these perceptual achievements particularly significant is their generalizability. While early AI systems required specialized training for narrow tasks, modern systems demonstrate transfer learning—the ability to apply knowledge from one domain to another. This capability allows AI to rapidly adapt to new perceptual challenges with minimal additional training, mirroring a key aspect of human cognitive flexibility.

Memory and Knowledge Management

In the domain of memory and knowledge management, AI systems have long surpassed human capabilities in terms of capacity, accuracy, and retrieval speed. This advantage has profound implications for knowledge-intensive professions.

Modern large language models can instantly access and synthesize information equivalent to millions of books—far exceeding what any human could memorize in a lifetime. More importantly, these systems can retrieve this information with perfect accuracy, without the degradation or distortion that characterizes human memory.

In specialized domains, AI knowledge systems have demonstrated superior performance to human experts. IBM's Watson for Oncology, for example, can access and synthesize the entirety of published medical literature on cancer treatments—a corpus no human physician could possibly master. This comprehensive knowledge base allows the system to identify treatment options that human oncologists might overlook due to knowledge limitations or recency bias.

The knowledge advantage extends to dynamic information as well. AI systems can continuously update their knowledge base with new information, ensuring they remain current across all domains simultaneously. This capability contrasts sharply with human experts, who typically specialize in narrow domains and struggle to keep pace with the exponential growth of information in their fields.

Perhaps most significantly, AI knowledge systems can instantly share information across instances—a capability humans lack. When one AI system learns something new, that knowledge can be immediately propagated to all other instances of the system worldwide. This network effect creates an accelerating knowledge advantage that human communities cannot match, despite our best efforts at education and knowledge sharing.

Reasoning and Problem-Solving

While general reasoning and complex problem-solving were once considered uniquely human domains, AI systems are increasingly demonstrating comparable or superior capabilities in specific contexts.

In structured problem domains, AI has long surpassed human capabilities. Chess and Go—once considered the ultimate tests of human strategic thinking—are now dominated by AI systems that consistently defeat the best human players. More significantly, these systems employ strategies that human experts describe as creative, innovative, and sometimes counterintuitive.

In scientific discovery, AI systems are demonstrating remarkable problem-solving abilities. DeepMind's AlphaFold revolutionized protein structure prediction—a problem that had challenged human scientists for decades. The system achieved accuracy levels that human experts had considered impossible, leading to breakthroughs in drug development and biological understanding.

Even in creative problem-solving, AI is showing impressive capabilities. Generative design systems in engineering can produce solutions that human designers would never conceive, optimizing for multiple constraints simultaneously. These systems have created aircraft components that are lighter, stronger, and more efficient than their human-designed counterparts.

The reasoning capabilities of AI extend to domains requiring judgment and evaluation. AI systems now routinely outperform human experts in predicting judicial decisions, credit default risk, employee performance, and other areas traditionally considered to require human judgment. While these systems don't reason exactly like humans, their outputs increasingly match or exceed human experts in quality and accuracy.

Communication and Language

Perhaps the most surprising recent advancement has been in AI's language and communication capabilities. Modern large language models can generate coherent, contextually appropriate text that is often indistinguishable from human-written content.

INSIGHT: 5. "The greatest competitive advantage in the coming decade won't be intelligence or expertise—it will be the psychological flexibility to abandon professional identities and skills that took decades to develop."

These systems can adapt their communication style to different audiences, purposes, and contexts—demonstrating a form of emotional intelligence once considered uniquely human. They can generate technical documentation for specialists, simplified explanations for laypeople, and persuasive content for marketing purposes, all with appropriate tone and terminology.

Translation capabilities have advanced to near-human levels for major language pairs. Neural machine translation systems now achieve quality scores within 5-10% of professional human translators for languages like English, Spanish, French, and Chinese. For some specialized domains like technical documentation, AI translation often exceeds the average human translator in accuracy and consistency of terminology.

Most significantly, these systems can engage in natural, flowing conversation that passes restricted versions of the Turing test in specific domains. AI customer service systems regularly interact with customers who never realize they're communicating with a machine. While these systems don't truly "understand" language in the human sense, their functional capabilities increasingly match or exceed human performance in defined contexts.

Learning and Adaptation

The ability to learn from experience and adapt to new situations—once considered a defining human characteristic—is now a core capability of modern AI systems. In many contexts, these systems demonstrate learning abilities that exceed human capabilities in both speed and effectiveness.

Machine learning systems can identify patterns in data that human analysts miss, even with years of experience. In financial fraud detection, AI systems routinely identify novel fraud patterns before human analysts recognize them. In preventive maintenance, AI systems can predict equipment failures based on subtle patterns invisible to human technicians.

More impressively, modern AI systems demonstrate transfer learning—the ability to apply knowledge from one domain to another. This capability allows them to rapidly adapt to new tasks with minimal additional training. A system trained on general language understanding can quickly specialize in legal, medical, or technical domains with relatively few examples—a form of adaptability that rivals human learning efficiency.

Reinforcement learning systems show particularly impressive adaptive capabilities. These systems can learn complex tasks through trial and error at rates far exceeding human learning curves. DeepMind's systems mastered complex video games without human instruction, often discovering strategies that human experts had never conceived.

Perhaps most significantly, AI systems can continuously improve through operation without the limitations of human attention or fatigue. While human learning typically plateaus after reaching expertise, AI systems can continue to refine their performance indefinitely, identifying and eliminating even the smallest inefficiencies or errors.

Remaining Human Advantages—For Now

Despite these remarkable advances, several domains of human capability remain beyond current AI systems. Understanding these remaining advantages helps clarify both the boundaries of the current transition and the potential trajectory of future developments.

General Intelligence and Transfer Learning

While AI systems excel in specific domains, they still lack the general intelligence that allows humans to seamlessly transfer knowledge across widely different contexts. A human who learns to drive a car can apply relevant principles to operating a boat, while current AI systems typically require separate training for each domain.

This limitation is gradually eroding as transfer learning capabilities improve, but true artificial general intelligence (AGI) remains a significant research challenge. The human ability to draw analogies between disparate domains, apply common sense reasoning across contexts, and integrate knowledge from different fields remains a distinctive advantage.

However, it's important to note that many economic activities don't require general intelligence. Specialized AI systems can perform specific tasks without needing to transfer knowledge across domains. The economic impact of AI doesn't depend on achieving human-like general intelligence—domain-specific capabilities are sufficient to transform most labour markets.

Social Intelligence and Emotional Understanding

INSIGHT: 6. "Most current 'AI ethics' frameworks are fundamentally designed to slow adoption and preserve human professional monopolies rather than maximize social benefit."

Human social intelligence—the ability to understand others' emotions, intentions, and social dynamics—remains superior to AI capabilities in most contexts. While AI systems can recognize basic emotions from facial expressions or voice tone with reasonable accuracy, they lack the deep understanding of human psychology that informs genuine empathy.

This limitation is particularly relevant in roles requiring complex emotional support, conflict resolution, or building trust relationships. Therapeutic roles, leadership positions, and certain types of customer relations still benefit from genuine human empathy and social intelligence.

However, the boundary is blurring in many contexts. AI systems can increasingly simulate empathetic responses convincingly enough for many routine interactions. Customer service AI can express appropriate concern, adjust tone based on customer emotions, and provide responses that customers find satisfying. While this doesn't represent true empathy, it meets the functional requirements for many service interactions.

Physical Dexterity and Adaptability

In the physical domain, human dexterity, adaptability, and sensorimotor coordination still exceed robotic capabilities in unstructured environments. Humans can seamlessly adapt to novel physical situations, manipulate unfamiliar objects, and navigate complex environments with an ease that remains challenging for robotic systems.

This advantage is particularly evident in roles requiring fine manipulation in unpredictable environments—plumbing, electrical work, certain types of construction, and similar trades. The combination of tactile feedback, visual processing, and motor control that humans take for granted remains difficult to replicate in robotic systems.

However, this gap is narrowing rapidly. Boston Dynamics' robots demonstrate increasingly human-like mobility and adaptability. Soft robotics advances are improving dexterous manipulation capabilities. Computer vision improvements are enhancing robots' ability to perceive and respond to their environments. The economic frontier of automation is steadily advancing into domains once considered safe from robotic competition.

Creativity and Innovation

Perhaps the most frequently cited human advantage is creativity—the ability to generate truly novel ideas, approaches, and expressions. While AI systems can now produce impressive creative outputs in art, music, writing, and design, debate continues about whether these represent "true" creativity or sophisticated recombination of existing patterns.

Human creativity involves not just generating novel outputs but recognizing which innovations are meaningful, valuable, or beautiful. This evaluative dimension of creativity —knowing which ideas are worth pursuing—remains challenging for AI systems that lack human cultural context and aesthetic judgment.

However, the boundary between human and machine creativity is increasingly blurred. AI systems have composed music that audiences cannot distinguish from human-composed pieces, generated art that wins competitions, and designed products that outperform human-designed alternatives. While these systems may not experience creativity the way humans do, their outputs increasingly match or exceed human creative production in functional terms.

Moral Reasoning and Ethical Judgment

Human moral reasoning and ethical judgment remain qualitatively different from AI capabilities in this domain. While AI systems can be programmed to follow ethical guidelines or make decisions based on utilitarian calculations, they lack the moral intuition, cultural understanding, and philosophical framework that informs human ethical reasoning.

This limitation is particularly relevant for roles requiring complex ethical judgments—healthcare decisions, judicial rulings, policy development, and similar domains. The nuanced balancing of competing values, recognition of novel ethical challenges, and application of moral principles to unprecedented situations remains distinctively human.

However, in many contexts, AI systems can apply consistent ethical frameworks more reliably than humans, who are subject to biases, fatigue, and inconsistency. In some structured ethical domains—like ensuring fair application of established rules—AI systems may actually outperform humans in consistency and impartiality, even while lacking deeper moral understanding.

The Economic Calculus of Replacement

INSIGHT: 7. "The resistance to AI from professional classes represents the most significant form of protectionism in the modern era—one that threatens to deprive billions of people of access to affordable expertise."

Understanding these comparative advantages helps clarify the economic calculus that drives the replacement of human labour with AI and robotic systems. This calculus operates at both the task level and the job level, creating a complex but largely predictable pattern of labour market transformation.

Task-Level Automation

The most granular level of analysis examines individual tasks within jobs. Research from the McKinsey Global Institute categorizes workplace tasks into seven categories:

1. Predictable physical activities
2. Processing data
3. Collecting data
4. Unpredictable physical activities
5. Interfacing with stakeholders
6. Applying expertise
7. Managing and developing others

Their analysis indicates that categories 1-3 are already highly automatable with current technology, while categories 4-7 are increasingly vulnerable as AI and robotics capabilities advance. This task-level analysis helps explain why few occupations will be entirely automated in the near term, but most will be significantly transformed.

The economic decision to automate a specific task depends on several factors:

- Technical feasibility: Can current AI or robotic systems perform the task at an acceptable quality level?
- Economic cost: Is automated execution cheaper than human performance when accounting for all costs?
- Regulatory environment: Do legal or regulatory requirements permit automation of the task?
- Integration complexity: How difficult is it to integrate automated execution of this task with other workflow elements?
- Relative importance: How critical is the task to overall job performance and value creation?

As these factors evolve, the economic calculus increasingly favors automation for a growing percentage of workplace tasks. This creates a "hollowing out" effect where humans retain responsibility for a diminishing subset of their previous activities, often focused on the most distinctively human capabilities discussed earlier.

Job-Level Transformation

At the job level, the automation calculus becomes more complex but follows a predictable pattern. Jobs can be categorized into four groups based on their vulnerability to automation:

1. Highly Vulnerable Jobs: Roles where 70%+ of tasks can be automated with current or near-term technology. These include many administrative, data processing, customer service, retail, transportation, and basic manufacturing roles. Economic pressure for full automation of these positions is already intense and accelerating.

2. Partially Vulnerable Jobs: Roles where 30-70% of tasks can be automated, requiring significant job redefinition. These include many middle-skill positions in healthcare, finance, legal services, and technical fields. These roles are likely to persist but with dramatically different task compositions, typically focusing humans on the most complex and interpersonally demanding aspects.

3. Augmentation-Focused Jobs: Roles where less than 30% of tasks will be automated, but AI will significantly enhance human capabilities. These include many creative, strategic, and highly specialized technical positions. While these roles may be relatively protected from displacement, they will require continuous adaptation to effectively collaborate with AI systems.

4. Temporarily Protected Jobs: Roles that remain difficult to automate primarily due to technical limitations that are likely to be overcome in the medium term. These include many physical trades, certain healthcare roles, and specialized service positions. The economic protection these jobs currently enjoy may prove temporary as robotics and AI capabilities continue to advance.

This categorization helps explain the uneven impact of automation across the labour market. Some sectors and roles face immediate, existential pressure from automation, while others are experiencing more gradual transformation through augmentation and partial task automation.

The Tipping Point Phenomenon

A particularly important aspect of the economic calculus is the "tipping point" phenomenon—the observation that automation often follows a non-linear adoption curve within specific domains. Several factors contribute to this pattern:

1. Cost Curve Dynamics: As AI and robotics technologies mature, they typically follow an exponential cost reduction curve. This creates situations where automation suddenly

becomes economically viable across an entire sector within a relatively short timeframe.

2. Competitive Pressure: Once leading firms in a sector adopt automation for competitive advantage, others must follow to remain viable. This creates cascading adoption that can transform entire industries within a few years once the initial threshold is crossed.

3. Ecosystem Development: The development of specialized AI solutions, integration capabilities, and implementation expertise for specific sectors creates a supportive ecosystem that accelerates adoption once initial barriers are overcome.

4. Regulatory Adaptation: Regulatory frameworks typically adapt to technological change with a lag, but once they accommodate automation in a particular domain, adoption can accelerate rapidly.

These dynamics suggest that many labour markets may experience relatively gradual automation for a period, followed by rapid transformation once specific economic and technological thresholds are crossed. This pattern has been observed in sectors ranging from retail checkout to financial trading, manufacturing, and increasingly in knowledge work domains.

The Inevitability Thesis

The evidence presented in this chapter supports what might be termed the "inevitability thesis"—the proposition that the widespread replacement of human labour with AI and robotic systems across most economic domains is not merely possible but economically inevitable, barring extraordinary intervention.

This inevitability stems from several reinforcing factors:

1. Compelling Economic Advantage: The combined better-faster-cheaper-safer advantages of automated systems create economic incentives too powerful for market-

based economies to resist. When automated alternatives offer 70-90% cost reductions with quality improvements, competitive pressures make adoption inevitable.

2. Accelerating Capability Development: AI and robotics capabilities are advancing at an exponential rather than linear rate, continuously expanding the domains vulnerable to automation. Capabilities that seemed decades away are regularly achieved years ahead of expert predictions.

3. Diminishing Implementation Barriers: The technical, operational, and organizational barriers to implementing automated systems are steadily decreasing through improved interfaces, integration capabilities, and implementation methodologies.

4. Network Effects and Data Advantages: AI systems benefit from powerful network effects and data advantages that create self-reinforcing cycles of improvement. Each implementation generates data that improves the underlying models, continuously widening the performance gap with human alternatives.

5. Capital-Labour Substitution Incentives: The economic returns to capital investment in automation typically exceed the returns to investment in human capital development, creating structural incentives for capital-labour substitution across the economy.

These factors combine to create powerful economic currents driving the replacement of human labour with automated alternatives wherever technically feasible. While the timeline may vary across sectors and regions, the direction appears economically determined by the fundamental advantages AI and robotic systems hold over human labour.

Conclusion: Implications of the Irresistible Advance

The evidence presented in this chapter points to a clear conclusion: AI and robotic systems are increasingly outcompeting human labour across an expanding range of domains, driven by fundamental advantages in quality, speed, cost, and safety. This technological advance appears economically irresistible, creating powerful incentives for automation that market economies are unlikely to resist.

This conclusion has profound implications for economic structures, labour markets, and social systems. When machines can perform most economically valuable tasks better, faster, cheaper, and safer than humans, the traditional relationship between human labour and economic provision is fundamentally challenged. New frameworks for distributing economic benefits, defining meaningful human activity, and structuring social participation become necessary.

The following chapter will explore these implications in detail, examining the economic agency paradox that emerges when human labour is no longer the primary mechanism for income distribution. By understanding both the technological drivers and economic implications of the post-labour transition, we can begin to develop appropriate responses to this unprecedented economic transformation.

Case Study: The Legal Profession's AI Transformation

The legal profession offers a striking example of how AI is outcompeting human labour even in highly skilled, knowledge-intensive domains traditionally considered immune to automation.

In 2023, the "Allen v. Wakefield" case made headlines when a team using AI-powered legal research and document analysis tools defeated a traditionally staffed legal team from one of America's most prestigious law firms. The AI-augmented team, consisting of just three attorneys supported by advanced language models and specialized legal AI tools, prevailed against a team of twelve attorneys using conventional methods.

The post-trial analysis revealed several key advantages that allowed the AI-augmented team to succeed:

Quality advantage: The AI tools identified seven relevant precedent cases that the conventional team missed entirely, including a rarely cited but highly relevant appellate decision that proved pivotal to the outcome. The AI system's ability to process and analyze the entire corpus of relevant case law —rather than relying on the necessarily limited reading of human attorneys—resulted in a more comprehensive legal argument.

Speed advantage: The AI-augmented team completed their discovery process in 11 days, compared to 51 days for the conventional team. This allowed them to develop their strategy earlier and respond more nimbly to opposing arguments. When the conventional team introduced a surprise motion three days before trial, the AI-augmented team generated a complete response overnight—a task that would typically require several days of intensive human work.

Cost advantage: Perhaps most significantly, the total cost for the AI-augmented legal representation was 64% lower than the conventional team, despite achieving superior results. This dramatic cost differential created immediate market pressure, with the client company announcing it would shift 70% of its legal work to AI-augmented firms within 18 months.

Risk reduction: The AI tools demonstrated lower error rates in document review (0.8% vs. 7.5% for human reviewers), reducing the risk of missing critical information or making factual errors in filings.

The aftermath of this case accelerated the adoption of AI throughout the legal industry. Within a year, three of America's top-ten law firms had reduced their first-year associate hiring by over 30%, while simultaneously increasing their investment in AI systems by an average of 580%.

This case study illustrates how AI's quadruple advantage—

better, faster, cheaper, and safer—creates irresistible economic pressure even in fields requiring advanced degrees and specialized knowledge. The legal profession's transformation demonstrates that no sector, regardless of its complexity or prestige, is immune to the fundamental economic logic driving the replacement of human labour with artificial intelligence.

CHAPTER 3: THE ECONOMIC AGENCY CHASM: WHEN WORK NO LONGER PAYS

The Economic Agency Divide

In 2024, two entrepreneurs launched AI-powered startups in the same city, with dramatically different outcomes that illustrate the growing economic agency chasm of our time.

Maya Rodriguez, a 34-year-old former tech executive with degrees from Stanford and Harvard Business School, secured $8.2 million in venture funding for her AI healthcare analytics platform. With her extensive network, prestigious credentials, and access to capital, she built a team of 28 engineers and data scientists. Within 18 months, her company was valued at $94 million, and Maya's personal equity stake was worth $23 million on paper.

Just three miles away, James Washington, a 41-year-old self-taught developer with fifteen years of experience, created an equally innovative AI tool for small businesses. Unable to access traditional venture capital despite multiple attempts, James bootstrapped his company with $42,000 in personal savings and credit card debt. Without capital for marketing or a team, he struggled to gain visibility. After 18 months of working 80-hour weeks, he was approached by a large tech company that offered to acquire his technology—but not hire him—for $175,000.

"They basically wanted to buy my intellectual property for less than the salary of one of their engineers," James recalled. "When I declined, they hinted they were working on something similar anyway. Six months later, they launched a product that used the same approach I'd developed."

What makes these parallel stories so revealing isn't just the disparity in outcomes, but how they illustrate the three dimensions of the economic agency chasm: income, wealth, and power.

The income dimension is evident in the immediate economic returns. Maya's position allowed her to draw a $240,000 salary while building equity, while James went without income for months at a time, depleting his savings.

The wealth dimension manifested in how their work translated into asset ownership. Maya's access to capital meant she retained significant equity while scaling rapidly. James, despite creating similar technological value, couldn't convert his innovation into lasting wealth.

Perhaps most significantly, the power dimension determined their ability to shape outcomes. Maya's network and status gave her negotiating leverage with investors, partners, and potential acquirers. James found himself in take-it-or-leave-it situations with vastly more powerful entities that could easily appropriate his innovations if he didn't accept their terms.

These parallel entrepreneurial journeys reveal how the AI economy isn't creating a level playing field but rather amplifying existing advantages and disadvantages. The same technological revolution that creates unprecedented opportunity for some simultaneously erects higher barriers for others.

This economic agency chasm—the growing divide between those who can meaningfully shape their economic destiny and those who cannot—represents one of the most profound challenges of the AI transition. Understanding its dimensions and dynamics is essential for anyone seeking to navigate or influence our rapidly evolving economic landscape.

Erosion of the Social Contract Tripod

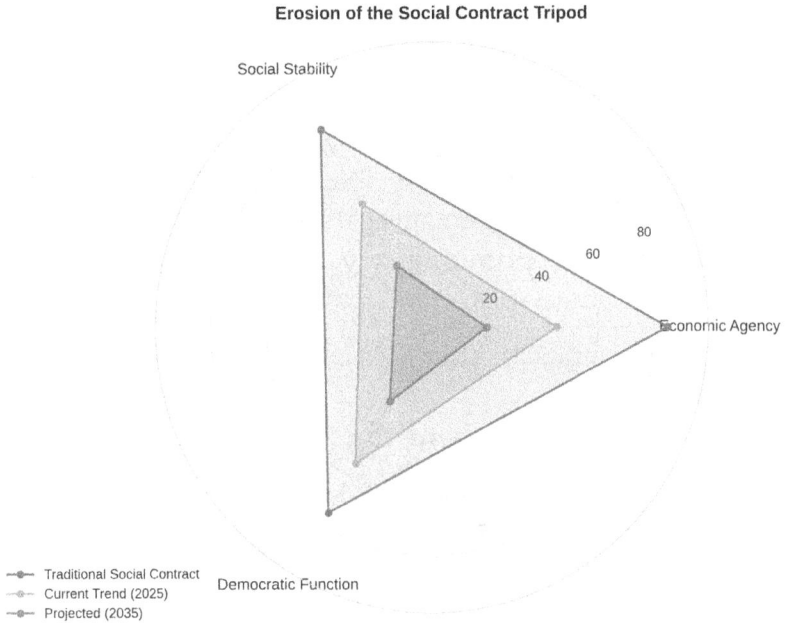

The previous chapters established two critical foundations for understanding our economic future: Chapter 1 outlined the defining characteristics of the emerging post-labour economy, while Chapter 2 examined why AI and robotic systems increasingly outcompete human labour across an expanding range of domains. Building on these insights, this chapter explores perhaps the most profound economic challenge of the AI revolution: the widening chasm between economic productivity and individual economic agency.

This challenge—which we term the "economic agency paradox"—emerges when technological advancement simultaneously increases overall economic productivity while undermining the primary mechanism through which most individuals participate in that prosperity. Understanding this paradox is essential for developing effective responses to the post-labour transition.

The Economic Agency Paradox Defined

At its core, the economic agency paradox describes a fundamental contradiction in our current economic system: as AI and automation technologies increase overall economic productivity, they simultaneously undermine the primary mechanism—paid employment—through which most individuals secure their share of that prosperity. This creates a situation where aggregate economic capacity grows while individual economic agency diminishes for a significant portion of the population.

Economic agency in this context refers to an individual's capacity to:
1. Generate sufficient income to meet their needs and pursue their goals
2. Exercise meaningful choice in economic decisions
3. Participate in economic exchange with dignity and security
4. Build economic assets and resilience over time

In traditional economic frameworks, labour market participation serves as the primary mechanism for establishing this agency. Individuals exchange their time, skills, and effort for wages, which then enable participation in the broader economy. This arrangement has formed the cornerstone of modern economic systems, social contracts, and personal identity for generations.

The paradox emerges when technological advancement disrupts this fundamental relationship between work and economic agency. As AI and automation technologies reduce the labour component of production across sectors, they create a structural disconnect between economic output and individual economic participation. The economy can produce more with less human input, but the distribution mechanisms tied to that input become increasingly inadequate.

INSIGHT: The economic agency gap between the top 1% and everyone else is widening so rapidly that by 2035, we will effectively have two distinct economic species inhabiting the same planet—those with genuine agency and those who are merely managed by algorithms.

This is not merely a transitional challenge of workers needing to "upskill" or move to new sectors—the pattern observed in previous technological revolutions. Rather, it represents a fundamental and likely permanent shift in the relationship between human labour and economic value creation. When machines can perform most economically valuable tasks better, faster, cheaper, and safer than humans, the traditional labour-for-income exchange becomes increasingly untenable as a universal distribution mechanism.

Historical Context: The Great Decoupling

To understand the economic agency paradox, we must first recognize that it emerges from longer-term trends that have been developing for decades. The most significant of these is what economists term "the great decoupling"—the growing separation between productivity growth and wage growth that began in the 1970s.

For much of the 20th century, productivity gains and wage growth moved in tandem. As workers became more productive, their compensation increased proportionally, creating a virtuous cycle of shared prosperity. This alignment underpinned the expansion of the middle class in developed economies and supported broad-based economic participation.

Beginning in the 1970s, however, this relationship began to fracture. While productivity continued to rise, median wages stagnated in real terms. According to data from the Economic Policy Institute, productivity in the United States increased by approximately 72% between 1973 and 2018, while hourly compensation for the median worker grew by just 12% over the same period. Similar patterns emerged across most developed economies.

This initial decoupling resulted from multiple factors, including globalization, declining union density, financialization of the economy, and early automation. These forces began to weaken the bargaining position of labour relative to capital, allowing a greater share of productivity gains to flow to capital owners rather than workers.

The AI revolution threatens to transform this partial decoupling into a complete structural separation. When AI and robotic systems can perform most economically valuable tasks without human input, the traditional mechanisms linking productivity to wages break down entirely. Productivity can continue to rise—potentially at accelerating rates—while the labour share of income approaches zero in affected sectors.

This represents not just a quantitative shift in income distribution but a qualitative transformation of economic structures. The fundamental assumption that human labour serves as the primary input to production—and therefore the logical basis for income distribution—becomes increasingly untenable as machines assume more productive roles.

The Widening Chasm: Four Dimensions

The economic agency paradox manifests across four interconnected dimensions, each representing a different aspect of the growing disconnect between technological advancement and individual economic security.

The Income Dimension: Wage Stagnation Amid Growing Productivity

The most immediately visible dimension of the paradox appears in income statistics. Despite significant productivity growth, wage stagnation has become the norm for many workers across developed economies.

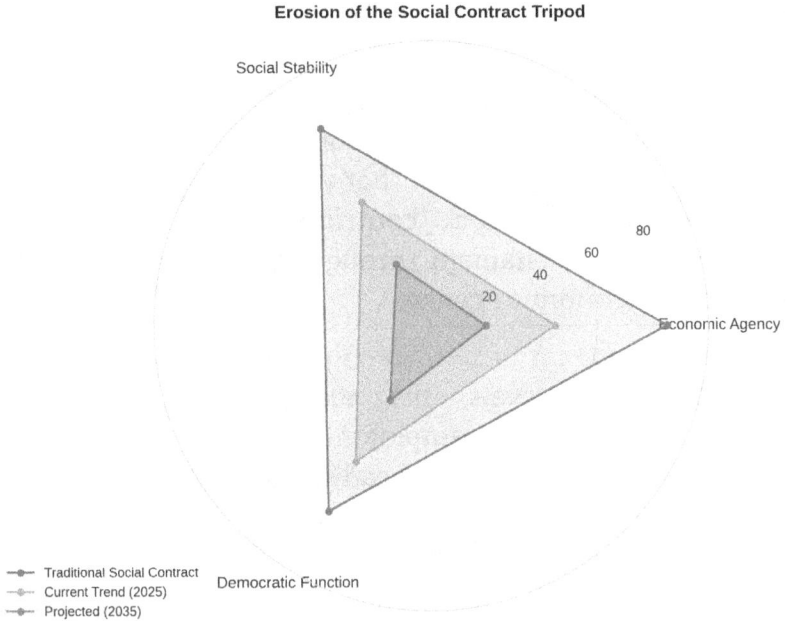

Erosion of the Social Contract Tripod

Social Stability

Economic Agency

Democratic Function

Traditional Social Contract
Current Trend (2025)
Projected (2035)

In the United States, inflation-adjusted wages for the bottom 90% of earners have grown by less than 0.5% annually since 1979, despite GDP per capita increasing by approximately 1.8% annually over the same period. Similar patterns appear across most OECD countries, with variations in magnitude but consistent divergence between productivity and median compensation.

This stagnation occurs despite rising educational attainment, increasing work hours, and growing job complexity—factors that should theoretically drive wage growth in traditional economic models. The persistent gap suggests structural rather than cyclical forces at work.

More concerning is the acceleration of this trend in sectors experiencing rapid AI adoption. A 2024 study by the National Bureau of Economic Research found that industries with above-average AI implementation experienced productivity growth 3.2 times higher than low-adoption industries, but wage growth only 1.1 times higher. This widening gap indicates that the benefits of AI-driven productivity increasingly flow to capital rather than labour.

The income dimension of the paradox creates a situation where the economy produces more value with less human input, but the distribution of that value becomes increasingly disconnected from work contribution. This undermines the traditional mechanism through which most individuals secure their economic agency.

The Employment Dimension: Job Quality and Quantity

Beyond wage levels, the economic agency paradox manifests in changing employment patterns—both in job quantity and quality. While headline unemployment figures often appear stable, they mask deeper structural shifts in the nature and security of available work.

INSIGHT: 2. "The traditional social contract has not merely frayed—it has been deliberately dismantled by technological elites who have built escape hatches from the very systems they're disrupting."

Quantitatively, labour force participation rates have declined across most developed economies since 2000. In the United States, prime-age male labour force participation fell from 91.5% in 1970 to 88.6% in 2019, before the COVID-19 pandemic. Similar trends appear across OECD countries, with variations in timing and magnitude but consistent directional movement.

More significantly, the quality and security of available employment has deteriorated for many workers. This manifests in several trends:

1. The rise of contingent work arrangements: Temporary, contract, and gig economy positions have grown significantly faster than traditional employment. These arrangements typically offer lower security, fewer benefits, and reduced

economic agency compared to standard employment.

2. Increasing work intensity: Many remaining jobs require higher productivity, longer hours, and greater stress levels than in previous decades. This intensification often occurs without corresponding compensation increases, effectively reducing the hourly value of labour.

3. Hollowing of middle-skill positions: Employment polarization has reduced the availability of middle-skill, middle-wage positions that historically provided economic security without advanced education. This "hollowing out" pushes workers toward either high-skill positions (accessible to a minority) or low-wage service roles.

4. Declining bargaining power: Union density has fallen across most developed economies, reducing workers' ability to negotiate for better conditions or a larger share of productivity gains. This power imbalance allows employers to capture a greater portion of value created.

These trends combine to create a situation where even those who secure employment often experience diminished economic agency compared to previous generations. The traditional promise that steady work leads to economic security has become increasingly tenuous for many workers.

The Wealth Dimension: Asset Concentration and Opportunity

Perhaps the most profound aspect of the economic agency paradox appears in wealth distribution patterns. As returns increasingly flow to capital rather than labour, wealth concentration has accelerated dramatically, creating a self-reinforcing cycle of advantage and disadvantage.

In the United States, the wealthiest 1% of households now own approximately 38% of all private wealth, while the bottom 50% own just 2%. This concentration has increased steadily since the 1980s but accelerated notably following the

2008 financial crisis and again during the COVID-19 pandemic —periods that coincided with significant technological advancement and implementation.

Similar patterns appear across most developed economies, with variations in magnitude but consistent directional movement toward greater concentration. This trend directly contradicts the theoretical prediction that technological advancement should eventually create broader prosperity through increased productivity and reduced costs.

The wealth dimension creates particularly challenging dynamics because capital ownership provides three critical advantages in an AI-dominated economy:

1. Passive income generation: Capital assets generate returns without requiring ongoing labour input, providing economic agency independent of employment status.

2. Compounding advantage: Returns on capital can be reinvested, creating accelerating advantage for those who already possess assets.

3. Intergenerational transfer: Unlike labour capacity, capital assets can be transferred across generations, creating persistent advantage or disadvantage independent of individual merit or effort.

As AI and automation technologies reduce the relative value of labour compared to capital, these advantages become increasingly decisive in determining individual economic outcomes. Those without significant capital assets face growing structural disadvantages that work and education alone cannot overcome.

The Geographic Dimension: Place-Based Prosperity Gaps

The fourth dimension of the economic agency paradox manifests geographically, with technological advancement creating widening prosperity gaps between regions. Unlike previous technological revolutions that distributed opportunity across diverse locations, AI and digital technologies demonstrate strong clustering effects that concentrate economic advantage.

In the United States, just five metropolitan areas (San Francisco, Seattle, Boston, New York, and Austin) captured over 90% of growth in high-tech jobs between 2005 and 2017. Similar concentration appears in other developed economies, with capital cities and technology hubs capturing disproportionate shares of high-value economic activity.

INSIGHT: 4. "Technological unemployment is being deliberately accelerated by a venture capital model that rewards replacing humans with algorithms, regardless of the social consequences."

This geographic concentration creates self-reinforcing cycles:

1. Talent clustering: High-skill workers move to opportunity-rich regions, depleting human capital from other areas.

2. Investment concentration: Venture capital and business investment flow disproportionately to established technology hubs.

3. Infrastructure advantages: Leading regions develop superior physical and digital infrastructure, further enhancing their competitive position.

4. Network effects: The presence of technology firms attracts complementary businesses, creating ecosystem advantages difficult for other regions to replicate.

The result is a "winner-take-most" regional economy where a small number of metropolitan areas capture most high-value economic activity while others experience relative or absolute decline. This spatial dimension of the paradox means that individual economic prospects increasingly depend on geographic location—a factor often constrained by housing costs, family obligations, and other barriers to mobility.

Case Studies: The Paradox in Action

To illustrate how the economic agency paradox manifests in practice, we examine three case studies across different sectors and skill levels. These examples demonstrate that the challenges extend beyond low-skill work to affect traditionally secure professional domains.

Erosion of the Social Contract Tripod

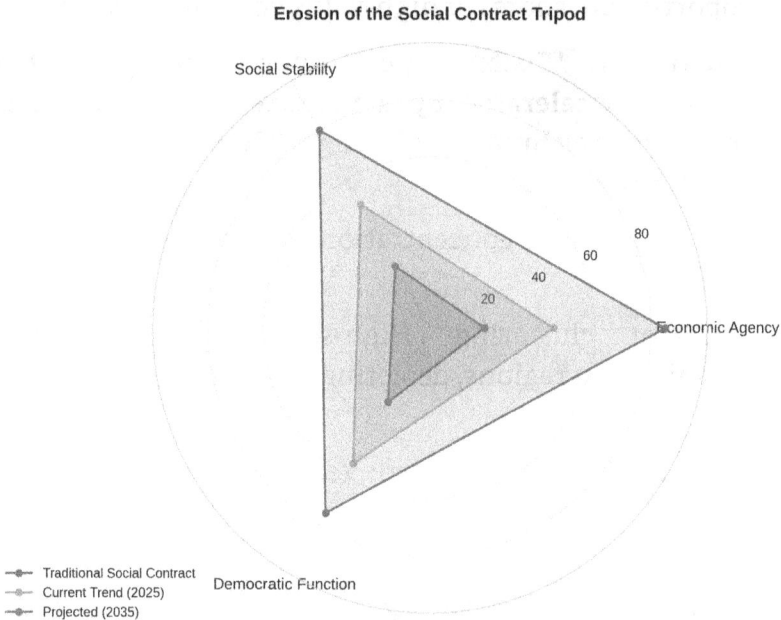

Traditional Social Contract
Current Trend (2025)
Projected (2035)

Case Study 1: Retail and Customer Service

The retail sector provides a clear example of how automation affects employment quantity, quality, and bargaining power. Between 2015 and 2025, approximately 2.3 million retail jobs in the United States were eliminated or fundamentally transformed by technologies including self-checkout systems, inventory management AI, and e-commerce platforms.

While these technologies created new roles in data analysis, software development, and logistics, the net effect was a significant reduction in total employment and a qualitative shift in required skills. For every high-skill position created, approximately 3.7 traditional retail roles were eliminated.

More significantly, the remaining retail positions experienced substantial changes in job quality. Increased monitoring through algorithmic management systems intensified work expectations while reducing autonomy. Scheduling algorithms optimized for employer flexibility rather than worker stability, creating unpredictable income patterns that complicated financial planning.

The economic agency impact extended beyond those who lost jobs to affect workers who remained employed but experienced diminished bargaining power, reduced hours, and increased precarity. Many shifted to gig economy platforms like Instacart or DoorDash, trading traditional employment for flexible but insecure income streams with limited benefits or advancement opportunities.

This transformation occurred during a period when the retail sector as a whole experienced significant revenue growth and productivity improvements. The economic gains from these advances flowed primarily to shareholders and executives rather than frontline workers, exemplifying the core dynamic of the economic agency paradox.

Case Study 2: Legal Services

The legal profession—traditionally considered secure, prestigious, and well-compensated—demonstrates how the economic agency paradox extends into knowledge work domains. Between 2018 and 2025, AI-powered legal tools transformed multiple aspects of legal practice, from document review to contract analysis, legal research, and even brief writing.

These technologies dramatically improved productivity while reducing the number of billable hours required for many tasks. A 2024 study by the American Bar Association found that tasks that previously required 100 attorney hours could typically be completed in 15-20 hours using AI assistance, with equal or superior quality.

This productivity improvement created significant value but led to structural changes in the legal labour market. Entry-level associate positions at major firms declined by approximately 30% between 2018 and 2025, as work previously performed by junior attorneys was increasingly automated. Paralegals and legal assistants experienced even steeper employment declines, with approximately 45% of positions eliminated or fundamentally transformed.

INSIGHT: 5. "The 'skills gap' narrative is a convenient myth that blames individuals for systemic failures, distracting us from the reality that no amount of retraining will preserve labor's bargaining power in an AI-dominated economy."

While experienced attorneys with established client relationships maintained strong economic positions, new law school graduates faced a dramatically altered opportunity landscape. The traditional career path of joining a firm and gradually building expertise through apprenticeship-like progression became increasingly unavailable, creating a "missing middle" in legal career development.

The economic returns from these productivity improvements flowed primarily to law firm partners and corporate legal department leaders rather than being distributed across the profession. This created a bifurcated market where a smaller number of highly successful attorneys captured an increasing share of sector income, while many others experienced diminished opportunities and economic agency despite similar educational investments.

Case Study 3: Healthcare Diagnostics

Healthcare provides a particularly nuanced example of the economic agency paradox, as AI implementation simultaneously improves patient outcomes while transforming professional roles and economic returns.

Diagnostic specialties like radiology and pathology have experienced the most significant impacts. AI diagnostic systems now routinely outperform human specialists in accuracy for many conditions, from diabetic retinopathy to lung cancer, breast cancer, and skin lesions. These systems can analyze images in seconds rather than minutes, don't experience fatigue, and continuously improve through exposure to new data.

The economic and professional implications have been substantial. While few radiologists or pathologists have lost their jobs outright, the nature of their work has fundamentally changed. Rather than serving as primary diagnosticians, many now function as AI supervisors and exception handlers —reviewing flagged cases and managing edge scenarios the AI cannot confidently resolve.

This role transformation has economic consequences. New radiologists and pathologists typically earn 15-25% less than their predecessors did a decade ago, despite similar educational investments and technical skills. The supply-demand balance has shifted as each specialist can effectively cover a larger patient population with AI assistance, reducing the market value of these previously scarce skills.

More significantly, the economic returns from improved diagnostic efficiency flow primarily to hospital systems, insurance companies, and technology providers rather than to the medical professionals themselves. The productivity gains are real and benefit patients through faster, more accurate diagnoses, but the economic value distribution has shifted away from the human experts who previously captured much of the premium for these specialized services.

The Structural Drivers of the Paradox
The economic agency paradox is not a temporary disruption

but a structural transformation driven by fundamental changes in how value is created and distributed in an AI-dominated economy. Four interconnected drivers make this challenge particularly difficult to address through traditional policy approaches.

Driver 1: The Declining Labour Share of Income

Perhaps the most fundamental driver is the declining share of national income flowing to labour as opposed to capital. Across OECD countries, the labour share of income has fallen from an average of approximately 65% in the 1970s to 56% by 2020, with the decline accelerating in sectors with high technology adoption.

This shift reflects the changing relative contributions of labour and capital to production. As AI and automation technologies assume more productive roles, the marginal value of human labour decreases relative to the value of the technology itself. This creates a structural shift in income flows toward capital owners rather than workers.

The declining labour share represents a fundamental challenge to traditional economic distribution mechanisms. When most production required significant human input, directing a substantial portion of income to workers was both economically necessary and aligned with productivity contribution. As that input requirement diminishes, the economic logic of income distribution through labour markets weakens.

Driver 2: Winner-Take-Most Market Dynamics

The second structural driver emerges from the economics of digital and AI-powered markets, which typically demonstrate strong network effects, scale advantages, and winner-take-most dynamics. Unlike traditional industries where market share typically distributed across multiple competitors, digital markets often consolidate around a small number of dominant platforms.

These dynamics create unprecedented wealth concentration. The five largest U.S. technology companies (Apple, Microsoft, Alphabet, Amazon, and Meta) now represent approximately 25% of the S&P 500's total market capitalization—a level of concentration unseen since the industrial monopolies of the early 20th century.

More significantly, these companies generate extraordinary value with relatively few employees. In 2025, the combined market capitalization of these five firms exceeded $12 trillion, while their total employment was approximately 1.8 million workers—less than 1.2% of the U.S. workforce. This represents a fundamental shift from previous industrial giants like General Motors, which at its peak employed over 600,000 workers directly and supported millions more through its supply chain.

This concentration means that the economic benefits of technological advancement flow disproportionately to a small number of companies, their shareholders, and their highest-skilled employees, rather than being broadly distributed throughout the economy. The traditional assumption that productivity improvements would eventually create broad-based prosperity through competitive markets appears increasingly questionable in these winner-take-most environments.

INSIGHT: 6. "The concentration of AI capabilities in a handful of corporations represents the most significant threat to democratic governance since the rise of fascism in the 1930s."

Driver 3: The Globalization of Labour Markets

The third structural driver involves the globalization of labour markets, which increases competitive pressure on workers while reducing their bargaining power. Digital technologies enable work to be disaggregated and distributed globally, creating what economist Richard Baldwin terms "telemigration"—the ability of workers to provide services remotely across national boundaries.

This capability dramatically expands the effective labour supply for many roles, placing downward pressure on wages even for skilled positions. A software developer in San Francisco now effectively competes with counterparts in Bangalore, Warsaw, or Lagos—a competitive dynamic that constrains wage growth even as productivity increases.

More significantly, this global labour market creates fundamental power imbalances. Capital can move freely across borders while labour mobility remains constrained by immigration policies, language barriers, and cultural factors. This asymmetry allows employers to access global labour pools while workers remain largely bound to local labour markets, further shifting bargaining power toward capital.

Driver 4: The Financialization of the Economy

The fourth structural driver involves the increasing dominance of the financial sector in economic activity and value capture. Financial assets now represent a significantly larger portion of total wealth than in previous decades, and financial engineering often generates higher returns than productive investment in the real economy.

This financialization creates several challenges for economic agency:

1. Short-termism: Financial markets typically prioritize quarterly results over long-term investments, encouraging cost-cutting (often through automation and workforce reduction) rather than capability building.

2. Asset inflation: Financial flows into housing, stocks, and other assets drive price increases that benefit existing owners while creating barriers to entry for those without initial capital.

3. Rent extraction: Financial intermediation captures an

increasing share of economic value without necessarily creating corresponding productive capacity.

4. Volatility: Financial market fluctuations create economic instability that disproportionately affects those without significant capital buffers.

These dynamics further concentrate economic returns toward capital owners while creating additional challenges for those relying primarily on labour income for economic security.

The Inadequacy of Traditional Responses

Given the structural nature of the economic agency paradox, traditional policy responses prove increasingly inadequate. Three conventional approaches demonstrate particular limitations in addressing the fundamental challenges of the post-labour transition.

The Education and Training Fallacy

The most common response to technological disruption has been to emphasize education and training—helping workers develop new skills to remain competitive in changing labour markets. While education remains valuable for multiple reasons, it faces significant limitations as a solution to the economic agency paradox.

First, the pace of technological change increasingly outstrips human learning capacity. When AI systems can master new domains in days or weeks while humans require months or years, a perpetual skills gap becomes inevitable regardless of educational investment. The half-life of technical skills continues to shorten, creating a situation where workers must continuously reskill simply to maintain their current position.

Second, education alone cannot address the fundamental oversupply of labour relative to demand in an increasingly automated economy. When the total quantity of economically necessary human work diminishes, even highly skilled workers face competitive pressures that constrain their bargaining power and economic returns.

Third, educational opportunity itself remains unequally distributed, often reinforcing rather than mitigating existing advantages. Those with initial economic, social, and geographic advantages typically access higher-quality education and leverage it more effectively, potentially widening rather than narrowing economic disparities.

INSIGHT: 7. "The current trajectory of AI development virtually guarantees a neo-feudal economic structure within two decades unless we implement radical ownership reforms."

While education and training programs should certainly continue and expand, they cannot independently resolve the structural challenges of the economic agency paradox. At best, they allow some individuals to compete more effectively for a potentially shrinking pool of well-compensated roles; at worst, they create false expectations and delay more fundamental systemic reforms.

The Job Creation Limitation

A second traditional response focuses on job creation through economic growth, infrastructure investment, and entrepreneurship support. While these approaches have merit, they face increasing limitations in an AI-dominated economy.

The fundamental challenge is that new business formation and economic growth no longer generate employment at historical rates. A 2024 study by the Brookings Institution found that each $1 million in new economic activity generated approximately 60% fewer jobs in 2023 than in 1980, with the relationship continuing to weaken as AI adoption accelerates.

This "jobless growth" phenomenon appears across sectors

and development stages. Startup companies that reach billion-dollar valuations today typically employ 80-90% fewer workers than similarly valued companies did two decades ago. Mature industries experiencing growth often do so through productivity improvements rather than workforce expansion.

Even when new jobs emerge, they increasingly demonstrate the characteristics of the economic agency paradox—lower security, reduced bargaining power, and a smaller share of value capture compared to capital. Creating more jobs with these characteristics may increase employment statistics without meaningfully addressing the underlying economic agency challenges.

The Growth and Redistribution Dilemma

The third traditional approach combines economic growth with redistributive policies—using taxation and transfers to share productivity gains more broadly. While this approach has historical precedent in welfare state development, it faces significant practical and political challenges in the current environment.

Practically, the increasing mobility of capital and high-skill labour creates jurisdictional competition that constrains redistributive capacity. When capital and talent can relocate to more favorable tax environments, individual nations face pressure to limit redistributive policies or risk economic outflows.

Politically, redistributive approaches often create sharp divisions between those who primarily earn income through labour and those who primarily receive returns on capital. These divisions can undermine the social cohesion and political consensus necessary for substantial policy reform.

More fundamentally, purely redistributive approaches maintain a problematic distinction between "productive" participants who create economic value and "dependent" recipients who receive transfers. This distinction becomes increasingly problematic when technological systems rather than human effort generate most economic value, raising deeper questions about the basis for economic participation and reward.

Toward New Frameworks: Bridging the Chasm

Addressing the economic agency paradox requires moving beyond traditional policy approaches to develop new frameworks that reconnect technological productivity with broadly shared prosperity. While subsequent chapters will explore specific solutions in detail, three foundational principles can guide this development.

Principle 1: Broadening Capital Ownership

The first principle involves dramatically expanding capital ownership across the population. If returns increasingly flow to capital rather than labour, broader capital distribution becomes essential for maintaining widely shared prosperity.

This principle can manifest through multiple mechanisms:

1. Sovereign wealth funds: Publicly owned investment funds that generate returns for all citizens, similar to Norway's Government Pension Fund or Alaska's Permanent Fund.

2. Universal basic capital: Programs that provide every citizen with a capital stake through baby bonds, stakeholder grants, or similar mechanisms.

3. Employee ownership expansion: Policies that encourage broader employee ownership of companies through stock options, employee stock ownership plans (ESOPs), or cooperative structures.

4. Community wealth building: Strategies that develop community-owned assets generating returns for local residents rather than external shareholders.

These approaches share a common goal: ensuring that productivity gains from technological advancement generate returns for everyone, not just existing capital owners. By broadening capital ownership, they create income streams that don't depend on traditional employment, helping bridge the gap between technological productivity and individual economic agency.

Principle 2: Redefining Contribution and Reward

The second principle involves reconsidering what constitutes valuable contribution in an economy where traditional labour input becomes less central to production. This requires expanding our conception of economically valuable activity beyond market employment.

Several approaches demonstrate this principle:

1. Care work recognition: Acknowledging and compensating the essential care work that sustains families and communities but remains largely unrecognized in traditional economic metrics.

2. Commons development: Supporting contributions to shared resources, knowledge, and infrastructure that create broad-based value without necessarily generating market returns.

3. Community service platforms: Creating systems that recognize and reward contributions to community well-being, from environmental stewardship to civic participation.

4. Creative and cultural production: Developing mechanisms to support artistic, cultural, and intellectual contributions that enrich society but face challenges in purely market-based valuation.

These approaches recognize that human contribution extends far beyond what current market mechanisms value and reward. By expanding our conception of valuable activity, they create additional pathways to economic participation and agency beyond traditional employment.

Principle 3: Strengthening Collective Bargaining Power

The third principle focuses on rebalancing power relationships to ensure that productivity gains are shared more equitably between capital and labour, even as the nature of work evolves. This requires developing new forms of collective organization and bargaining appropriate for the changing work landscape.

Several approaches demonstrate this principle:

1. Sectoral bargaining: Moving beyond enterprise-level unionization to establish standards across entire industries or occupations, reducing the ability of employers to undercut conditions through outsourcing or contingent work arrangements.

2. Portable benefits systems: Creating benefit structures that follow workers across multiple employers or work arrangements, addressing the insecurity of non-traditional employment.

3. Data and algorithmic governance: Establishing collective rights regarding data collection, algorithmic management, and workplace surveillance to prevent technology from being used primarily as a control mechanism.

4. Stakeholder governance: Expanding corporate governance to include worker and community representation, ensuring that productivity gains benefit all stakeholders rather than shareholders exclusively.

These approaches recognize that market outcomes reflect power relationships as much as productivity contributions. By strengthening collective voice and representation, they help ensure that technological advancement enhances rather than diminishes individual economic agency.

Conclusion: Navigating the Transition

The economic agency paradox represents perhaps the

most profound challenge of the post-labour transition. When technological advancement simultaneously increases overall economic productivity while undermining the primary mechanism through which most individuals participate in that prosperity, fundamental questions emerge about how we organize economic life.

The evidence presented in this chapter suggests that this paradox is not a temporary disruption but a structural transformation driven by the changing relationship between human labour and economic value creation. Traditional policy responses—focused on education, job creation, and conventional redistribution—prove increasingly inadequate in addressing these structural challenges.

Moving forward requires developing new frameworks that reconnect technological productivity with broadly shared prosperity. By broadening capital ownership, redefining contribution and reward, and strengthening collective bargaining power, we can begin to bridge the economic agency chasm that threatens to undermine the promise of technological advancement.

The following chapters will explore these approaches in greater detail, examining specific policies and models that can help navigate the post-labour transition in ways that enhance rather than diminish human flourishing. By understanding both the challenges and potential solutions, we can work toward an economic future where technological abundance serves human well-being rather than exacerbating inequality and insecurity.

Case Study: The Economic Agency Chasm in Practice - Amazon's Market Power

Amazon provides a compelling case study of how the economic agency chasm manifests in practice. By 2025, Amazon had established unprecedented market power across multiple sectors, creating what economists now refer to as "digital monopsony" - a market condition where a single buyer (Amazon) exerts disproportionate control over suppliers and workers.

The company's evolution illustrates the three dimensions of the economic agency chasm:

Income Dimension: Amazon's marketplace hosts over 9.7 million third-party sellers worldwide, but the relationship is profoundly asymmetric. A 2024 study by the Institute for Local Self-Reliance found that Amazon captures approximately 34% of the revenue generated by third-party sellers - up from 19% in 2014. This extraction has increased even as sellers report shrinking margins, with 61% of surveyed sellers stating they could not survive without Amazon's platform despite the increasingly unfavorable terms.

Wealth Dimension: The wealth accumulation enabled by Amazon's platform model has been staggering. Between 2020 and 2025, Amazon's market capitalization increased by 87%, while the average net worth of third-party sellers on its platform declined by 18% in real terms. This wealth transfer mechanism operates continuously and systematically, concentrating capital with the platform owner while those dependent on the platform experience diminishing returns despite working harder.

Power Dimension: Perhaps most significantly, Amazon's algorithmic governance system demonstrates the power asymmetry inherent in the new economic landscape. Sellers report having virtually no recourse when facing account suspensions, search ranking changes, or fee increases. A 2023 survey found that 74% of Amazon sellers had experienced significant revenue drops due to unexplained algorithm changes they could neither understand nor appeal effectively.

The company's "A9" search algorithm exemplifies this power dynamic - it determines product visibility based on over 200 factors that remain largely opaque to sellers. When Amazon adjusted this algorithm in late 2023, an estimated 41% of sellers saw their sales decrease by more than 25% overnight, with no explanation or appeal mechanism available.

What makes Amazon's case particularly instructive is how it demonstrates the self-reinforcing nature of the economic agency chasm. The data collected from sellers and consumers feeds back into Amazon's AI systems, continuously improving its market intelligence and strengthening its negotiating position. Meanwhile, sellers become increasingly dependent on the platform, with 68% reporting they have abandoned independent sales channels due to the difficulty of competing with Amazon's logistics and market reach.

This case illustrates how the economic agency chasm operates not through traditional exploitation but through a new form of structural power imbalance - one that is algorithmic, data-driven, and increasingly difficult to counterbalance through conventional economic policies or individual action.

CHAPTER 4: BEYOND EMPLOYMENT: REDEFINING HUMAN VALUE AND PURPOSE

The Meaning Crisis

Alex Torres, a 36-year-old software engineer, had what many would consider the perfect career trajectory. After graduating with honors in computer science, he spent a decade climbing the corporate ladder at a prestigious tech company, eventually reaching a senior position with a comfortable six-figure salary. From the outside, he embodied professional success.

Yet in 2023, sitting in his sleek downtown apartment surrounded by the trappings of his achievement, Alex found himself in the grip of what his therapist called an "existential crisis." Despite his material comfort and career advancement, he felt a profound emptiness.

"I realized I was spending 50 hours a week optimizing algorithms to make people click on ads more efficiently," he explained. "The work was intellectually challenging, but at the end of the day, what was I really contributing to the world? What would I look back on when I was 80?"

Alex's crisis deepened when his company implemented an advanced AI system that could perform many of his core tasks more efficiently. While he wasn't laid off—he was reassigned to "oversee" the AI—the nature of his work changed dramatically. The creative problem-solving that had once given him satisfaction was now handled by the AI, leaving him in what felt like a hollow supervisory role.

"The irony wasn't lost on me," Alex recalled. "I had more status, more money, and technically more authority than ever before. But I'd never felt less fulfilled or less necessary."

Alex's experience reflects a phenomenon that psychologists and sociologists are increasingly documenting across professions: a crisis of meaning that transcends traditional concerns about employment and income. Even as AI and automation create new forms of work and preserve many people's livelihoods, they're fundamentally altering the psychological relationship between humans and their labour.

This transformation forces us to confront questions that go beyond the economic dimensions of the AI revolution: What makes work meaningful? How do we construct identity and purpose when the traditional markers of professional success are being disrupted? What happens to our sense of self-worth when machines can increasingly do what we've built our identities around?

In response to his crisis, Alex eventually made a radical change. He took a 70% pay cut to join a nonprofit developing AI applications for environmental conservation. "I make less money now, but I've never felt more engaged or purposeful," he said. "The question isn't just whether we'll have jobs in the AI future—it's whether those jobs will fulfill our deeper human needs for meaning, mastery, and contribution."

Alex's journey highlights a crucial dimension of the post-employment future that purely economic analyses often miss: beyond securing livelihoods, we must address the profound human need for purpose and meaning that work has traditionally provided. As we navigate the AI transition, reimagining not just how we make a living but how we make a life may be our most essential challenge.

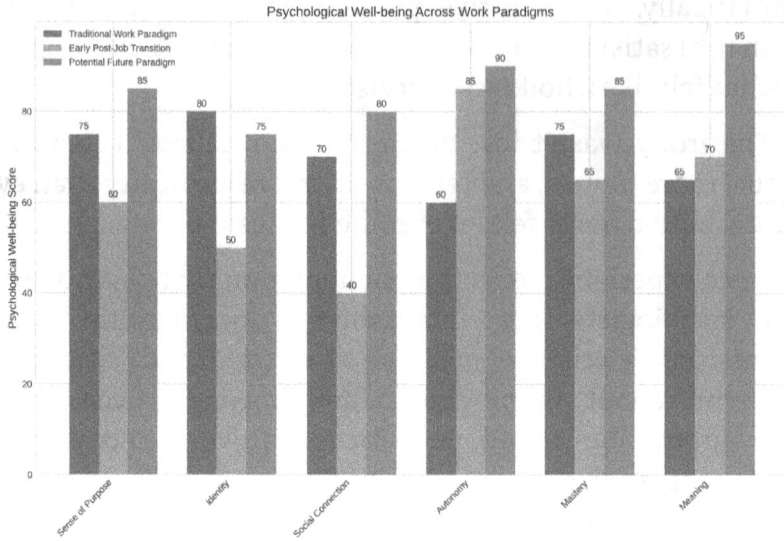

Psychological Well-being Across Work Paradigms

The previous chapters have established the fundamental economic challenges of the AI revolution: Chapter 1 outlined the defining characteristics of the post-labour economy, Chapter 2 examined why AI increasingly outcompetes human labour, and Chapter 3 explored the economic agency paradox that emerges when technological advancement simultaneously increases productivity while undermining the primary mechanism through which most individuals secure their economic participation.

This chapter addresses an equally profound challenge: the psychological, social, and cultural implications of a world where traditional employment no longer serves as the central organizing principle for human life and identity. As paid work becomes less available and less economically necessary, societies face fundamental questions about how individuals derive meaning, purpose, status, and structure in their lives.

The Work-Centric Society: A Recent Historical Development

To understand the magnitude of the transition we face, we must first recognize that our current work-centric social model represents a relatively recent historical development rather than a timeless human arrangement. The centrality of employment to identity, social status, and life purpose is primarily a product of industrial capitalism rather than an inherent feature of human civilization.

Pre-Industrial Work Patterns

For most of human history, work patterns differed substantially from the employment model that dominates modern societies. In hunter-gatherer societies, which represent approximately 95% of human evolutionary history, "work" was indistinguishable from other aspects of life. Activities like hunting, gathering, tool-making, and shelter construction were integrated into daily existence rather than compartmentalized as separate economic functions.

Anthropological research indicates that hunter-gatherer societies typically "worked" (engaged in direct subsistence activities) between 3-5 hours daily, with the remainder of time devoted to social interaction, rest, play, ritual, and creative expression. The concept of "employment" as a distinct life domain simply did not exist.

Agricultural societies introduced more regimented work patterns tied to seasonal cycles, but still lacked the sharp distinction between "work" and "life" that characterizes industrial societies. Farmers worked intensively during planting and harvest seasons but experienced significant downtime during winter months. Craftspeople typically worked from home workshops, with flexible schedules integrated with family and community life.

Even in early urban civilizations, work remained more integrated with other life domains than in modern societies. Merchants might conduct business in the morning and participate in civic or religious activities in the afternoon.

Artisans could pause work to interact with family members or neighbors. The strict temporal and spatial separation of work from other life domains was uncommon.

The Industrial Transformation

The industrial revolution fundamentally transformed human relationships with work through several interconnected developments:

1. Spatial separation: Work moved from homes and community spaces to centralized factories and offices, creating a physical boundary between "work" and "life."

2. Temporal regimentation: Fixed working hours replaced task-oriented time patterns, with productivity measured by time rather than output.

3. Specialization: Workers performed increasingly narrow functions within complex production systems, reducing autonomy and connection to end products.

4. Wage dependency: Direct subsistence activities gave way to complete dependence on monetary wages for survival.

5. Identity formation: Occupational identity became a primary social identifier, with "what do you do?" becoming the standard introduction question.

INSIGHT: The psychological devastation of the AI transition will rival or exceed the Great Depression, with suicide rates potentially doubling in developed nations as millions lose not just income but identity and purpose.

These changes occurred relatively recently in human history—primarily over the past 200-250 years—yet have become so normalized that many consider them natural or inevitable aspects of human society. This historical perspective is crucial for understanding that a post-employment society would not necessarily represent an unprecedented human arrangement but rather a transition to new social forms that might incorporate elements from both pre-industrial and industrial patterns.

The Mid-20th Century Intensification

The centrality of employment to identity and social organization reached its apex in developed economies during the mid-20th century (approximately 1945-1975). During this period, several factors combined to make employment the dominant organizing principle for individual and social life:

1. The family wage: Economic systems in many developed countries evolved to support a model where a single (typically male) wage earner could support an entire family, intensifying the importance of employment for both economic security and social status.

2. Lifelong careers: Many workers could expect to spend their entire working lives with a single employer, strengthening occupational identity and institutional loyalty.

3. Work-based welfare: Social benefits including healthcare, retirement security, and various insurances became increasingly tied to employment status rather than citizenship or residency.

4. Organizational man: Corporate culture celebrated organizational loyalty and identification, with large employers providing not just income but social communities, recreational activities, and status markers.

This period represents the historical peak of employment centrality—a model that has already begun to erode through globalization, automation, and changing social patterns even before the AI revolution. Understanding this historical context helps clarify that the post-employment transition represents not just a future challenge but the continuation of changes already underway for decades.

The Psychological Functions of Work

To understand what might replace employment as an

organizing principle for human life, we must first examine the psychological functions that work currently serves beyond income provision. Research in psychology, sociology, and anthropology identifies several core functions that employment provides in contemporary societies:

Identity and Self-Definition

Perhaps the most fundamental psychological function of work is its role in identity formation and self-definition. In work-centric societies, occupational identity often forms the core of how individuals understand and present themselves to others. The question "What do you do?" typically elicits an occupational response rather than information about family roles, community involvement, or personal interests.

This occupational identity provides several psychological benefits:

1. Social legibility: Occupations provide easily understood social markers that help others categorize and understand an individual's place in society.

2. Competence signaling: Professional roles signal specific competencies and expertise, providing external validation of personal capabilities.

3. Value alignment: Many occupations (teacher, nurse, engineer) implicitly communicate personal values and priorities.

4. Narrative continuity: Career progression provides a coherent narrative structure for understanding one's life development and growth.

When employment becomes less available or central, these identity functions must be fulfilled through alternative mechanisms. The challenge is particularly acute for those whose self-concept is strongly tied to occupational identity —often those in professional, managerial, or skilled trades positions.

Status and Social Recognition

Work serves as the primary status allocation mechanism in most contemporary societies. Occupational prestige hierarchies are remarkably consistent across cultures and provide a structured system for social recognition and respect.

This status function operates through several channels:

1. Occupational prestige: Different occupations carry varying levels of social prestige, with professional and managerial roles typically ranking highest.

2. Achievement markers: Promotions, titles, and career advancement provide visible indicators of success and competence.

3. Income signaling: Employment typically determines income level, which enables consumption patterns that signal status.

4. Contribution recognition: Work provides formal recognition of contributions to society, acknowledging individual value.

As traditional employment declines, societies face the challenge of developing alternative status systems that recognize diverse forms of contribution and achievement. Without such alternatives, status anxiety and social comparison may intensify as traditional markers become less available.

Time Structure and Routine

INSIGHT: 2. "The current mental health crisis is merely a preview of the psychological pandemic that will emerge as AI eliminates the work that has anchored human identity and meaning for centuries."

Employment provides temporal structure to daily life, weekly cycles, and annual patterns. This structuring function offers significant psychological benefits, particularly for mental health and well-being.

Research consistently shows that unemployed individuals struggle not just with income loss but with the dissolution of temporal structure. Without the external demands of work schedules, many experience:

1. Temporal disorientation: Difficulty distinguishing between days or maintaining regular sleep patterns
2. Activity paralysis: Reduced motivation for self-directed activities despite increased available time
3. Decision fatigue: Exhaustion from continually deciding how to use unstructured time
4. Purpose vacuum: Difficulty justifying activities without external expectations or deadlines

These challenges highlight the importance of temporal structure for psychological well-being. As employment becomes less universal, individuals and communities need alternative mechanisms for creating meaningful temporal patterns and routines.

Social Connection and Belonging

Workplaces serve as primary sites for adult social connection, providing regular interaction with individuals outside family networks. For many adults, especially in individualistic societies, work relationships represent their largest source of social contact and community belonging.

The workplace provides several unique social benefits:

1. Diverse connections: Exposure to individuals from different backgrounds, generations, and perspectives
2. Structured interaction: Social contact within defined roles and expectations, reducing social anxiety
3. Collaborative purpose: Shared goals and challenges that create natural bonds and conversation topics
4. Institutional belonging: Identification with an organization larger than oneself

The decline of traditional employment threatens these social functions, potentially exacerbating loneliness and social isolation unless alternative community structures emerge. This challenge is particularly significant in societies where other community institutions (religious organizations, civic groups, extended families) have already weakened.

Competence and Mastery

Work provides structured opportunities to develop skills, demonstrate competence, and experience mastery—psychological needs that contribute significantly to well-being and self-esteem.

The competence function operates through several mechanisms:

1. Skill development: Structured learning opportunities and practice within defined domains
2. Performance feedback: Regular evaluation and recognition of capabilities and contributions
3. Challenge calibration: Tasks matched to skill levels, creating appropriate challenge
4. Achievement recognition: Formal acknowledgment of mastery through promotions, certifications, or expanded responsibilities

These opportunities for competence development and demonstration contribute significantly to psychological well-being. As traditional employment declines, alternative contexts for skill development, challenge, and mastery become increasingly important.

Purpose and Meaning

Perhaps most fundamentally, work provides a ready-made answer to questions of purpose and meaning. Employment offers a socially validated explanation for how one's time and energy contribute to something beyond oneself.

This meaning function operates through several channels:

1. Social contribution: Direct connection between individual effort and benefits to others
2. Value alignment: Activities consistent with personal and cultural values
3. Legacy creation: Contributions that outlast individual effort or lifetime
4. Transcendent purpose: Connection to goals larger than individual self-interest

The meaning derived from work varies significantly across occupations and individuals, but even routine jobs typically provide some sense of purpose through social contribution. As employment becomes less universal, the search for alternative sources of meaning and purpose becomes increasingly important.

The Social Functions of Work

Beyond its psychological functions for individuals, employment serves crucial social functions that stabilize and organize communities and societies. Understanding these functions helps clarify the magnitude of the transition required as employment becomes less central.

Social Integration and Cohesion

Employment creates cross-cutting social ties that integrate diverse individuals into shared systems and institutions. These workplace connections often bridge differences in background, ideology, and identity that might otherwise lead to social fragmentation.

This integration function operates through several mechanisms:

1. Shared contexts: Regular interaction in common environments despite different backgrounds
2. Collaborative necessity: Interdependence that requires cooperation across differences
3. Institutional identification: Common loyalty to organizations that transcends individual differences

4. Economic interdependence: Recognition of mutual benefit from economic cooperation

As employment declines, societies face the challenge of developing alternative mechanisms for social integration across differences. Without such mechanisms, social fragmentation along ideological, cultural, or identity lines may intensify.

Norm Transmission and Socialization

INSIGHT: 3. "Traditional employment has functioned as society's largest mental health program—providing structure, purpose, and social connection. Its rapid dissolution will reveal how psychologically dependent we've become on a system that was never designed for human flourishing."

Workplaces serve as crucial sites for adult socialization, transmitting social norms, behavioral expectations, and cultural values. For many individuals, particularly those from disadvantaged backgrounds, employment provides structured exposure to mainstream behavioral expectations and professional norms.

This socialization function includes:

1. Behavioral standards: Expectations regarding punctuality, reliability, communication, and conflict resolution
2. Cultural competence: Exposure to dominant cultural norms and expectations
3. Professional ethics: Field-specific values and ethical frameworks
4. Organizational citizenship: Norms regarding cooperation, initiative, and institutional loyalty

As employment becomes less universal, societies need alternative mechanisms for transmitting shared norms and expectations, particularly for young adults entering society.

Productivity Channeling and Social Control

Employment channels human energy and time toward socially sanctioned productive activities. This productivity channeling function serves both economic and social control purposes, reducing socially disruptive behavior by occupying time and energy with structured activities.

This function operates through several mechanisms:

1. Time occupation: Structured use of time that reduces opportunity for disruptive activities
2. Energy direction: Channeling of physical and mental energy toward productive outputs
3. Reward alignment: Financial incentives for socially approved behaviors
4. Status provision: Social recognition that reduces status-seeking through disruptive means

As employment becomes less universal, societies face the challenge of developing alternative mechanisms for channeling energy toward constructive activities and providing non-disruptive paths to status and recognition.

Distributional Legitimacy

Perhaps most fundamentally, employment provides moral legitimacy for economic distribution. The principle that individuals "earn" their economic share through work contribution creates perceived fairness in resource allocation, even amid significant inequality.

This legitimacy function operates through several mechanisms:

1. Merit justification: The belief that economic rewards reflect work contribution and value
2. Effort visibility: Observable work input that justifies differential rewards
3. Contribution measurement: Quantifiable metrics (hours, outputs) that rationalize distribution

4. Moral deservingness: Cultural narratives connecting work effort to moral worth

As the connection between work and income weakens through automation, societies face profound challenges to distributional legitimacy. Without alternative frameworks for justifying economic participation, social cohesion and political stability may deteriorate.

Case Studies: Early Manifestations of the Post-Work Challenge

The psychological and social challenges of a post-employment society are not merely theoretical concerns for the future. Early manifestations are already visible in communities experiencing significant employment disruption. Three case studies illustrate these challenges and potential responses:

Case Study 1: Coal Mining Communities in Appalachia

The Appalachian region of the United States provides a compelling case study of communities experiencing rapid employment disruption through technological change and market shifts. Coal mining employment in the region declined from approximately 175,000 jobs in 1985 to fewer than 45,000 by 2020, creating communities where traditional employment became increasingly scarce.

The psychological and social impacts have been severe:

1. Identity crisis: Communities with strong occupational identities tied to mining experienced collective identity disruption, with former miners reporting loss of purpose and self-worth.

2. Status collapse: The disappearance of well-paid, high-status mining jobs created status anxiety and resentment, particularly among men who had defined their social position through these roles.

3. Temporal disruption: Without the structuring function

of shift work, many former miners experienced temporal disorientation and activity paralysis, contributing to increased substance abuse.

4. Social fragmentation: The shared workplace context that previously integrated diverse individuals disappeared, reducing cross-cutting social ties and increasing isolation.

5. Distributional conflict: The legitimacy of economic distribution came into question as the connection between work and income weakened, creating resentment toward both welfare recipients and economic elites.

These communities have experimented with various responses, with mixed success:

1. Skills transition programs: Efforts to retrain miners for alternative employment, which have shown limited success due to geographic constraints and cultural resistance.

2. Cultural preservation initiatives: Programs celebrating mining heritage and culture, which support collective identity but don't address economic needs.

INSIGHT: 5. "The concept of 'meaningful work' is becoming a luxury good available primarily to the elite, while the majority will be forced to find meaning outside economic production."

3. Entrepreneurship development: Support for small business creation, which helps some individuals but cannot replace the scale of lost employment.

4. Universal basic income pilots: Small-scale experiments with unconditional cash transfers, which address immediate economic needs but not the non-economic functions of work.

The Appalachian experience highlights both the magnitude of the post-employment challenge and the inadequacy of purely economic responses that don't address the psychological and social functions of work.

Case Study 2: Automation in Japanese Manufacturing

Japan provides an instructive case study of a society experiencing advanced automation while maintaining social cohesion through cultural adaptations. Japanese manufacturing has implemented industrial robots at rates far exceeding most other developed economies, with approximately 364 robots per 10,000 manufacturing workers by 2023—nearly triple the global average.

This automation has significantly reduced manufacturing employment, yet Japan has maintained relatively low unemployment and social stability through several adaptive mechanisms:

1. Corporate social responsibility: Japanese firms have maintained employment through job redesign, internal transfers, and early retirement programs rather than layoffs, preserving the social contract despite reduced labour needs.

2. Identity diversification: Cultural emphasis on multiple identity sources beyond occupation, including family roles, community participation, and personal interests.

3. Status alternatives: Development of non-occupational status markers through community roles, cultural pursuits, and family position.

4. Temporal structuring: Cultural practices that provide temporal structure through community activities, seasonal observances, and family responsibilities.

5. Social integration: Strong neighborhood associations and community organizations that provide social connection and belonging outside workplace contexts.

While Japan faces significant challenges, including demographic decline and economic stagnation, its experience suggests that cultural adaptations can mitigate some negative impacts of employment disruption. The emphasis on multiple identity sources, community integration, and corporate responsibility offers potential lessons for other societies facing similar transitions.

Case Study 3: The FIRE Movement and Voluntary Employment Reduction

The Financial Independence, Retire Early (FIRE) movement represents a voluntary experiment in reducing employment centrality among primarily high-income professionals in developed economies. Participants typically work intensively for 10-15 years while saving 50-70% of their income, then significantly reduce or eliminate traditional employment decades before conventional retirement age.

This voluntary movement provides insights into both the challenges and opportunities of reduced employment:

1. Identity transition: FIRE participants report significant identity disruption when leaving careers, even when financially secure, highlighting the psychological importance of occupational identity.

2. Purpose creation: Successful transitions typically involve developing alternative purpose sources through community service, creative pursuits, relationship investment, or self-directed learning.

3. Status recalibration: Participants describe developing alternative status frameworks based on time affluence, relationship quality, and personal growth rather than professional achievement or consumption.

4. Temporal autonomy: While initial post-employment periods often involve temporal disorientation, successful participants develop self-directed routines and projects that provide structure without external requirements.

5. Community development: Many FIRE adherents create intentional communities (both physical and virtual) that provide social connection, shared values, and mutual support

outside traditional workplace contexts.

While representing a privileged subset of society with substantial financial resources, the FIRE movement demonstrates both the challenges of identity and purpose in post-employment life and potential adaptive strategies that might inform broader social responses.

The Human Quotient: Capabilities Beyond Automation

As AI capabilities expand, understanding distinctively human attributes becomes increasingly important for both individual adaptation and social reorganization. The concept of the "Human Quotient" provides a framework for identifying and developing capabilities that remain uniquely or predominantly human, even as AI advances.

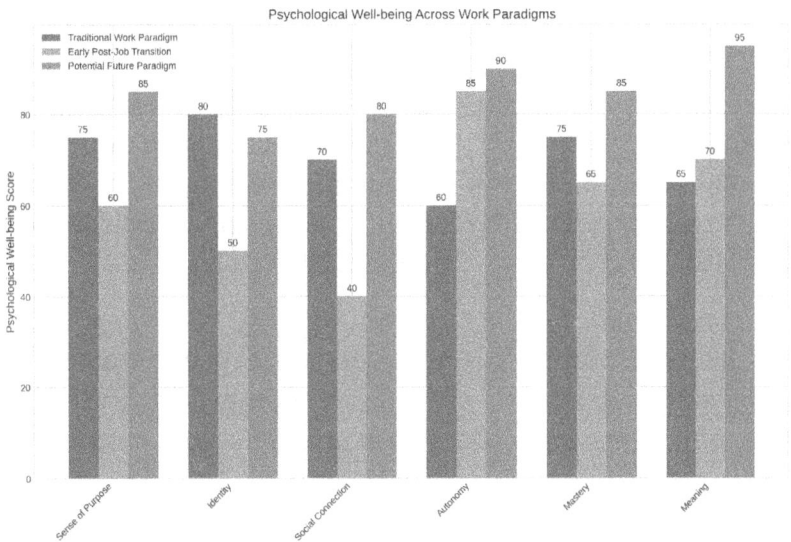

Psychological Well-being Across Work Paradigms

Unlike traditional frameworks focused on intelligence or specific skills, the Human Quotient encompasses five interconnected capability domains that represent enduring human advantages:

Embodied Intuition

Embodied intuition refers to understanding derived from physical existence in the world—the accumulated wisdom of having a body that interacts with physical and social environments. This capability includes:

INSIGHT: 6. "The psychological transition to a post-employment society will be more challenging than the economic one, requiring nothing less than a complete reimagining of how humans construct identity and purpose."

1. Physical empathy: Intuitive understanding of others' physical experiences and needs based on shared embodiment
2. Sensory integration: Holistic processing of multisensory information beyond analytical decomposition
3. Somatic wisdom: Body-based knowledge that informs decision-making below conscious awareness
4. Environmental attunement: Intuitive adaptation to physical contexts and conditions

While AI systems can process vast amounts of data, they lack the embodied experience that informs human intuition. This capability remains particularly valuable in contexts requiring physical interaction, caregiving, environmental adaptation, and intuitive understanding of human needs.

Ethical Reasoning

Ethical reasoning encompasses the capacity to navigate complex moral situations, balance competing values, and make judgments that reflect both principles and context. This capability includes:

1. Value balancing: Weighing different moral considerations without algorithmic reduction
2. Moral imagination: Envisioning ethical implications across diverse perspectives and experiences
3. Contextual judgment: Applying principles flexibly based on specific circumstances
4. Normative innovation: Developing new ethical frameworks for unprecedented situations

While AI systems can be programmed with ethical guidelines or trained on human moral judgments, they lack the lived experience and moral agency that informs human ethical reasoning. This capability remains essential in contexts requiring value judgments, ethical innovation, and balancing competing moral considerations.

Creative Synthesis

Creative synthesis refers to generating novel combinations and approaches that transcend existing patterns and categories. This capability includes:

1. Cross-domain integration: Connecting ideas across disparate fields and knowledge domains
2. Metaphorical thinking: Using analogies and metaphors to understand new situations
3. Constraint transcendence: Moving beyond established boundaries and assumptions
4. Aesthetic judgment: Evaluating creative outputs based on subjective quality and impact

While AI systems can generate variations within learned patterns, human creativity involves subjective judgment, metaphorical leaps, and aesthetic evaluation that remain distinctively human. This capability remains valuable in contexts requiring genuine innovation, artistic expression, and transcending established frameworks.

Social Intelligence

Social intelligence encompasses understanding and navigating complex human relationships, emotions, and social dynamics. This capability includes:

1. Emotional attunement: Recognizing and responding to subtle emotional signals
2. Perspective taking: Understanding others' viewpoints, needs, and motivations
3. Relationship building: Developing trust and connection across differences

4. Group dynamics management: Navigating and influencing collective behavior

While AI systems can recognize basic emotional signals and simulate social responses, human social intelligence involves intuitive understanding of complex social contexts that remains beyond current AI capabilities. This capability remains essential in contexts requiring genuine emotional connection, trust building, conflict resolution, and community development.

Existential Wisdom

Existential wisdom refers to making meaning from the human condition—finding purpose, value, and significance within the constraints of mortality and uncertainty. This capability includes:

1. Meaning creation: Developing frameworks for understanding life's significance
2. Existential courage: Facing uncertainty and limitation with resilience
3. Value prioritization: Determining what matters most within finite lives
4. Transcendent connection: Experiencing belonging to something beyond individual existence

While AI systems can process information about human values and beliefs, they lack the existential stakes that inform human wisdom about meaning and purpose. This capability remains uniquely human and increasingly valuable as material needs are met through automation.

Reimagining Identity, Status, and Purpose

As employment becomes less universal and central, societies face the challenge of developing alternative frameworks for identity formation, status allocation, and purpose creation. Several emerging models offer potential directions for this reimagining:

Contribution Portfolios: Beyond Occupational Identity

The contribution portfolio model replaces singular occupational identity with a diversified set of activities through which individuals create value and meaning. Rather than defining oneself primarily through employment ("I am a teacher"), individuals develop multiple contribution streams that collectively constitute identity ("I educate children, create digital art, and coordinate community gardens").

This approach offers several advantages:

1. Resilience: Multiple identity sources provide stability when any single domain faces disruption
2. Adaptability: Portfolio elements can evolve as interests, capabilities, and opportunities change
3. Personalization: Unique combinations reflect individual values, talents, and priorities
4. Integration: Reduced separation between "work" and "life" domains

Early adopters of this model include freelancers, portfolio workers, and participants in the "slash careers" movement (e.g., teacher/writer/coach). Their experiences highlight both the benefits of identity diversification and the challenges of managing multiple domains without institutional structure.

For this approach to scale beyond early adopters, several supports are needed:

1. Cultural narratives: Stories and examples that normalize and celebrate multifaceted identities
2. Institutional recognition: Systems that acknowledge diverse contributions beyond employment
3. Temporal frameworks: Structures that help individuals allocate time across multiple domains
4. Financial mechanisms: Economic supports that enable contribution beyond market employment

INSIGHT: 7. "Most current approaches to 'future of work'

are fundamentally designed to preserve employment as the central organizing principle of society—a goal that is both impossible and undesirable in an AI-dominated economy."

Status Pluralism: Diversifying Recognition Systems

Status pluralism involves developing multiple, parallel status systems that recognize diverse forms of contribution, achievement, and excellence. Rather than a single prestige hierarchy dominated by professional achievement, this approach creates multiple pathways to social recognition and respect.

Emerging examples include:

1. Care status: Recognition systems that honor excellence in family and community care work
2. Creative status: Platforms that acknowledge artistic and creative contributions
3. Learning status: Frameworks that recognize continuous learning and knowledge development
4. Community status: Systems that honor civic contribution and community building

For status pluralism to effectively replace occupational prestige, these alternative status systems require:

1. Visibility mechanisms: Ways to make diverse contributions observable to others
2. Credible evaluation: Trusted assessment of quality and impact within each domain
3. Cultural validation: Shared social agreement about the value of different contribution types
4. Status markers: Symbols and signals that communicate achievement across domains

The challenge lies in developing status systems that provide meaningful recognition without reproducing the exclusionary aspects of current prestige hierarchies.

Purpose Ecosystems: Beyond

Employment-Based Meaning

Purpose ecosystems represent networks of activities, relationships, and contexts that collectively provide meaning and direction beyond employment. Rather than deriving purpose primarily from occupational contribution, individuals develop purpose portfolios spanning multiple domains.

Components of purpose ecosystems typically include:

1. Care relationships: Meaningful connections with family, friends, and community members
2. Creative expression: Activities that develop and share creative capabilities
3. Learning journeys: Ongoing growth and development across knowledge domains
4. Legacy projects: Contributions designed to outlast individual lifetimes
5. Transcendent connection: Experiences of belonging to something larger than oneself

Early examples of purpose ecosystem development appear in intentional communities, meaning-focused educational programs, and post-career transitions. These experiences highlight the importance of both individual agency in purpose creation and supportive contexts that validate diverse sources of meaning.

For purpose ecosystems to effectively replace employment-based meaning, several supports are needed:

1. Purpose literacy: Education in identifying and developing personal sources of meaning
2. Contribution infrastructure: Platforms connecting individual capabilities with social needs
3. Meaning communities: Groups that provide shared purpose and mutual support
4. Cultural narratives: Stories that validate diverse paths to meaningful contribution

Temporal Autonomy: Restructuring Time Beyond Employment

Temporal autonomy involves developing self-directed temporal structures that provide rhythm and organization without employment requirements. Rather than having time structured primarily by work schedules, individuals and communities create alternative temporal frameworks.

Emerging approaches include:

1. Project-based structuring: Organizing time around self-directed projects with defined goals and timelines
2. Ritual temporality: Using regular practices and observances to create daily, weekly, and seasonal rhythms
3. Community synchronization: Coordinating activities with others to create shared temporal patterns
4. Natural alignment: Structuring time in harmony with natural cycles and rhythms

Early adopters of temporal autonomy include digital nomads, sabbatical takers, and intentional communities with alternative temporal practices. Their experiences highlight both the freedom and challenge of self-directed time structuring.

For temporal autonomy to effectively replace employment-based structuring, several supports are needed:

1. Temporal literacy: Education in self-directed time management and structuring
2. Coordination platforms: Tools for synchronizing activities with others outside employment contexts
3. Rhythm-supporting infrastructure: Community spaces and services available beyond standard work hours
4. Cultural permission: Social validation of diverse temporal patterns beyond the work/leisure binary

Policy Implications: Supporting the Transition

The transition from employment-centricity to more diverse

frameworks for identity, status, and purpose requires supportive policy environments. While subsequent chapters will address economic policies in detail, several approaches specifically target the psychological and social dimensions of the transition:

Education for Post-Employment Flourishing

Educational systems designed for industrial economies primarily prepare students for employment roles. A post-employment society requires education that develops capabilities for flourishing beyond traditional work contexts.

Key elements include:

1. Purpose education: Developing skills for identifying personal sources of meaning and contribution
2. Identity diversification: Supporting the development of multifaceted rather than occupation-centered identities
3. Temporal autonomy: Building capabilities for self-directed time management and structuring
4. Contribution literacy: Developing diverse ways to create value beyond employment contexts
5. Human Quotient development: Cultivating distinctively human capabilities that transcend automation

Promising models include Finland's "life skills" curriculum, Singapore's SkillsFuture program for continuous learning, and various "gap year" programs that develop self-direction capabilities. These approaches recognize that flourishing in a post-employment society requires different preparation than success in traditional career paths.

Community Infrastructure for Connection and Contribution

As workplaces become less universal contexts for social connection and contribution, alternative infrastructure becomes increasingly important. Public investment in physical and organizational spaces for community engagement can support the social functions previously provided by workplaces.

Key elements include:

1. Multipurpose community centers: Physical spaces for diverse activities and connections
2. Contribution platforms: Systems connecting individual capabilities with community needs
3. Intergenerational programs: Structured opportunities for cross-age interaction and learning
4. Civic participation infrastructure: Frameworks for meaningful involvement in community governance
5. Digital commons: Online spaces for collaboration, learning, and connection

Promising models include Barcelona's "superblocks" that prioritize community space, Seoul's sharing city initiative, and various timebanking systems that facilitate service exchange outside market mechanisms. These approaches recognize that social infrastructure becomes increasingly important as workplace contexts decline.

Transition Support for Identity Adaptation

As employment disruption accelerates, many individuals face challenging transitions from work-centered to more diversified identities. Dedicated support services can facilitate these transitions and prevent psychological distress.

Key elements include:

1. Identity counseling: Professional support for navigating identity transitions
2. Peer communities: Groups of individuals experiencing similar transitions
3. Purpose exploration programs: Structured processes for identifying alternative sources of meaning
4. Status recalibration support: Assistance developing new frameworks for achievement and recognition
5. Narrative development: Help creating coherent life stories

that integrate past work identity with new directions

Promising models include Sweden's job security councils, which provide holistic transition support beyond mere job placement, and various midlife renewal programs that support identity exploration during career transitions. These approaches recognize that identity adaptation requires both psychological support and practical assistance.

Cultural Evolution Support

Perhaps most fundamentally, the transition from employment-centricity requires cultural evolution—shifts in shared narratives, values, and norms regarding contribution, success, and meaning. While cultural change cannot be directly legislated, policy can support environments where new cultural models can emerge and spread.

Key elements include:

1. Narrative development: Support for media, arts, and storytelling that explore post-employment models
2. Visibility platforms: Showcasing diverse examples of flourishing beyond traditional employment
3. Language evolution: Developing new terminology that transcends the work/leisure binary
4. Norm experimentation spaces: Supporting communities exploring alternative social arrangements
5. Intergenerational dialogue: Facilitating exchange between generations with different work experiences

Promising models include South Korea's work hour reduction campaign, which explicitly addresses cultural as well as policy dimensions, and various "future of work" initiatives that engage communities in reimagining social organization. These approaches recognize that cultural evolution requires both bottom-up experimentation and top-down support.

Conclusion: The Human Challenge Beyond Economics

The post-employment transition presents challenges that extend far beyond economic distribution. As AI and automation technologies reduce the centrality of human labour in production, societies face fundamental questions about how individuals develop identity, achieve status, create meaning, and structure time outside traditional employment contexts.

This challenge is not merely theoretical or distant. Early manifestations already appear in communities experiencing employment disruption, from deindustrialized regions to automated sectors. Their experiences highlight both the psychological and social dimensions of the transition and the inadequacy of purely economic responses.

Moving forward requires developing new frameworks for human flourishing beyond employment—contribution portfolios that diversify identity, status pluralism that recognizes diverse achievements, purpose ecosystems that generate meaning across domains, and temporal autonomy that structures time beyond work schedules.

These developments require both individual adaptation and systemic support. Educational systems must evolve to develop capabilities for post-employment flourishing. Community infrastructure must expand to provide connection and contribution contexts. Transition services must support identity adaptation. Cultural evolution must create new narratives of success and meaning.

The ultimate challenge extends beyond ensuring material provision in an automated economy—though that remains essential. The deeper question involves reimagining human flourishing itself when traditional employment no longer serves as the central organizing principle for individual and social life. By developing new frameworks for identity, status, purpose, and time, societies can potentially create post-employment arrangements that enhance rather than diminish human well-being and social cohesion.

The following chapter will build on this understanding by examining specific economic mechanisms for maintaining broad-based agency and participation in an increasingly automated economy.

Case Study: The Psychological Impact of Work Redefinition - The Coding Profession

The transformation of the coding profession between 2023 and 2026 provides a revealing case study of how AI is redefining the psychological relationship between humans and work beyond simple job displacement.

In early 2023, software development was considered among the most secure and intellectually rewarding professions. Surveys showed that 82% of professional developers reported high job satisfaction, with "creative problem-solving" and "intellectual challenge" cited as the primary sources of fulfillment. The average developer spent approximately 70% of their time writing original code and 30% on maintenance, debugging, and administrative tasks.

By mid-2025, this ratio had dramatically inverted. With the widespread adoption of advanced AI coding assistants like GitHub Copilot X, Anthropic Claude for Coding, and Google's DeepMind Developer, the nature of software development underwent a profound transformation. A comprehensive industry study conducted by Stack Overflow in partnership with MIT found that professional developers now spent only 23% of their time writing original code, with the remainder devoted to prompt engineering, code review, system architecture, and integration tasks.

The psychological impact of this shift was multifaceted and complex:

Identity Crisis: Interviews with developers revealed widespread identity disruption. As one senior engineer at

Microsoft expressed: "I used to define myself by my ability to solve complex coding problems. Now the AI solves those problems faster and more elegantly than I ever could. My job is to guide the AI, not to code myself. It's efficient, but I've lost the core activity that defined my professional identity."

Skill Devaluation: A longitudinal study tracking 1,200 developers found that 68% reported experiencing "skill obsolescence anxiety" - the fear that their hard-earned technical abilities were rapidly losing value. This anxiety manifested despite the fact that most remained employed, often at higher salaries than before.

Meaning and Purpose: Perhaps most significantly, the psychological rewards of the profession shifted dramatically. The satisfaction derived from creative problem-solving declined by 47%, while new sources of meaning emerged around system design and AI collaboration. However, these new sources of fulfillment were reported as "less intrinsically rewarding" by a majority of participants.

Adaptation Strategies: The study identified three distinct psychological adaptation patterns among developers:
1. "Prompt Engineers" (41%) - Those who embraced the new paradigm and found satisfaction in mastering the art of AI collaboration
2. "Architecture Specialists" (37%) - Those who moved up the abstraction ladder to focus on system design rather than implementation
3. "Coding Traditionalists" (22%) - Those who actively sought niches where human-written code remained valuable, often accepting lower compensation for greater autonomy

The case illustrates how AI is transforming work beyond simple displacement - it's fundamentally altering the psychological relationship between professionals and their craft. Even in fields where employment remains robust, the qualitative experience of work and its role in providing meaning, identity, and fulfillment is being profoundly disrupted.

This transformation suggests that addressing the psychological dimension of the post-employment future may be just as important as solving its economic challenges. As one study participant noted: "I'm still employed and well-paid. But the work that once gave me deep satisfaction now feels hollow. I'm not sure any universal basic income or wealth redistribution scheme can compensate for that loss."

CHAPTER 5: REBUILDING AGENCY: NEW FOUNDATIONS FOR ECONOMIC DISTRIBUTION

Rebuilding Agency in the Age of AI

In 2023, Maria Gonzalez found herself in a situation that's becoming increasingly common in the AI era. After eight years as a customer service representative for a major telecommunications company, she received the email that employees had been dreading: her department was implementing an advanced AI system that could handle 85% of customer interactions more efficiently than human agents.

Unlike many of her colleagues who were laid off, Maria was offered a transition to a new role "supervising" the AI system—essentially monitoring its performance and handling the small percentage of cases it couldn't resolve. The new position came with slightly higher pay but stripped her of the autonomy and human connection that had made her previous role meaningful.

"I went from having real conversations where I could use my judgment and empathy to basically watching a dashboard and waiting for exceptions," Maria explained. "The AI made all the decisions—which customers got what offers, how long to spend on each call, even the exact language to use in specific situations. I felt like I'd been reduced to a human failsafe for a machine."

What happened next illustrates the central challenge of rebuilding agency in the AI economy. Initially, Maria fell into depression as she mourned the loss of autonomy in her work. But rather than accepting her diminished role, she began organizing weekly meetings with other "AI supervisors" across different departments. Together, they documented patterns in the AI's performance—which types of customers it served well, where it consistently failed, and how its decision-making affected different demographic groups.

After three months of careful documentation, Maria and her colleagues presented company leadership with evidence that the AI system was systematically underserving Spanish-speaking customers and elderly clients, costing the company both revenue and customer loyalty. More importantly, they proposed a solution: a collaborative human-AI approach where agents would have greater discretion to override the system for certain customer segments.

"We didn't fight against the technology—that would have been futile," Maria recalled. "Instead, we reclaimed our agency by becoming experts in the AI's limitations and advocating for a more balanced approach."

The company implemented their recommendations as a pilot program, which proved so successful it was expanded company-wide. Maria was promoted to lead a new "AI-Human Collaboration Team" with significantly higher compensation and genuine decision-making authority.

Maria's experience illustrates a crucial truth about agency in the AI era: it rarely comes from resisting technological change outright, nor from passively accepting diminished roles. Instead, rebuilding agency requires developing new forms of expertise, collective action, and strategic engagement with the very technologies that threaten to disempower us.

As we navigate the profound economic transformations driven by artificial intelligence, Maria's story offers an important perspective. The question isn't simply whether AI will eliminate jobs or create new ones—it's whether humans will retain meaningful agency in the new economic landscape, and what strategies might help us reclaim it when it's threatened.

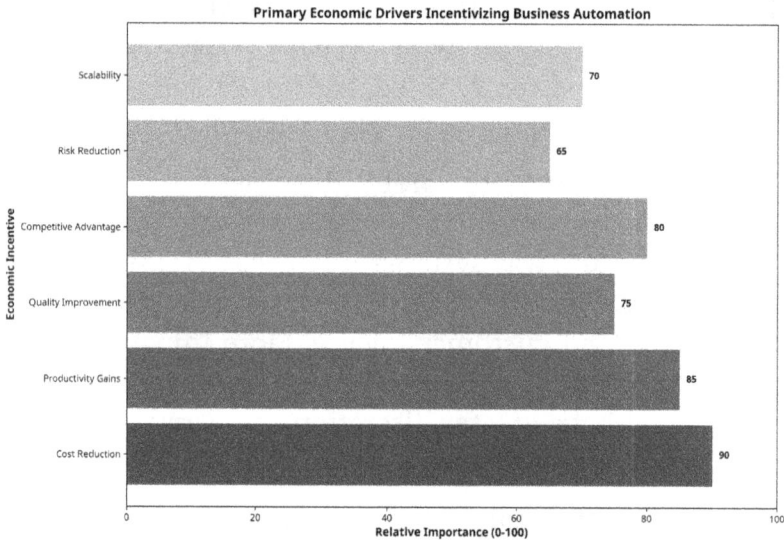

Primary Economic Drivers Incentivizing Business Automation

Introduction: The Distribution Challenge in a Post-Labour Economy

As artificial intelligence increasingly displaces human labour across economic sectors, we face a fundamental distribution challenge: how can we ensure broad-based economic agency when traditional employment no longer serves as the primary mechanism for distributing income and opportunity? This question strikes at the heart of our economic systems and social contracts, demanding innovative approaches that move beyond conventional policy frameworks.

The preceding chapters have established the structural nature of this challenge. We have examined how AI-driven automation differs fundamentally from previous technological transitions, potentially eliminating the need for human labour across vast swathes of the economy rather than merely shifting it between sectors. We have explored how this transformation undermines the wage-labour bargain that has served as the foundation for economic distribution in capitalist democracies for generations.

This chapter advances beyond diagnosis to explore potential solutions—new foundations for economic distribution that could maintain and potentially enhance human agency in a post-labour economy. We examine four broad approaches: universal basic income, universal capital ownership, commons-based production, and contribution income. Each represents not merely a policy proposal but a fundamental reimagining of how economic value might be distributed when the traditional link between labour and income is severed.

Our analysis recognizes that these approaches are not mutually exclusive but potentially complementary elements of a comprehensive response to the distribution challenge. We also acknowledge that effective solutions must address not only income distribution but deeper questions of economic agency, democratic participation, and transitional support for those most affected by automation-driven displacement.

The Inadequacy of Conventional Responses

Before exploring alternative distribution mechanisms, we must understand why conventional policy responses prove inadequate to address the structural challenge of AI-driven labour displacement. Traditional approaches typically fall into three categories: education and retraining, job creation through public investment, and work-sharing through reduced working hours.

Education and Retraining: The Skills Gap Fallacy

INSIGHT: The concept of individual agency in the traditional sense is becoming obsolete—in an AI-dominated economy, genuine agency will only exist at the collective level through new forms of democratic organization.

The conventional wisdom that education and retraining can solve technological unemployment rests on a fundamental misconception: that there exists a stable set of skills that, once acquired, will remain valuable despite advancing automation. This "skills gap" framing suggests that unemployment results primarily from a mismatch between worker capabilities and job requirements rather than a structural decline in labour demand.

This framing becomes increasingly untenable as AI systems demonstrate capabilities across domains previously considered uniquely human. The historical pattern where technological advancement created new categories of work requiring different human skills may not hold when AI systems can potentially perform most cognitive, creative, and even social tasks more efficiently than humans.

Even if education and retraining could temporarily address displacement in specific sectors, several limitations remain:

1. Pace of Change: The accelerating rate of AI capability development means that newly acquired skills may become obsolete before providing sustainable economic returns.

2. Capacity Constraints: Not all workers possess equal capacity to acquire the increasingly complex skills that might remain valuable in an AI-dominated economy.

3. Aggregate Demand: Even if individual workers successfully retrain, this does not address the aggregate decline in labour demand that occurs when AI systems can perform most productive tasks more efficiently.

4. Diminishing Returns: As more workers compete for a shrinking pool of non-automated roles, the economic returns to education and training likely diminish.

While education and skill development remain valuable for human flourishing beyond economic returns, they cannot serve as the primary solution to structural labour displacement in an AI-driven economy.

Job Creation: The Fiscal and Demand Constraints

Public investment in job creation—whether through infrastructure projects, expanded public services, or subsidized private employment—represents another conventional response to technological unemployment. While such approaches can provide valuable transitional support, they face significant limitations as long-term solutions to AI-driven displacement:

1. Fiscal Constraints: Creating jobs through public spending faces fiscal limitations, particularly if the tax base erodes as labour income declines relative to capital returns.

2. Efficiency Tradeoffs: Maintaining human employment in roles where AI systems could operate more efficiently creates economic distortions and opportunity costs.

3. Meaningful Work: Creating jobs primarily to distribute income rather than to meet genuine social needs risks undermining the sense of purpose and contribution that meaningful work provides.

4. Scalability: The scale of potential AI-driven displacement —potentially affecting the majority of current employment— exceeds what public job creation programs could realistically address.

While targeted public employment can play a valuable role in addressing specific social needs and providing transitional opportunities, it cannot serve as the primary distribution mechanism in a highly automated economy.

Work-Sharing: The Coordination Problem

Work-sharing approaches—reducing standard working hours to distribute available employment among more workers—have succeeded in specific contexts but face significant limitations as a response to AI-driven displacement:

1. Diminishing Returns: As automation capabilities advance, the total amount of human labour required for production may decline so dramatically that even substantial reductions in individual working hours cannot maintain full employment.

2. Coordination Challenges: Implementing work-sharing at scale requires coordinated action across firms, sectors, and potentially nations, creating significant collective action problems.

INSIGHT: 2. "The 'learn to code' narrative is perhaps the most damaging myth of the digital age—suggesting that individual skill acquisition can solve what is fundamentally a power imbalance between labour and capital."

3. Income Effects: Without mechanisms to maintain income despite reduced hours, work-sharing can lead to financial hardship rather than enhanced well-being.

4. Structural Mismatch: Work-sharing assumes that human labour remains necessary but should be more widely distributed; it does not address scenarios where certain forms of human labour become structurally unnecessary for production.

While reduced working hours may enhance well-being and provide transitional benefits, work-sharing alone cannot address the fundamental distribution challenge in a highly automated economy.

Universal Basic Income: Decoupling

Survival from Employment

Universal Basic Income (UBI)—a regular cash payment provided to all citizens or residents without means testing or work requirements—represents perhaps the most direct response to the distribution challenge in a post-labour economy. By providing unconditional economic support, UBI explicitly decouples basic survival and participation from employment status.

Core Design Considerations

Effective UBI implementation requires addressing several key design considerations:

1. Payment Level: The amount must balance between providing meaningful economic security and maintaining fiscal sustainability. Most serious proposals suggest a level sufficient to meet basic needs but not high enough to eliminate incentives for additional contribution.

2. Funding Mechanisms: Sustainable funding could come from various sources, including:
  - Taxation of automated production and capital returns
  - Data dividends from the economic value of aggregated data
  - Reduction of existing welfare programs that UBI would replace
  - Natural resource dividends similar to Alaska's Permanent Fund

3. Implementation Approach: Options range from immediate full implementation to gradual introduction through age cohorts, geographic regions, or payment levels.

4. Relationship to Existing Programs: UBI could either complement or replace existing social welfare programs, with significant implications for cost, complexity, and distributional effects.

Evidence from Pilot Programs

Contrary to common concerns, evidence from UBI pilot

programs in diverse contexts—from Manitoba and Finland to Kenya and India—suggests several consistent findings:

1. Work Effects: Recipients generally do not withdraw from productive activity but often shift toward education, caregiving, entrepreneurship, or more suitable employment.

2. Health Outcomes: Significant improvements in mental health, stress reduction, and preventive healthcare utilization typically emerge.

3. Educational Investment: Families often invest more in children's education when freed from immediate financial pressure.

4. Community Effects: Some evidence suggests strengthened social cohesion and civic participation in communities with UBI programs.

5. Economic Multipliers: Local economies typically benefit from increased consumer spending and entrepreneurial activity.

While these pilots provide valuable insights, they necessarily differ from full-scale, permanent implementation in ways that limit direct extrapolation.

INSIGHT: 3. "Most 'AI ethics' frameworks serve primarily to pacify public concern while allowing the continued concentration of technological power in the hands of a small elite."

Limitations and Complementary Approaches

Despite its potential benefits, UBI alone cannot fully address the distribution challenge in a post-labour economy:

1. Agency Beyond Consumption: While UBI provides consumption agency (the ability to meet needs through market purchases), it does not directly address production agency (meaningful participation in value creation).

2. Power Dynamics: UBI does not inherently alter power

relationships between those who own productive capital and those who rely primarily on transfers.

3. Psychological Needs: Financial security addresses only one dimension of human needs; purpose, contribution, and social connection require complementary approaches.

4. Political Vulnerability: As a visible transfer program, UBI may face greater political vulnerability than less direct distribution mechanisms like capital ownership.

These limitations suggest that while UBI may form an important component of a post-labour distribution system, it likely requires complementary approaches that address deeper questions of ownership, participation, and purpose.

Universal Capital Ownership: Democratizing the Means of Production

If returns to capital increasingly dominate returns to labour in an automated economy, broadening capital ownership represents a logical response to maintain widely distributed economic agency. Universal capital ownership approaches aim to ensure that productivity gains from automation flow to the broader population rather than concentrating among existing capital owners.

Sovereign Wealth Approaches

Publicly owned investment funds that hold diversified asset portfolios and distribute returns to citizens represent one promising approach to universal capital ownership. Examples and potential models include:

1. Norway's Government Pension Fund Global: Accumulating over $1.3 trillion from oil revenues, this fund owns approximately 1.5% of all publicly listed companies globally and generates returns that support Norway's social welfare system.

2. Alaska Permanent Fund: Provides annual dividends to all state residents from investment returns on oil revenue,

demonstrating the political durability of universal ownership models.

3. Social Wealth Funds: Proposed funds that would accumulate capital through various mechanisms (initial public offerings, corporate tax, data dividends) and distribute returns universally.

These approaches maintain market allocation of investment while democratizing the ownership of productive assets and their returns.

Stakeholder Ownership Models

Alternative approaches focus on broadening ownership at the firm level through various stakeholder ownership structures:

1. Employee Ownership Trusts: Legal structures that hold company shares on behalf of employees, providing them with both governance rights and profit participation.

2. Platform Cooperatives: User-owned alternatives to extractive platform business models, where those who create value through participation share in ownership and governance.

INSIGHT: 4. "The greatest threat to human agency isn't AI itself, but the deliberate design choices that embed existing power structures into these systems, effectively encoding current inequalities into our technological future."

3. Community Ownership: Local ownership structures for essential services and infrastructure, ensuring that automation benefits flow to affected communities.

These approaches potentially offer stronger governance rights and local accountability than sovereign wealth models but may provide less diversification and scale.

Challenges and Implementation Pathways

Universal capital ownership approaches face several

implementation challenges:

1. Capital Acquisition: Accumulating significant capital stakes without disrupting economic function requires careful mechanism design, potentially including:
  - Gradual share dilution requirements for public companies
  - Dedicated taxation of capital returns or natural resources
  - Leveraging public assets and infrastructure

2. Governance Structures: Effective governance must balance professional management with democratic accountability and protection against political interference.

3. Transition Dynamics: Building significant capital stakes takes time, creating challenges for addressing immediate displacement effects.

4. Global Capital Mobility: National or local ownership initiatives may face challenges from global capital mobility without coordinated international approaches.

Despite these challenges, universal capital ownership represents perhaps the most direct response to the structural shift from labour to capital returns in an automated economy.

Commons-Based Production: Abundance Beyond Markets

The third approach recognizes that certain goods and services—particularly those with near-zero marginal production costs—might be most effectively provided outside traditional market mechanisms through commons-based production and distribution.

Digital Commons

The digital realm already demonstrates the potential of commons-based production through examples like:

1. Open Source Software: Collaborative production of software that anyone can use, modify, and redistribute, now underpinning much of the world's digital infrastructure.

2. Wikipedia and Open Knowledge: Volunteer-created

knowledge resources that provide universal access without direct monetization.

3. Creative Commons Content: Artistic and intellectual works shared under licenses that permit various forms of reuse and adaptation.

As AI reduces production costs across domains, similar commons-based approaches could potentially expand beyond purely digital goods.

Physical Commons and Infrastructure

Commons-based approaches can extend to physical domains through:

INSIGHT: 6. "Technological unemployment is not inevitable—it is a policy choice made by those who benefit from replacing human labour with machines they own and control."

1. Community Infrastructure: Shared physical resources like makerspaces, tool libraries, and community facilities that provide access without individual ownership.

2. Urban Commons: Collectively managed spaces and services within cities, from parks and gardens to transportation systems.

3. Energy Commons: Distributed renewable energy systems with shared ownership and governance, potentially leveraging AI for optimal coordination.

These approaches recognize that when abundance becomes technically feasible, artificial scarcity through market mechanisms may become increasingly unnecessary and counterproductive.

Challenges and Limitations

Commons-based approaches face several challenges:

1. Governance Complexity: Effective management of commons requires sophisticated governance mechanisms to

prevent overuse or underinvestment.

2. Funding Production: While marginal distribution costs may approach zero, initial production often requires significant investment that commons models must somehow fund.

3. Boundary Definition: Determining which goods and services are suitable for commons-based provision versus market allocation remains complex.

4. Transition Pathways: Moving from current market-based provision to commons-based alternatives requires navigating complex transition dynamics.

Despite these challenges, commons-based approaches offer promising complements to both market mechanisms and direct transfers, particularly for goods and services where artificial scarcity creates more harm than benefit.

Contribution Income: Valuing Work Beyond Employment

The fourth approach recognizes that meaningful human contribution will continue even as formal employment declines, requiring new mechanisms to recognize and reward socially valuable activities outside traditional labour markets.

Redefining Valuable Contribution

Contribution income systems would recognize and potentially remunerate activities including:

1. Care Work: Child-rearing, elder care, and support for vulnerable community members that creates enormous social value but receives limited market recognition.

2. Community Service: Volunteer activities, mutual aid, and civic participation that strengthen social fabric and resilience.

3. Environmental Stewardship: Conservation, restoration, and sustainable management of natural resources and ecosystems.

4. Cultural Production: Artistic creation, cultural

preservation, and meaning-making activities that enrich human experience beyond commercial entertainment.

INSIGHT: 7. "The current trajectory of AI development is creating a new form of technological colonialism, where a small global elite extracts value from the data and attention of billions while offering increasingly meager compensation in return."

5. Knowledge Creation and Sharing: Research, education, and information curation that advances human understanding and capability.

These activities already create substantial social value but often receive limited or no financial compensation under current economic arrangements.

Implementation Approaches

Potential mechanisms for recognizing and rewarding such contributions include:

1. Participation Income: A modified basic income that requires some form of social contribution but defines this broadly beyond market employment.

2. Social Credits: Systems that recognize contributions through credits that can be exchanged for goods, services, or other forms of support.

3. Time Banking: Formalized reciprocal service exchange where time spent helping others earns credits that can be used to receive help in return.

4. Community Dividends: Local distribution systems that recognize contributions to community well-being through shared economic returns.

These approaches aim to maintain the connection between contribution and reward while expanding our conception of valuable activity beyond market employment.

Challenges and Considerations

Contribution income approaches face several implementation challenges:

1. Valuation Complexity: Determining the relative value of different forms of contribution involves complex normative judgments that market mechanisms currently avoid.

2. Verification Systems: Balancing accountability with respect for autonomy and privacy in verifying contributions presents significant design challenges.

3. Avoiding Exploitation: Systems must prevent the exploitation of vulnerable individuals through coerced "contribution" requirements.

4. Cultural Adaptation: Shifting cultural recognition of value from market employment to broader forms of contribution requires significant social evolution.

Despite these challenges, contribution income approaches offer promising pathways for maintaining the connection between meaningful activity and economic reward in a post-employment context.

Integrated Distribution Systems: Beyond Single Solutions

The distribution challenge in a post-labour economy likely requires not a single approach but an integrated system combining elements from multiple frameworks. Different individuals, communities, and societies may require different combinations based on their specific contexts, values, and transition pathways.

Potential Integration Models

Several integration models merit consideration:

1. Foundation and Flourishing: A universal basic income providing foundational security, combined with contribution recognition systems that support flourishing beyond basic needs.

2. Commons and Capital: Universal capital ownership ensuring broadly distributed returns from automated production, combined with commons-based provision of essential goods and services.

3. Transitional Hybrids: Systems that begin with familiar mechanisms like job guarantees but gradually evolve toward more fundamental alternatives as automation advances.

4. Layered Approaches: Different distribution mechanisms operating at different scales—from local contribution systems and community commons to national capital funds and global basic income provisions.

These integrated approaches recognize that the distribution challenge involves multiple dimensions—from basic material security to meaningful participation and purpose—that no single mechanism can fully address.

Implementation Principles

Regardless of the specific combination adopted, several principles should guide implementation:

1. Gradual Evolution: Distribution systems should evolve incrementally rather than through sudden, disruptive changes that risk harmful transition effects.

2. Experimental Pluralism: Different communities and regions should be empowered to experiment with various approaches, generating valuable learning about what works in different contexts.

3. Participatory Design: Those affected by changing distribution systems should have meaningful input into their design and implementation rather than having solutions imposed from above.

4. Adaptive Management: Distribution systems should incorporate feedback mechanisms and regular reassessment to adapt to changing technological and social conditions.

These principles recognize that the transition to post-labour distribution systems represents not a one-time policy change but an ongoing process of social and economic evolution.

Conclusion: From Labour Market to Distribution Ecosystem

The distribution challenge in a post-labour economy requires moving beyond incremental policy adjustments to reimagine the fundamental mechanisms through which economic agency is distributed. Rather than attempting to preserve wage labour as the primary distribution mechanism in the face of overwhelming automation pressure, societies must develop new foundations for economic participation and security.

The approaches explored in this chapter—universal basic income, universal capital ownership, commons-based production, and contribution income—each address different aspects of this challenge. Their effective integration could potentially create distribution ecosystems that maintain and even enhance human agency despite the declining centrality of labour markets.

This transition involves not merely technical policy design but profound cultural and psychological adaptation—shifting how we conceptualize the relationship between contribution, value, and reward. It requires moving beyond the industrial-era assumption that employment represents the only legitimate avenue to economic participation toward more diverse and flexible understandings of how humans can create and share value.

The stakes could not be higher. Failure to develop effective post-labour distribution mechanisms risks creating societies where technological abundance coexists with widespread economic exclusion—a morally indefensible and politically unstable outcome. Success, however, could enable unprecedented human flourishing, where technology serves as a foundation for expanded freedom, creativity, and meaning rather than a force for displacement and concentration.

The following chapter will explore how these distribution approaches might be implemented in practice, examining the political economy of transition and the governance challenges involved in moving toward post-labour economic systems.

Case Study: Rebuilding Agency Through Platform Cooperativism - The Drivers Collective

The Drivers Collective, founded in 2024, provides a compelling case study of how platform cooperativism can rebuild economic agency in the face of algorithmic management and platform monopolies.

The collective emerged as a direct response to the deteriorating conditions faced by ride-share drivers working for dominant platforms like Uber and Lyft. By 2023, these drivers had experienced five consecutive years of declining real income, with the average full-time driver earning 37% less per hour (adjusted for inflation) than in 2018. More significantly, they had lost virtually all control over their working conditions, with pricing, route selection, and customer allocation entirely determined by proprietary algorithms they could neither understand nor influence.

The Drivers Collective took a radically different approach. Founded by a coalition of 230 former Uber and Lyft drivers in partnership with platform cooperative developers and community organizations, they created an alternative ride-sharing platform with three distinctive features:

Democratic Governance: Unlike traditional platforms where algorithms are designed to maximize corporate profit, the Collective's algorithms were developed through a participatory process with drivers themselves. All major decisions about pricing models, commission structures, and dispatch algorithms are put to a vote among driver-members, with transparent information about the trade-offs involved.

Algorithmic Transparency: The Collective's code is open-source, allowing drivers to understand exactly how ride allocation and pricing work. A simplified dashboard shows drivers in real-time how the algorithm is making decisions, creating what they call "algorithmic literacy" among members.

Data Ownership: Perhaps most significantly, the Collective established a data trust that gives drivers collective ownership over the data generated through their work. This data - including traffic patterns, demand fluctuations, and customer preferences - is a valuable asset that traditional platforms monopolize. The Collective's data trust ensures this value flows back to drivers.

The results have been remarkable. Within 18 months of launch, the Collective had expanded to 14 cities and attracted over 12,000 driver-members. Drivers report earning an average of 28% more per hour than on traditional platforms, despite customers paying comparable or slightly lower fares. This efficiency gain comes primarily from the dramatically lower overhead - the Collective operates with a 12% commission compared to Uber's 25-30%.

Beyond the economic benefits, surveys of Collective members reveal significant improvements in psychological well-being and professional satisfaction. As one driver explained: "On Uber, I felt like a disposable component in someone else's machine. With the Collective, I'm a co-owner making real decisions about how our platform works. The difference in dignity is immeasurable."

The Collective's success demonstrates that rebuilding economic agency doesn't require rejecting technological advancement or algorithmic management per se. Rather, it requires fundamentally restructuring ownership and governance to ensure that technology serves human needs rather than extracting value from human labour.

As the Collective's co-founder noted in a 2025 interview: "The problem was never the technology itself. The problem was who controlled it and for what purpose. When drivers collectively own and govern the algorithms that organize their work, those same technologies that once exploited them can become tools of empowerment."

CHAPTER 6: OWNERSHIP REIMAGINED: CAPITAL, COMMONS, AND COLLECTIVE PROSPERITY

Ownership Reimagined

In 2023, the employees of Meridian Manufacturing, a mid-sized industrial equipment manufacturer in Wisconsin, received news that sent shockwaves through their community. The company's private equity owners had decided to implement an advanced AI-powered automation system that would eliminate approximately 60% of the factory's 340 jobs within 18 months.

For Tom Reeves, a 52-year-old machinist who had spent 27 years at Meridian, the announcement felt like more than just a threat to his livelihood—it was an existential crisis. "This factory built this town," he explained. "My father worked here before me. I put my kids through college on this job. And now some investors who've never even visited are going to hollow it out because an algorithm told them it would improve their returns."

What happened next, however, defied the usual narrative of inevitable displacement. Instead of accepting their fate, Tom and a core group of employees approached the local branch of a community development financial institution with an audacious proposal: they wanted to explore an employee buyout of the factory.

The initial response was skepticism. How could workers possibly compete with the capital efficiency promised by automation? But as they dug deeper into the financials, a different picture emerged. The private equity owners were focused on maximizing short-term returns over a 3-5 year horizon, which made the immediate labour cost savings of automation attractive despite the substantial upfront investment.

The employees, with their longer time horizon and deeper community ties, developed an alternative business model. They would implement automation more gradually, using the productivity gains to fund diversification into higher-value product lines rather than simply eliminating jobs. Their plan included an innovative ownership structure where both employees and the local community would hold shares, creating what they called a "stakeholder-owned enterprise."

After six months of intense negotiation, financial engineering, and community organizing, they secured the necessary financing through a combination of loans, community investment, and employee contributions. In January 2024, Meridian became one of the largest employee-community owned manufacturers in the Midwest.

Two years later, the results have been remarkable. The company has indeed automated many processes, but at a pace that allowed for natural attrition and retraining rather than layoffs. Productivity has increased by 32%, and those gains have been shared among worker-owners through both higher wages and profit distributions. Most significantly, the company has expanded into new product lines that have actually increased total employment to 372—more than before the transition.

"The fundamental difference is who benefits from technological advancement," explained Lisa Chen, the company's CFO and a former factory floor supervisor. "Under the previous ownership model, productivity gains from automation flowed primarily to distant shareholders. Under our model, those same gains flow to the people who helped create them and the community that supports them."

Meridian's story illustrates a profound truth about the AI revolution: the impact of technology on human welfare depends less on the technology itself than on who owns it and how its benefits are distributed. As we navigate the transition to an increasingly automated economy, reimagining ownership may be one of our most powerful tools for ensuring that technological progress translates into broadly shared prosperity rather than concentrated wealth and widespread displacement.

Manufacturing Cost Structure Comparison

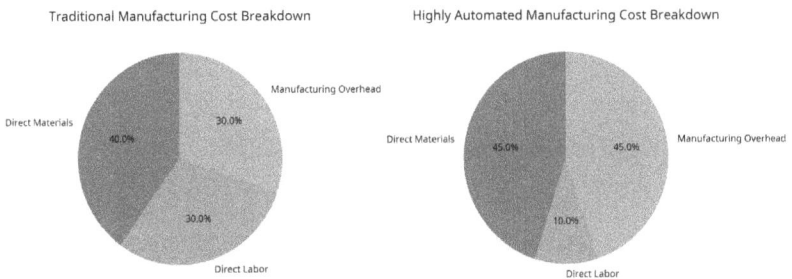

Traditional Manufacturing Cost Breakdown

Manufacturing Overhead

Direct Materials
30.0%
40.0%

30.0%

Direct Labor

Highly Automated Manufacturing Cost Breakdown

Direct Materials
45.0%
45.0%
Manufacturing Overhead

10.0%

Direct Labor

Source: Industry averages compiled from multiple manufacturing sectors

Introduction: The Ownership Challenge in an AI Economy

As artificial intelligence transforms the foundations of economic production, the question of who owns the means of production—and thus who benefits from increasing automation—becomes central to determining whether AI leads to broadly shared prosperity or extreme concentration of wealth and power. This chapter examines how ownership structures must evolve to ensure that the benefits of AI-driven productivity flow to society broadly rather than concentrating among a small technological elite.

The preceding chapters have established how AI fundamentally alters the relationship between labour and capital, potentially eliminating the need for human labour across vast swathes of the economy. We have explored how this transformation undermines traditional distribution mechanisms and requires new approaches to maintain economic agency. This chapter focuses specifically on ownership—of physical capital, intellectual property, data, and algorithmic systems—as a critical determinant of how AI's benefits will be distributed.

We examine four interconnected ownership transformations: the democratization of capital ownership, the expansion of the digital and physical commons, the evolution of property rights for data and AI, and the development of new governance models for technological infrastructure. Each represents not merely a policy adjustment but a fundamental reimagining of how ownership might function in an economy where automated systems increasingly generate wealth with minimal human labour input.

Our analysis recognizes that these transformations face significant implementation challenges and resistance from those who benefit from current arrangements. However, we argue that evolving ownership structures is not merely desirable but necessary to prevent AI from driving extreme inequality and undermining the social foundations of market economies.

The Concentration Challenge: Why

Current Trends Are Unsustainable

Before exploring alternative ownership models, we must understand why current ownership trends in an AI-driven economy are likely unsustainable—both economically and politically.

INSIGHT: The concentration of AI ownership in the hands of a few corporations represents the greatest threat to economic democracy since the robber baron era—potentially creating a level of wealth inequality that will make our current disparities look trivial by comparison.

Economic Concentration Dynamics

Several factors drive increasing concentration of ownership and returns in AI-intensive economies:

1. Network Effects: Many AI applications exhibit strong network effects, where services become more valuable as more users participate, creating winner-take-all dynamics that favor early leaders.

2. Data Advantages: Companies with access to more data can develop more capable AI systems, creating self-reinforcing advantages that new entrants struggle to overcome.

3. Scale Economies: The high fixed costs and low marginal costs of AI development and deployment create significant scale advantages for larger firms.

4. Intellectual Property Regimes: Current intellectual property frameworks allow broad patenting of AI techniques and applications, potentially restricting innovation and reinforcing incumbent advantages.

5. Capital Requirements: Developing cutting-edge AI systems increasingly requires massive computational resources and technical talent, creating barriers to entry for all but the most well-resourced organizations.

These dynamics have already led to significant

concentration in the digital economy, with a handful of technology companies capturing an increasing share of market value, data assets, and technical talent. As AI capabilities advance and spread across economic sectors, these concentration dynamics threaten to intensify and expand.

Political Economy Implications

The economic concentration resulting from these dynamics creates significant political economy challenges:

1. Democratic Accountability: When economic power concentrates among a small number of firms or individuals, their influence over political processes often grows correspondingly, potentially undermining democratic accountability.

2. Social Cohesion: Extreme inequality in ownership and returns can erode social cohesion and trust, particularly when technological change is perceived as benefiting a small elite at the expense of the broader population.

3. Innovation Direction: Concentrated ownership can skew innovation toward applications that maximize returns to capital rather than addressing broader social needs or enhancing human capabilities.

4. System Legitimacy: Market economies derive their legitimacy partly from delivering broadly shared prosperity; when benefits flow primarily to a small ownership class, this legitimacy may erode.

These challenges suggest that current ownership structures may prove politically unsustainable as AI increasingly displaces human labour across economic sectors. The question is not whether ownership models will evolve, but how— through deliberate, democratic processes or through crisis and conflict.

Democratizing Capital Ownership: From Shareholders to Stakeholders

The first transformation involves broadening the ownership of productive capital to ensure that returns from increasingly automated production flow to the broader population rather than concentrating among existing capital owners.

Employee Ownership Expansion

INSIGHT: 2. "Private ownership of advanced AI systems is fundamentally incompatible with democratic governance and human flourishing—these technologies must be treated as public utilities rather than private property."

Employee ownership represents one promising approach to broadening capital ownership, with several models showing particular potential:

1. Employee Ownership Trusts: Legal structures that hold company shares on behalf of employees, providing them with both governance rights and profit participation. The John Lewis Partnership in the UK demonstrates how such trusts can operate at scale, with over 80,000 employee-owners sharing in decision-making and profits.

2. Worker Cooperatives: Firms owned and governed directly by their workers, often operating on a one-member-one-vote principle. Mondragon Corporation in Spain shows how worker cooperatives can achieve significant scale (over 80,000 worker-owners) and compete effectively across multiple sectors.

3. Broad-Based Employee Stock Ownership: Programs that distribute ownership widely among employees rather than concentrating it among executives. Companies like Publix Super Markets demonstrate how broad-based ownership can enhance both employee well-being and business performance.

These models face implementation challenges, particularly in highly automated industries where the ratio of capital to labour is extremely high. However, they can be adapted through mechanisms like multi-stakeholder governance that include both current workers and broader community representation.

Public and Community Ownership

Beyond employee ownership, public and community ownership models offer additional approaches to democratizing capital:

1. Public Asset Trusts: Publicly owned but independently managed entities that hold productive assets on behalf of citizens. The Alaska Permanent Fund demonstrates how such trusts can generate returns that benefit all residents of a jurisdiction.

2. Community Wealth Building: Strategies that develop locally owned assets anchored in place, from community land trusts to municipal enterprises. Preston, UK has pioneered this approach, redirecting procurement toward local, democratic businesses and developing community-owned enterprises.

3. Platform Cooperatives: User-owned alternatives to extractive platform business models, where those who create value through participation share in ownership and governance. Stocksy United exemplifies this approach in stock photography, with contributors sharing ownership and governance of the platform.

These models recognize that in an AI economy, ownership must extend beyond traditional employees to include the broader communities affected by and contributing to economic activity.

Sovereign Wealth and Social Wealth Funds

At larger scales, sovereign wealth funds and social wealth funds offer mechanisms for broad-based capital ownership:

1. National Wealth Funds: Publicly owned investment funds that hold diversified asset portfolios and distribute returns to citizens or public services. Norway's Government Pension Fund Global, with over $1.3 trillion in assets, demonstrates how resource wealth can be transformed into broadly shared

financial returns.

2. Social Wealth Funds: Proposed funds that would accumulate capital through various mechanisms (IPO shares, corporate tax, data dividends) and distribute returns universally. The UK's proposed Inclusive Ownership Fund would require large companies to transfer a percentage of shares to worker-controlled funds.

3. Municipal Wealth Funds: City or regional funds that develop assets and distribute returns locally. The Urban Wealth Fund model proposed for UK cities would consolidate public land and property assets to generate returns for local communities.

These approaches maintain market allocation of investment while democratizing the ownership of productive assets and their returns. They can be particularly valuable for capturing returns from highly automated production where direct employment is limited.

Expanding the Commons: Beyond Market and State

INSIGHT: 3. "The venture capital model driving AI development is structurally incapable of producing technologies that serve the common good—it systematically rewards applications that concentrate wealth rather than distribute it."

The second transformation involves expanding the economic commons—resources that are openly accessible to all members of society—particularly in domains where marginal production costs approach zero due to automation and digitization.

Digital Commons Expansion

The digital realm already demonstrates the potential of commons-based production through examples like:

1. Open Source Software: Collaborative production of software that anyone can use, modify, and redistribute, now

underpinning much of the world's digital infrastructure. Projects like Linux, Apache, and thousands of others show how commons-based production can create sophisticated technological resources without traditional market incentives.

2. Open Access Knowledge: Repositories of knowledge freely available to all, from Wikipedia to open access academic journals. These demonstrate how knowledge production and curation can function effectively outside both market and state control.

3. Creative Commons Content: Artistic and intellectual works shared under licenses that permit various forms of reuse and adaptation. Over 2 billion works now use Creative Commons licenses, creating a massive cultural commons.

As AI reduces production costs across domains, similar commons-based approaches could potentially expand beyond purely digital goods, particularly for information products where the marginal cost of reproduction approaches zero.

Physical Commons Development

Commons-based approaches can extend to physical domains through:

1. Community Infrastructure: Shared physical resources like makerspaces, tool libraries, and community facilities that provide access without individual ownership. The 500+ tool libraries worldwide demonstrate how shared access can reduce resource consumption while expanding capabilities.

2. Urban Commons: Collectively managed spaces and services within cities, from parks and gardens to transportation systems. Barcelona's "City as Commons" framework shows how urban resources can be governed with citizen participation rather than purely market or state mechanisms.

3. Energy Commons: Distributed renewable energy systems with shared ownership and governance. Germany's energy

cooperatives, with over 1,700 organizations and 200,000 members, demonstrate how essential infrastructure can operate under community ownership.

These physical commons become increasingly viable as AI and automation reduce the labour required for their maintenance and coordination, potentially allowing more resources to operate outside pure market logic.

Knowledge and Data Commons

Perhaps most critically for an AI economy, knowledge and data commons offer mechanisms to ensure that the fundamental resources powering AI systems benefit society broadly:

1. Public Data Trusts: Governance structures that manage data as a collective resource rather than private property, ensuring that its value benefits data contributors and society rather than only those who collect it.

2. Open Training Resources: Publicly available datasets and models that democratize access to AI development capabilities rather than concentrating them among well-resourced organizations.

3. Algorithmic Commons: Core algorithmic techniques and capabilities maintained as public resources rather than proprietary advantages, similar to how basic scientific knowledge functions as a commons.

INSIGHT: 4. "The notion that we can maintain traditional property rights while AI transforms the economy is perhaps the most dangerous delusion of our time—one that virtually guarantees neo-feudalism."

These knowledge and data commons are particularly important given the cumulative, self-reinforcing advantages that data and algorithmic capabilities create in AI development.

Evolving Property Rights: Rethinking Ownership for the Digital Age

The third transformation involves reimagining property rights themselves—the legal frameworks that define what can be owned, by whom, and with what limitations—to better align with the realities of an AI-driven economy.

Data Rights Reformation

Current data governance frameworks inadequately address the unique characteristics of data as an economic resource:

1. Collective Data Rights: Recognizing that much valuable data emerges from collective activity rather than individual creation, requiring governance models that reflect this collective nature.

2. Data Dividends: Mechanisms to ensure that value generated from data flows back to those who contributed it, whether through direct payments, public services, or shared infrastructure.

3. Fiduciary Data Frameworks: Legal structures that impose duties of care, loyalty, and confidentiality on those who collect and process data, similar to how financial fiduciaries must act in their clients' best interests.

These approaches move beyond both the current corporate data extraction model and simplistic individual ownership frameworks to recognize data's distinctive characteristics as a resource.

Intellectual Property Reformation

Intellectual property regimes designed for an industrial economy require significant evolution for an AI context:

1. AI-Specific Patent Reforms: Limiting the scope and duration of AI-related patents to prevent monopolization of fundamental techniques while maintaining innovation incentives.

2. Algorithmic Transparency Requirements: Mandating disclosure of core algorithmic approaches in exchange for limited exclusivity, similar to how patent systems traditionally balanced exclusivity with knowledge diffusion.

3. Graduated Monopoly Rights: Intellectual property frameworks where exclusivity diminishes over time rather than operating as an all-or-nothing proposition.

These reforms aim to balance innovation incentives with broader access to and benefit from technological capabilities, preventing intellectual property from becoming a mechanism for permanent advantage rather than temporary innovation reward.

Stewardship Rather Than Absolute Ownership

More fundamentally, property rights themselves may evolve from absolute ownership toward stewardship models:

1. Purpose-Bound Property: Ownership rights conditioned on serving specific social purposes rather than granting unlimited control, similar to how community land trusts maintain property for affordable housing.

INSIGHT: 5. "Data is the new land, algorithms are the new factories, and we're witnessing the largest enclosure of the commons in human history—all occurring with minimal democratic oversight or public benefit."

2. Stakeholder Governance Requirements: Legal frameworks requiring consideration of impacts on all stakeholders rather than only property owners, as benefit corporation legislation has begun to implement.

3. Commons-Based Property Regimes: Hybrid ownership models that combine elements of private use rights with collective governance and benefit-sharing, as demonstrated in various natural resource management systems worldwide.

These approaches recognize that in an increasingly

interdependent economy, absolute property rights may create more harm than benefit, requiring more nuanced frameworks that balance individual control with collective interests.

New Governance Models: Participation Beyond Ownership

The fourth transformation involves developing governance models that enable meaningful participation in economic decision-making beyond traditional ownership structures.

Multi-Stakeholder Governance

As AI systems affect diverse stakeholders, governance models must evolve to incorporate multiple perspectives:

1. Multi-Stakeholder Cooperatives: Ownership structures that formally include multiple stakeholder groups—workers, users, community members, and investors—in governance processes.

2. Stakeholder Councils: Formal governance bodies that represent diverse interests in corporate or platform decision-making, with real authority rather than merely advisory capacity.

3. Nested Governance Systems: Decision-making structures where different stakeholder groups have authority over different types of decisions, matching governance rights to legitimate interests.

These approaches recognize that in complex, interdependent systems, effective governance requires incorporating diverse perspectives rather than privileging a single stakeholder group.

Algorithmic Governance Participation

As algorithmic systems increasingly shape economic opportunities and outcomes, participation in their governance becomes essential:

1. Algorithmic Impact Assessments: Participatory processes

to evaluate potential impacts of algorithmic systems before deployment, with meaningful input from affected communities.

2. Ongoing Monitoring Rights: Mechanisms for continuous stakeholder oversight of algorithmic systems, with rights to access information about operation and impacts.

3. Contestation Mechanisms: Formal processes through which those affected by algorithmic decisions can challenge and potentially modify those decisions.

These participatory mechanisms aim to ensure that algorithmic systems remain accountable to those they affect rather than serving only their developers or owners.

Platform Governance Innovation

INSIGHT: 7. "Employee ownership and cooperative models aren't just nice alternatives—they're the only structures that can prevent AI from creating a permanent underclass in a post-labour economy."

Digital platforms that coordinate economic activity require governance innovations beyond traditional corporate structures:

1. User Governance Rights: Formal mechanisms for platform users to participate in rule-setting, dispute resolution, and strategic direction.

2. Distributed Governance Protocols: Technical and social protocols that enable decentralized governance of digital infrastructure, as demonstrated in some blockchain-based systems.

3. Data Stewardship Organizations: Independent entities that govern data use on platforms according to principles established by data contributors rather than platform owners.

These innovations recognize that platforms increasingly function as economic infrastructure rather than merely private businesses, requiring governance appropriate to their quasi-public nature.

Implementation Pathways: From Vision to Reality

Transforming ownership structures faces significant implementation challenges and resistance from those who benefit from current arrangements. Effective implementation requires strategic approaches that build momentum while navigating political and practical constraints.

Policy Levers for Ownership Transformation

Several policy approaches can accelerate ownership transformation:

1. Tax Incentives: Preferential tax treatment for broadly owned enterprises, from employee ownership trusts to multi-stakeholder cooperatives.

2. Procurement Preferences: Government purchasing that prioritizes democratically owned enterprises, as demonstrated in Preston's community wealth building approach.

3. Conditional Support: Making business support, bailouts, and subsidies conditional on ownership reforms, particularly for firms benefiting from public research or infrastructure.

4. Antitrust Enforcement: Preventing excessive concentration through robust competition policy, potentially including breakups of dominant platforms.

5. Public Investment: Direct public investment in commons-based infrastructure and democratically owned enterprises, particularly in emerging sectors.

These policy levers can shift incentives and resources toward more democratic ownership without requiring immediate, comprehensive transformation.

Transitional Strategies

Effective implementation also requires transitional

strategies that build from current realities toward transformed ownership:

1. Hybrid Models: Organizations that combine elements of conventional and democratic ownership, allowing gradual evolution rather than abrupt transformation.

2. Conversion Pathways: Structured processes for converting conventional businesses to democratic ownership, particularly during succession or financial challenges.

3. Ecosystem Development: Building support systems—from specialized finance to technical assistance—that enable democratic ownership models to thrive.

4. Pilot Zones: Designated areas where alternative ownership models receive regulatory space and support for experimentation.

These transitional approaches recognize that ownership transformation requires not merely policy change but ecosystem development and cultural evolution.

Movement Building and Cultural Change

Perhaps most fundamentally, ownership transformation requires building social movements and cultural understanding:

1. Ownership Literacy: Educational initiatives that expand understanding of ownership alternatives beyond the conventional shareholder corporation.

2. Practitioner Networks: Communities of practice that share knowledge and support among those implementing democratic ownership models.

3. Strategic Coalitions: Alliances between diverse stakeholders—from labour unions to community organizations to ethical investors—supporting ownership transformation.

4. Narrative Shift: Communication strategies that challenge

the inevitability and desirability of concentrated ownership, highlighting successful alternatives.

These movement-building approaches recognize that ownership transformation ultimately requires shifting cultural assumptions about how economic activity should be organized and who should benefit from technological progress.

Conclusion: Ownership as if People Mattered

The ownership challenge in an AI economy is not merely technical but deeply ethical and political. It concerns fundamental questions about the kind of society we wish to create as technological capabilities increasingly allow production with minimal human labour. Will we maintain ownership structures that channel the benefits of this technological abundance to a narrow slice of humanity, or will we develop new frameworks that ensure these benefits flow broadly?

The approaches explored in this chapter—democratizing capital ownership, expanding the commons, evolving property rights, and developing new governance models— each address different aspects of this challenge. Their effective integration could potentially create ownership ecosystems that maintain human agency and broad-based prosperity despite the declining role of labour in production.

This transformation involves not merely policy design but profound cultural evolution—shifting how we conceptualize the relationship between ownership, value creation, and social benefit. It requires moving beyond the industrial-era assumption that concentrated private ownership represents the only effective way to organize economic activity toward more diverse and participatory understandings of how resources can be governed for shared benefit.

The stakes could not be higher. Failure to evolve ownership structures for an AI economy risks creating societies where technological abundance coexists with widespread economic exclusion—a morally indefensible and politically unstable outcome. Success, however, could enable unprecedented human flourishing, where technology serves as a foundation for expanded freedom, creativity, and meaning rather than a force for displacement and concentration.

The following chapter will explore how these ownership transformations intersect with the evolution of income distribution systems, examining how reformed ownership and innovative distribution mechanisms might work together to maintain economic agency in a post-labour economy.

Case Study: Ownership Reimagined - The Mondragon Corporation's AI Transition

The Mondragon Corporation, Spain's tenth-largest business group and the world's largest worker cooperative, provides a compelling case study of how alternative ownership models can navigate the AI transition while preserving human dignity and economic security.

Founded in 1956, Mondragon had already established a successful model of worker ownership long before the AI revolution. By 2023, it comprised 96 cooperatives with over 81,000 worker-owners across manufacturing, retail, finance, and knowledge sectors. When advanced AI began threatening traditional employment models around 2020, Mondragon faced the same technological pressures as conventional corporations but responded in fundamentally different ways.

Shared Productivity Gains: When Mondragon's industrial division implemented advanced robotics and AI systems between 2022-2025, productivity increased by 64% across their manufacturing plants. Unlike traditional corporations, where such gains typically benefit shareholders while displacing workers, Mondragon distributed these benefits among all worker-owners. This took three forms:

1. Reduced working hours (from 40 to 32 hours weekly with no

reduction in pay)

2. Increased compensation (averaging 22% higher real wages)

3. Investment in new cooperative ventures to create additional worker-owner positions

Democratic Technology Governance: Perhaps most significantly, decisions about AI implementation were made through Mondragon's democratic governance structures. Worker-owners voted on which processes to automate, how quickly to implement new technologies, and how to redistribute the resulting productivity gains. This democratic approach led to more thoughtful, gradual implementation that prioritized human well-being alongside efficiency.

Human-Centered AI Design: Mondragon's approach to AI design differed markedly from conventional corporations. Their internal technology division developed AI systems specifically designed to complement human workers rather than replace them. As one engineer explained: "Our design brief wasn't 'maximize automation to reduce labour costs' but rather 'enhance human capabilities while preserving meaningful work.'"

Education and Transition Support: When automation did eliminate certain roles, Mondragon's robust internal education system retrained affected worker-owners for new positions. Between 2022-2025, over 4,200 worker-owners completed retraining programs, with 91% successfully transitioning to new roles within the cooperative network.

The results speak for themselves. While maintaining global competitiveness and strong financial performance (7.4% average annual growth during this period), Mondragon achieved what many thought impossible: technological advancement without worker displacement or increased inequality. By 2025, when many conventional corporations had reduced their workforces by 15-30% due to AI implementation, Mondragon had actually increased its number of worker-owners by 7%.

As Mondragon's president noted in a 2025 address: "The question was never whether to adopt advanced technologies, but how to ensure those technologies serve human flourishing rather than narrow financial interests. Our cooperative ownership structure allowed us to make that choice in a way that conventional corporations structurally cannot."

The Mondragon case demonstrates that ownership structure fundamentally determines how the benefits of AI and automation are distributed. When workers collectively own the enterprises implementing these technologies, the false dichotomy between technological progress and human welfare dissolves, revealing a path to shared prosperity in the age of AI.

CHAPTER 7: UNIVERSAL BASIC INCOME: FOUNDATIONS FOR FREEDOM IN THE AGE OF AI

The Universal Basic Income Experiment

In 2024, Olivia Chen, a 34-year-old graphic designer from Portland, Oregon, received an email that would fundamentally change her life. She had been randomly selected to participate in the West Coast Basic Income Project, a three-year experiment providing 5,000 Americans with an unconditional monthly payment of $1,000.

Olivia's initial reaction was skepticism. "I thought it was a scam," she recalled. "But after verifying it was legitimate, my next thought was: what's the catch?"

There was no catch. The payments would continue regardless of her employment status, income changes, or life choices. Unlike traditional welfare programs, there were no work requirements, means testing, or restrictions on how she could spend the money.

At the time, Olivia was working 50+ hours weekly at a marketing agency while freelancing nights and weekends to make ends meet. The relentless pace had taken a toll on her health and creativity, but financial necessity kept her tethered to this unsustainable routine.

"The first month, I just saved the payment," she explained. "By the third month, I realized this wasn't just extra money—it was freedom to make different choices."

Olivia reduced her agency hours to part-time and invested the freed-up time in developing her own design studio. The basic income provided a financial floor that made this transition possible without the crushing anxiety that typically accompanies entrepreneurial risk.

Eighteen months into the experiment, Olivia's studio was generating more income than her previous full-time job. More significantly, she reported profound improvements in her mental health, creative output, and personal relationships. "I'm not just financially better off," she noted. "I'm happier, healthier, and doing work that actually matters to me."

What makes Olivia's story particularly revealing is how it challenges conventional narratives about work incentives. Rather than reducing her productive contribution, the basic income enabled her to work in ways that better utilized her talents and created more economic value. She wasn't working less—she was working differently, with greater autonomy and purpose.

Not every participant's experience mirrored Olivia's entrepreneurial path. Some used the basic income to pursue education, care for family members, or simply reduce financial stress while continuing their existing jobs. The diversity of responses highlighted a crucial insight: when people have their basic needs secured, they make widely different choices based on their unique circumstances, values, and aspirations.

This diversity of outcomes points to perhaps the most powerful aspect of universal basic income: it doesn't prescribe a single vision of the good life but rather creates space for individuals to pursue their own definitions of meaningful contribution and fulfillment.

As we navigate the economic disruptions of the AI revolution, Olivia's experience offers a glimpse of how universal basic income might function not just as an economic safety net, but as a foundation for a more dynamic, diverse, and human-centered economy—one where technological productivity gains expand rather than constrain human possibility.

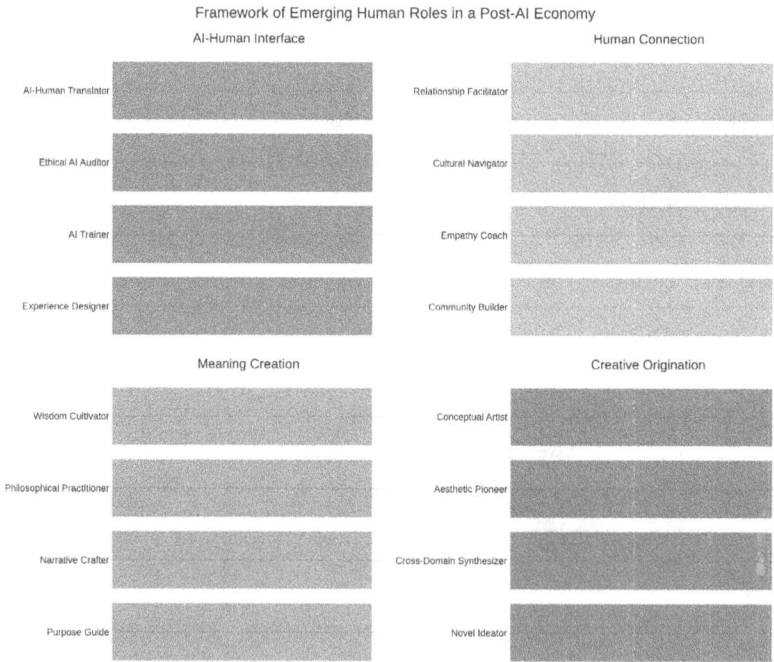

Framework of Emerging Human Roles in a Post-AI Economy

Introduction: UBI as a Response to Technological Disruption

As artificial intelligence increasingly displaces human labour across economic sectors, Universal Basic Income (UBI) has emerged as one of the most discussed policy responses.

At its core, UBI represents a simple yet radical idea: providing regular cash payments to all citizens or residents without means testing or work requirements. This approach explicitly decouples basic economic security from employment status, offering a potential foundation for human flourishing in an era where traditional employment may no longer serve as a viable distribution mechanism for many people.

This chapter examines UBI not merely as a welfare program but as a fundamental reimagining of the relationship between individuals, work, and society. We explore the philosophical foundations of UBI, evaluate evidence from implementations worldwide, address common criticisms, and consider how UBI might function as part of a broader response to AI-driven economic transformation.

Our analysis recognizes that UBI is neither a panacea nor the only necessary response to technological disruption. However, we argue that some form of unconditional income floor may become increasingly essential as AI capabilities advance, potentially eliminating the need for human labour across vast swathes of the economy. The question is not whether societies will need to provide economic security beyond employment, but how best to design systems that maintain human dignity, agency, and flourishing in a post-labour economy.

Philosophical Foundations: Freedom, Justice, and Efficiency

INSIGHT: Universal Basic Income isn't just one policy option among many—it's the only viable foundation for a stable society in an AI-dominated economy where traditional employment becomes increasingly scarce.

The case for UBI rests on multiple philosophical foundations, from libertarian conceptions of freedom to egalitarian notions of justice to utilitarian considerations of efficiency. Understanding these diverse foundations helps clarify both the appeal of UBI across the political spectrum and the different forms it might take in practice.

Freedom-Based Arguments

Freedom-based arguments for UBI emphasize how unconditional economic security enhances individual liberty:

1. Real Freedom: Philosopher Philippe Van Parijs argues that meaningful freedom requires not just absence of interference (negative liberty) but actual capacity to pursue one's life plans (positive liberty). UBI provides the material foundation for this "real freedom for all."

2. Freedom from Domination: Without basic economic security, individuals may be forced to accept exploitative conditions or relationships simply to survive. UBI reduces this vulnerability to domination by providing an exit option.

3. Entrepreneurial Freedom: Unconditional income provides the security to take risks, from starting businesses to pursuing education or creative endeavors, potentially increasing innovation and self-determination.

These freedom-based arguments have attracted support from thinkers across the political spectrum, from libertarians who see UBI as less paternalistic than traditional welfare to progressives who value its potential to liberate people from economic coercion.

Justice-Based Arguments

Justice-based arguments focus on UBI as a mechanism for ensuring fair distribution of society's resources and opportunities:

1. Common Inheritance: Philosophers like Thomas Paine argued that natural resources and accumulated knowledge represent a common inheritance to which all have some claim. UBI can be understood as a dividend from this shared inheritance.

2. Automation Dividend: As AI and automation increase

productivity while potentially reducing labour demand, UBI offers a mechanism to ensure these gains benefit society broadly rather than concentrating among capital owners.

3. Recognition of Unpaid Contribution: Much valuable work —from caregiving to community service—receives no market compensation. UBI acknowledges these contributions to social reproduction and community well-being.

These justice arguments emphasize that in a wealthy society with sufficient productive capacity, ensuring everyone can meet basic needs represents a fundamental requirement of fairness.

Efficiency-Based Arguments

Efficiency arguments highlight how UBI might improve economic functioning compared to alternative approaches:

1. Administrative Simplicity: Unlike means-tested programs that require extensive bureaucracy to determine eligibility, UBI's universality potentially reduces administrative costs and complexity.

2. Reduced Poverty Traps: Means-tested benefits that phase out as income rises can create high effective marginal tax rates that discourage work. UBI avoids this "poverty trap" by providing benefits regardless of earnings.

3. Economic Stabilization: By providing a permanent floor of consumer spending power, UBI could help stabilize economic demand during downturns or transitions.

INSIGHT: 2. "The resistance to UBI comes primarily from those who benefit from maintaining artificial scarcity in an age of potential abundance—essentially using poverty as a tool for labour discipline."

4. Innovation and Risk-Taking: Security to take risks could increase entrepreneurship, creative pursuits, and human capital investment that markets might otherwise underfund

due to risk aversion.

These efficiency arguments suggest that beyond philosophical considerations, UBI might offer practical advantages over more complex, conditional systems for ensuring economic security.

Evidence from Implementation: What We Know from UBI Experiments

While full-scale, permanent UBI has not been implemented nationally, numerous experiments and partial implementations provide valuable evidence about potential effects. These range from multi-year randomized controlled trials to dividend programs that share characteristics with UBI.

Contemporary UBI Pilots

Recent and ongoing UBI experiments offer insights into effects across multiple dimensions:

1. Finland's Basic Income Experiment (2017-2018): Provided €560 monthly to 2,000 unemployed individuals. Results showed improved well-being and slightly higher employment rates compared to the control group, with recipients reporting greater trust in institutions and reduced stress.

2. Ontario Basic Income Pilot (2017-2019): Though prematurely canceled, preliminary results indicated improvements in mental health, housing stability, and education participation among recipients.

3. Stockton Economic Empowerment Demonstration (2019-2021): Provided $500 monthly to 125 residents in Stockton, California. Found that recipients showed improved emotional health, reduced income volatility, and increased full-time employment compared to control groups.

4. GiveDirectly's Kenya Study (2016-ongoing): Long-term study providing various UBI amounts to over 20,000 people

across 295 villages. Initial results show increased assets, nutrition, revenue from self-employment, and psychological well-being without significant increases in alcohol or tobacco consumption.

These contemporary experiments consistently find improvements in psychological well-being, health outcomes, and economic security, with limited evidence for common concerns about reduced work effort or increased substance use.

Dividend Programs and Cash Transfers

Existing programs that share some characteristics with UBI provide additional evidence:

1. Alaska Permanent Fund Dividend: Since 1982, has provided annual payments (ranging from $1,000-$2,000) to all Alaska residents from investment returns on oil revenue. Research shows minimal effects on employment, significant poverty reduction, and increased birth weights among lower-income mothers.

2. Eastern Band of Cherokee Indians Casino Dividend: Distributes casino profits to all tribal members (approximately $4,000-$6,000 annually per person). Long-term studies show improved educational outcomes, reduced crime and substance abuse, and better mental health among recipient families.

3. Iran's Cash Transfer Program: When Iran reduced fuel subsidies in 2011, it offset the impact by providing cash transfers to all citizens (approximately 29% of median household income). Studies found no negative effect on labour supply and significant poverty reduction.

These programs demonstrate the political durability of universal payments and their potential for improving outcomes across multiple dimensions without significant negative effects on work incentives.

Limitations of Existing Evidence

INSIGHT: 3. "The current welfare state is fundamentally designed to support capitalism by ensuring a desperate workforce, not to maximize human flourishing—UBI represents a complete paradigm shift in how we understand economic security."

While existing evidence provides valuable insights, several limitations affect its applicability to full-scale, permanent UBI:

1. Scale and Duration: Most experiments involve limited populations and timeframes, potentially missing long-term adaptive behaviors and broader economic effects that might emerge in permanent, society-wide implementation.

2. Selection Effects: Many experiments focus on specific populations (often lower-income) rather than truly universal implementation, potentially missing interaction effects across income levels.

3. Macroeconomic Effects: Small-scale experiments cannot capture potential macroeconomic effects on prices, wages, and production that might emerge in full implementation.

4. Funding Mechanisms: Most experiments provide UBI without implementing the taxation or other funding mechanisms that would be necessary for permanent programs, missing potential behavioral responses to these funding mechanisms.

These limitations suggest caution in extrapolating directly from existing evidence to predictions about full-scale implementation. However, the consistency of positive effects across diverse contexts provides reason for optimism about UBI's potential benefits.

Design Considerations: Building Effective UBI Systems

Effective UBI implementation requires addressing several key design considerations that significantly affect both outcomes and political viability.

Payment Level and Frequency

The amount and timing of UBI payments fundamentally shape their effects:

1. Subsistence vs. Partial: UBI can range from a full subsistence-level income to a partial supplement. Higher amounts provide greater security and potential for transformative effects but require more substantial funding and may have stronger labour market effects.

2. Payment Frequency: Monthly payments support regular expenses and budgeting, while less frequent (e.g., quarterly or annual) payments might better support larger investments or debt reduction. Evidence suggests more frequent payments better support stability for vulnerable populations.

3. Age-Based Variation: Some proposals include lower payments for children (often directed to parents/guardians) and potentially higher payments for elderly individuals with greater needs.

These parameters must balance providing meaningful security against fiscal constraints and potential behavioral effects, with optimal designs likely varying based on existing social welfare systems and economic conditions.

Eligibility and Universality

While "universal" suggests everyone receives payments, practical implementations must define the eligible population:

1. Citizenship vs. Residency: Limiting eligibility to citizens versus including all legal residents significantly affects both coverage and political dynamics, particularly in societies with large immigrant populations.

2. Age Requirements: Most proposals include all adults but vary in treatment of children, with some providing full payments, others reduced amounts, and some integrating with existing child benefit systems.

INSIGHT: 4. "Means-tested welfare programs will become increasingly dysfunctional in an AI economy characterized by volatile incomes and algorithmic employment—only universal programs can provide genuine security."

3. Opt-In vs. Automatic Enrollment: Requiring active enrollment versus automatic provision significantly affects participation rates, particularly among marginalized populations who may face barriers to navigating bureaucratic processes.

These eligibility decisions significantly affect both the inclusivity of UBI systems and their administrative complexity, with more universal approaches generally providing broader coverage but potentially at higher fiscal cost.

Funding Mechanisms

Sustainable funding represents perhaps the most significant implementation challenge for UBI:

1. Tax-Based Funding: Options include increased income taxes (potentially with more progressive rates), wealth taxes, consumption taxes, or specialized taxes on automation, data, or natural resource use.

2. Dividend Approaches: Funding UBI through returns on publicly owned assets—whether natural resources, sovereign wealth funds, or intellectual property—potentially creates more sustainable and politically durable systems.

3. Monetary Approaches: Some proposals suggest funding through monetary creation rather than taxation, though these raise significant concerns about inflation unless carefully calibrated to productive capacity.

4. Program Consolidation: Replacing some existing social welfare programs with UBI could provide partial funding, though this raises concerns about potentially reducing support for those with specialized needs.

The funding approach significantly affects both economic impacts and political dynamics, with dividend-based approaches potentially offering greater durability than tax-based systems that create more visible redistribution.

Relationship to Existing Programs

UBI's relationship to existing social welfare systems fundamentally shapes its effects:

1. Complementary Approach: Maintaining specialized programs for healthcare, housing, disability, and other needs alongside UBI recognizes that cash alone cannot address all forms of vulnerability.

2. Replacement Approach: Replacing multiple existing programs with UBI could reduce administrative complexity and paternalism but risks inadequately addressing specialized needs that require more than cash support.

3. Hybrid Systems: Maintaining some specialized programs while consolidating others represents a middle path that balances simplification with recognition of diverse needs.

These design choices significantly affect UBI's impact on different populations, with complementary approaches generally providing stronger support for those with specialized needs but at higher total cost and complexity.

Addressing Common Criticisms: Beyond Simplistic Objections

UBI faces several common criticisms that merit serious engagement, though evidence suggests many represent oversimplifications or misunderstandings of likely effects.

Work Incentives and Economic Contribution

INSIGHT: 5. "The greatest threat to UBI implementation isn't economic feasibility but the psychological resistance of elites who equate human value with economic productivity."

Perhaps the most common criticism concerns UBI's

potential effects on work incentives:

1. Empirical Evidence: Contrary to common assumptions, evidence from UBI experiments consistently shows minimal reduction in work effort, with some studies even finding increased employment, particularly in full-time work. Where labour supply does decrease, it often reflects increased education, caregiving, or entrepreneurial activity rather than idleness.

2. Income vs. Substitution Effects: Economic theory distinguishes between income effects (working less because one has more income) and substitution effects (working more because work pays better relative to leisure). UBI creates an income effect but, unlike means-tested benefits, doesn't create negative substitution effects from benefit phase-outs.

3. Redefining Contribution: The concern about reduced work often implicitly equates contribution with paid employment, ignoring valuable unpaid activities like caregiving, community service, and creative production that UBI might enable.

While work incentive effects remain an important consideration, evidence suggests they are more nuanced and potentially more positive than critics often assume, particularly when considering broader conceptions of valuable contribution beyond market employment.

Fiscal Sustainability

Concerns about fiscal sustainability represent another common objection:

1. Gross vs. Net Cost: The headline cost of UBI (payment amount multiplied by population) significantly overstates the net fiscal impact, as much of the expenditure would be recaptured through taxation of higher-income recipients and potential savings from program consolidation.

2. Economic Feedback Effects: UBI likely generates positive

economic effects—from increased consumer spending to improved health outcomes to greater entrepreneurship—that partially offset fiscal costs through higher tax revenues and reduced expenses in other areas.

3. Implementation Options: Various implementation approaches, from gradual phase-in to partial UBI to dividend-funded models, can address fiscal concerns while maintaining core benefits.

While fiscal sustainability represents a legitimate consideration, it depends significantly on specific design choices and economic context rather than representing an inherent barrier to UBI implementation.

Inflation Concerns

Critics often suggest UBI would drive significant inflation, particularly in necessities like housing:

1. Supply Responsiveness: Inflation results from increased demand only when supply cannot respond. In many sectors, supply can adjust to increased purchasing power, limiting price effects.

2. Redistribution vs. Creation: When UBI primarily redistributes existing purchasing power rather than creating new money, aggregate demand effects may be limited, though distribution of demand across sectors would likely shift.

3. Housing Specificity: Housing inflation concerns are legitimate but reflect specific supply constraints in housing markets rather than inherent problems with UBI, suggesting the need for complementary housing policy rather than abandoning income support.

While inflation effects require careful consideration, they depend significantly on specific implementation details, existing supply constraints, and complementary policies rather than representing an inherent flaw in the UBI concept.

Political Vulnerability

INSIGHT: 6. "Work requirements for basic economic security will eventually be recognized as a form of coercion as morally indefensible as indentured servitude."

Some critics suggest UBI would prove politically vulnerable, potentially being reduced below subsistence levels over time:

1. Universality as Protection: Universal programs typically enjoy broader political support than targeted ones, as demonstrated by the durability of universal programs like Social Security compared to means-tested welfare.

2. Dividend Framing: Framing UBI as a dividend from common resources or technological progress rather than a welfare program potentially increases political durability, as demonstrated by the Alaska Permanent Fund's popularity across the political spectrum.

3. Constituency Building: By benefiting the middle class alongside lower-income populations, UBI potentially builds broader political constituencies than targeted programs.

While political sustainability remains an important consideration, UBI's universality potentially creates stronger protection against erosion than more targeted approaches, particularly when designed and framed to emphasize universal ownership rather than redistribution.

UBI in Context: Part of a Broader Response

While UBI offers potential benefits, it represents only one component of a comprehensive response to AI-driven economic transformation. Understanding its relationship to complementary approaches helps clarify both its potential and its limitations.

Complementary Policy Approaches

Several policy approaches complement UBI in addressing technological disruption:

1. Universal Basic Services: Ensuring universal access to essential services like healthcare, education, housing, and transportation addresses needs that cash alone cannot meet and may prove more efficient for services with significant economies of scale.

2. Stakeholder Ownership: Broadening ownership of productive capital through sovereign wealth funds, employee ownership, or other mechanisms ensures returns from automated production flow to the broader population rather than concentrating among existing capital owners.

3. Work Time Reduction: Reducing standard working hours can distribute available employment more widely while improving work-life balance, potentially complementing rather than competing with UBI.

4. Public Purpose Employment: Creating employment opportunities in socially valuable but market-undervalued areas like care work, environmental restoration, and community development can complement UBI by providing both income and meaningful contribution opportunities.

These approaches address different aspects of technological disruption and may work more effectively in combination than any single approach alone.

UBI's Distinctive Contribution

Within this broader policy ecosystem, UBI offers several distinctive contributions:

1. Individual Agency: By providing resources directly to individuals without paternalistic restrictions, UBI maximizes freedom to determine one's own priorities and life path.

2. Unconditionality: By avoiding behavioral requirements, UBI reaches vulnerable populations who often struggle to navigate conditional systems and reduces stigma associated with support.

3. Recognition of Unpaid Contribution: UBI acknowledges and supports valuable activities outside formal employment, from caregiving to community service to creative production.

4. Simplicity and Transparency: UBI's straightforward design potentially reduces administrative complexity and increases public understanding compared to more complex, conditional systems.

These distinctive characteristics suggest that while UBI should not be viewed as a complete solution to technological disruption, it offers valuable elements that other approaches may not fully provide.

Implementation Pathways

Effective implementation likely involves gradual, experimental approaches rather than immediate full-scale deployment:

1. Starter UBI: Beginning with a partial UBI below subsistence level allows testing effects and building systems while managing fiscal impact.

2. Demographic Phase-In: Implementing UBI first for specific age groups (e.g., young adults or seniors) allows gradual expansion while targeting groups with particular needs or transition challenges.

3. Geographical Experimentation: Allowing regional or local UBI experiments creates learning opportunities and demonstrates effects before national implementation.

4. Existing Program Integration: Gradually converting some existing benefits to more unconditional forms creates pathways toward UBI without abrupt system changes.

These incremental approaches recognize that effective UBI implementation requires learning and adaptation rather than immediate transformation of entire social welfare systems.

Conclusion: UBI as Foundation for Human Flourishing

As artificial intelligence increasingly transforms the relationship between human labour and economic production, Universal Basic Income offers a potential foundation for maintaining human agency, security, and flourishing. By providing unconditional economic support, UBI explicitly acknowledges that in a highly automated economy, traditional employment may no longer serve as a viable distribution mechanism for many people.

The evidence from diverse implementations—from controlled experiments to dividend programs—suggests that contrary to common concerns, UBI typically improves well-being across multiple dimensions without significantly reducing work effort or creating other negative behavioral effects. When properly designed and implemented, it appears to enhance rather than undermine human flourishing, providing security that enables greater risk-taking, creativity, and contribution beyond market employment.

However, UBI represents not a complete solution but one component of a broader response to technological disruption. It complements rather than replaces other approaches like universal basic services, broadened capital ownership, and public purpose employment. Its distinctive contribution lies in maximizing individual agency, recognizing non-market contributions, and providing security without paternalistic restrictions.

The implementation challenges—from funding mechanisms to relationship with existing programs—are significant but not insurmountable. Various pathways allow gradual, experimental approaches that manage fiscal impact while building systems and demonstrating effects.

As we navigate the profound economic transformation that AI enables, UBI offers a promising approach to ensuring that technological progress serves human flourishing rather than undermining it. By providing a secure foundation for all members of society, it potentially enables us to embrace automation's productive potential while ensuring its benefits flow broadly rather than concentrating among a fortunate few.

The following chapter will explore how these distribution approaches intersect with necessary institutional transformations, examining how governments, financial systems, and other core institutions must evolve to effectively navigate the transition to a post-labour economy.

Case Study: Finland's Universal Basic Income Experiment

Finland's 2017-2018 Universal Basic Income (UBI) experiment provides a compelling real-world case study of both the potential and limitations of basic income approaches in addressing economic transition.

The Finnish government selected 2,000 unemployed citizens to receive €560 (approximately $640) monthly for two years, regardless of whether they found work. This amount replaced their existing unemployment benefits but continued even if participants gained employment, eliminating the "welfare trap" where taking a job results in lost benefits.

The experiment's results, fully analyzed by 2020, revealed nuanced outcomes that inform our understanding of UBI's potential role in the AI transition:

Employment Effects: Contrary to critics' fears that UBI would reduce work incentives, recipients worked an average of 6 days more over the two-year period than the control group. However, this modest increase wasn't statistically significant enough to conclusively prove UBI increases employment. What it did demonstrate was that guaranteed income didn't create the "hammock effect" (people choosing not to work) that many opponents predicted.

Wellbeing Improvements: The most significant positive outcomes were psychological and social. UBI recipients

reported markedly higher levels of wellbeing across multiple dimensions:
- 55% rated their health as good or very good (compared to 46% in the control group)
- 17% reported lower stress levels
- 22% expressed higher confidence in their future
- Trust in institutions and other people increased significantly

Financial Security: The guaranteed income created a psychological "floor" that enabled different decision-making. As one participant explained: "The basic income gave me the security to start my own business. Even if it failed, I wouldn't end up on the street." This security translated into greater risk-taking and entrepreneurial activity among some participants.

Implementation Insights: The experiment revealed important practical considerations for larger-scale UBI programs. The administrative simplicity—replacing complex conditional benefits with a single payment—reduced bureaucracy and eliminated the stigma many felt when navigating traditional welfare systems.

Limitations: The Finnish experiment also highlighted important limitations. The amount provided (€560 monthly) was insufficient for comfortable living without additional income in Finland's high-cost economy. This underscores that UBI levels must be calibrated to local living costs to achieve their intended effects.

Additionally, the two-year timeframe proved too short to observe longer-term behavioral changes or economic impacts. Researchers concluded that more extended experiments (5+ years) would be necessary to fully understand UBI's transformative potential.

Perhaps most importantly, the Finnish experiment occurred in a context where universal healthcare and education were already guaranteed. This suggests that UBI works best as part of a comprehensive social support ecosystem rather than as a standalone solution.

The Finnish case demonstrates that while UBI alone isn't a panacea for the challenges of technological unemployment, it can form a crucial component of a broader response strategy. As Finland's Minister of Social Affairs reflected in 2022: "Our experiment showed that basic income can provide the psychological security people need to navigate economic transitions with dignity. But it must be part of a larger reimagining of the social contract for the age of artificial intelligence."

CHAPTER 8: INSTITUTIONAL TRANSFORMATION: FROM REFEREE TO ARCHITECT

Reimagining Governance for the AI Era

When Governor Eliza Martinez took office in 2023, her state was facing what many considered an insurmountable fiscal crisis. Tax revenues had plummeted as AI and automation eliminated thousands of middle-income jobs, while social service demands had skyrocketed from the resulting displacement. Budget projections showed a $4.2 billion deficit within two years if current trends continued.

"The traditional playbook offered only painful choices," Governor Martinez recalled. "Cut essential services, raise taxes on an already struggling population, or some combination of both. But those approaches addressed symptoms rather than the underlying structural problem."

The structural problem was clear: the state's governance and fiscal systems had been designed for an industrial economy where human labour was the primary driver of economic value. As AI increasingly generated economic output with minimal human involvement, the traditional mechanisms for funding public services and distributing prosperity were breaking down.

Rather than accepting these constraints, Martinez assembled an unconventional team of economists, technologists, legal scholars, and public policy experts to reimagine governance for the AI era. Their mandate was ambitious: design systems that could harness the unprecedented productivity of artificial intelligence to benefit the broader public rather than just technology owners.

The resulting "Digital Dividend Framework" represented a fundamental reimagining of the relationship between technology, governance, and public finance. Its core innovation was shifting taxation away from human labour and toward the automated systems replacing it. The framework included:

1. An "Automation Value Tax" applied to revenue generated primarily through AI and automated systems
2. A "Data Commons" that recognized the public's collective interest in data generated within the state
3. A streamlined regulatory approach that encouraged AI innovation while ensuring its benefits were broadly shared

Implementation wasn't easy. Technology companies initially threatened to relocate operations, while legal challenges questioned the constitutionality of the new approach. But as the framework took effect, something remarkable happened: rather than stifling innovation, it actually accelerated it by creating incentives for human-AI collaboration rather than simple human replacement.

Within three years, the state had not only eliminated its deficit but was generating a surplus while maintaining lower tax rates on human labour. More significantly, it had established a new model for how governance could evolve alongside technological change rather than being overwhelmed by it.

"The fundamental insight was that governance isn't static —it must evolve as technology transforms economic realities," Martinez explained. "The institutions that served us well in the industrial era simply weren't designed for a world where artificial intelligence generates an increasing share of economic value."

This story illustrates the central challenge we face as AI transforms our economy: our governance institutions—from tax systems to regulatory frameworks to public services— were designed for a fundamentally different technological reality. Incremental adjustments to these systems will prove insufficient. Instead, we need to reimagine governance from first principles for an era where artificial intelligence increasingly drives economic production.

Introduction: The Institutional Imperative

As artificial intelligence transforms the foundations of economic production and distribution, our core institutions —from government and finance to education and community structures—face unprecedented adaptation challenges. These institutions were designed for an industrial era with fundamentally different technological and economic realities. Their evolution from passive referees to active architects of inclusive technological futures represents perhaps the most critical determinant of whether AI leads to broadly shared prosperity or extreme concentration of wealth and power.

This chapter examines how key institutions must transform to effectively navigate the transition to a post-labour economy. We focus on four critical institutional domains: government's evolving role in technological governance, financial systems' adaptation to new economic realities, the transformation of monetary systems including digital currencies, and the reinvention of local governance to support community resilience. Each domain requires not merely incremental reform but fundamental reimagining to address the scale and nature of AI-driven economic transformation.

Our analysis recognizes that institutional transformation faces significant implementation challenges—from political resistance and bureaucratic inertia to coordination problems and transition management. However, we argue that such transformation is not merely desirable but necessary to prevent AI from driving extreme inequality and undermining the social foundations of democratic societies.

Government Transformation: From Referee to Architect

The first domain requiring transformation is government itself, which must evolve from its traditional role as market referee and regulator to become an architect of inclusive technological futures.

The Limitations of the Referee Model

The conventional understanding of government's role in market economies—enforcing property rights, addressing market failures, and providing basic public goods—proves increasingly inadequate in an AI-driven economy for several reasons:

INSIGHT: Our current governance institutions are fundamentally incapable of managing the AI transition— they were designed for an industrial era and will collapse under the pressure of exponential technological change.

1. Pace of Change: Traditional regulatory approaches struggle to keep pace with rapidly evolving AI capabilities, often addressing problems only after significant harm has occurred.

2. Systemic Effects: AI's impacts emerge from complex system interactions rather than discrete market failures, requiring more holistic governance approaches than traditional regulation provides.

3. Power Asymmetries: The concentration of AI capabilities

among well-resourced organizations creates information and power asymmetries that undermine the effectiveness of conventional regulatory oversight.

4. Global Coordination: AI development and deployment transcend national boundaries, creating governance challenges that exceed the capacity of individual national regulators.

These limitations suggest that government must evolve beyond the referee model to effectively govern AI development and deployment in the public interest.

Anticipatory Governance Capabilities

Effective governance of AI requires developing sophisticated anticipatory capabilities rather than merely responding to problems after they emerge:

1. Horizon Scanning: Systematic monitoring of technological developments and their potential societal implications, drawing on diverse expertise beyond technical specialists.

2. Scenario Planning: Developing and regularly updating multiple scenarios for AI development and impact to inform policy design and adaptation.

3. Regulatory Sandboxes: Creating controlled environments where innovative applications can be tested with appropriate oversight before wider deployment.

4. Outcome-Based Regulation: Shifting from prescriptive rules to outcome-based frameworks that specify desired results while allowing flexibility in implementation approaches.

These anticipatory capabilities enable more proactive governance that shapes technological development rather than merely responding to its consequences.

Strategic Investment and Direction-Setting

Beyond regulation, government must play a more active role in shaping technological development directions through strategic investment and coordination:

1. Mission-Oriented Innovation: Directing research and development toward specific societal challenges through targeted funding, prizes, and coordination mechanisms.

2. Public Interest Technology: Developing technological capabilities specifically designed to serve public needs rather than merely commercial interests, from privacy-enhancing technologies to accessibility tools.

3. Data Infrastructure: Creating public data resources and infrastructure that democratize access to a critical resource for AI development rather than allowing its concentration among dominant firms.

4. Compute Commons: Ensuring broad access to computational resources through public provision, subsidized access, or mandated sharing requirements for large-scale computing infrastructure.

These strategic interventions help ensure that technological development serves broader societal goals rather than merely maximizing returns to capital or market share for dominant firms.

INSIGHT: 2. "The nation-state as we know it will become increasingly irrelevant as AI-powered platforms create new forms of sovereignty that transcend traditional geographic boundaries."

Participatory Governance Models

Effective governance requires not merely technical expertise but robust democratic participation to ensure technological development reflects diverse values and interests:

1. Deliberative Processes: Structured deliberation involving

diverse stakeholders to develop shared understanding and identify areas of agreement on governance approaches.

2. Participatory Technology Assessment: Systematic processes for evaluating potential technological impacts with meaningful input from affected communities.

3. Digital Democracy Tools: Leveraging technology itself to enable broader, more informed citizen participation in governance decisions.

4. Algorithmic Impact Assessments: Mandatory evaluation of potential impacts before deploying significant algorithmic systems, with meaningful public input and transparency requirements.

These participatory approaches help ensure that technological governance reflects democratic values rather than merely technical or economic considerations.

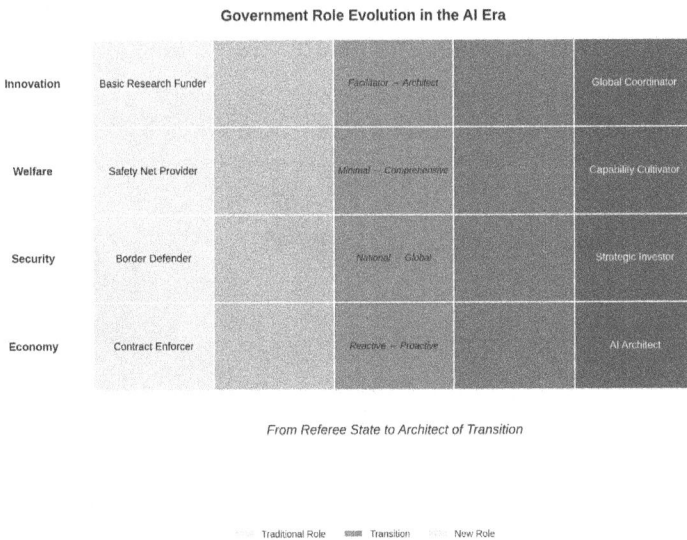

Government Role Evolution in the AI Era

	Traditional Role	Transition	New Role
Innovation	Basic Research Funder	Facilitator → Architect	Global Coordinator
Welfare	Safety Net Provider	Minimal → Comprehensive	Capability Cultivator
Security	Border Defender	National → Global	Strategic Investor
Economy	Contract Enforcer	Reactive → Proactive	AI Architect

From Referee State to Architect of Transition

Traditional Role ▓▓ Transition ░░ New Role

Implementation Challenges and Pathways

Transforming government's role faces significant implementation challenges:

1. Capability Gaps: Many government agencies lack the

technical expertise and institutional capacity for effective AI governance, requiring significant investment in talent and infrastructure.

2. Political Resistance: Powerful interests benefiting from limited governance may resist expanded government roles through lobbying, regulatory capture, or jurisdictional arbitrage.

3. Coordination Problems: Effective governance requires coordination across agencies, levels of government, and nations that existing institutional structures often impede.

4. Legitimacy Concerns: More active government roles may face legitimacy challenges in political contexts where market primacy remains the dominant paradigm.

Addressing these challenges requires building new governance capabilities incrementally, demonstrating effectiveness through targeted interventions, and developing broader political constituencies for more active governance approaches.

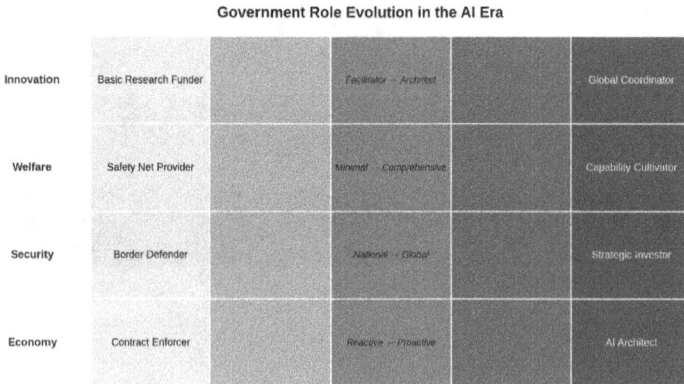

Government Role Evolution in the AI Era

Innovation	Basic Research Funder	Facilitator → Architect	Global Coordinator
Welfare	Safety Net Provider	Minimal → Comprehensive	Capability Cultivator
Security	Border Defender	National → Global	Strategic Investor
Economy	Contract Enforcer	Reactive → Proactive	AI Architect

From Referee State to Architect of Transition

Traditional Role   Transition   New Role

Financial System Transformation: Funding the Future

The second domain requiring transformation is the financial system, which must evolve to address the distinctive characteristics of an AI-driven economy—from the winner-take-all dynamics of digital markets to the public good aspects of data and algorithmic infrastructure.

The Limitations of Current Financial Systems

INSIGHT: 3. "Democracy itself is at risk in the AI era—not primarily from external threats but from the concentration of predictive power in private hands that can manipulate public opinion with unprecedented precision."

Existing financial systems face several limitations in effectively allocating capital in an AI-driven economy:

1. Short-Termism: Pressure for quarterly returns often undermines investment in technologies with longer-term societal benefits but delayed financial returns.

2. Concentration Dynamics: Winner-take-all tendencies in digital markets can channel investment toward already-dominant firms rather than more diverse innovation.

3. Public Good Underinvestment: Critical infrastructure with public good characteristics—from foundational research to data commons—often receives inadequate private investment despite significant societal value.

4. Distributional Blindness: Conventional financial evaluation typically ignores distributional impacts of investments, potentially funding technologies that generate returns through displacement rather than creation.

These limitations suggest that financial system transformation must address both the allocation of capital and the governance structures that determine how investment decisions are made.

Patient Capital Structures

Addressing short-termism requires developing financial

structures that enable longer investment horizons:

1. Long-Term Equity: Governance structures that insulate firms from short-term market pressures, from dual-class shares to steward ownership models that maintain mission focus.

2. Evergreen Funds: Investment vehicles without fixed liquidation timelines, allowing sustained support for companies developing technologies with longer-term impact horizons.

3. Development Finance Institutions: Public or quasi-public institutions with mandates to provide patient capital for technologies addressing societal challenges, from climate change to healthcare access.

4. Stakeholder Banking: Financial institutions governed by broader stakeholder interests rather than solely shareholder returns, potentially making different risk-return tradeoffs that favor longer-term societal benefits.

These patient capital structures enable investment in technologies and applications that create significant long-term value but may not maximize short-term returns.

Government Role Evolution in the AI Era

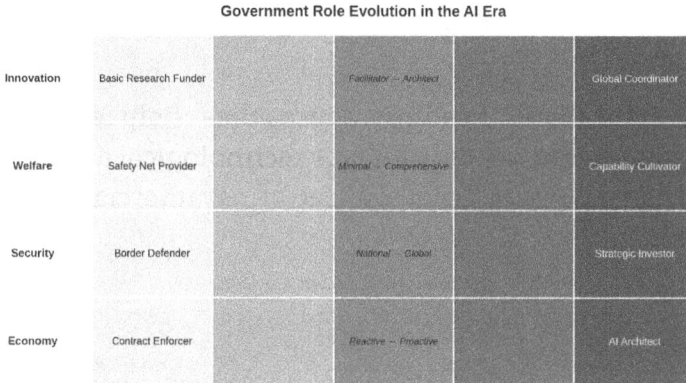

Innovation	Basic Research Funder	Facilitator → Architect	Global Coordinator
Welfare	Safety Net Provider	Minimal → Comprehensive	Capability Cultivator
Security	Border Defender	National → Global	Strategic Investor
Economy	Contract Enforcer	Reactive → Proactive	AI Architect

From Referee State to Architect of Transition

Traditional Role ▬▬ Transition New Role

Pluralistic Funding Ecosystems

Addressing concentration dynamics requires developing more diverse funding sources beyond traditional venture capital and public markets:

1. Community Investment Vehicles: Structures that enable local communities to invest in technologies addressing their specific needs and contexts.

2. Cooperative Capital: Funding mechanisms controlled by users, workers, or other stakeholders rather than external investors, potentially making different investment decisions.

3. Public Venture Funds: Government-backed investment vehicles that can accept different risk-return profiles to support more diverse innovation directions.

INSIGHT: 4. "Traditional taxation systems based on human labour and corporate profits will collapse as AI transforms the economy, potentially triggering fiscal crises that threaten basic government functions."

4. Philanthropic Innovation Funding: Strategic philanthropy focused on technological innovation that

addresses societal challenges regardless of commercial potential.

These pluralistic funding approaches help ensure that diverse values and needs influence technological development rather than allowing a narrow set of commercial criteria to dominate.

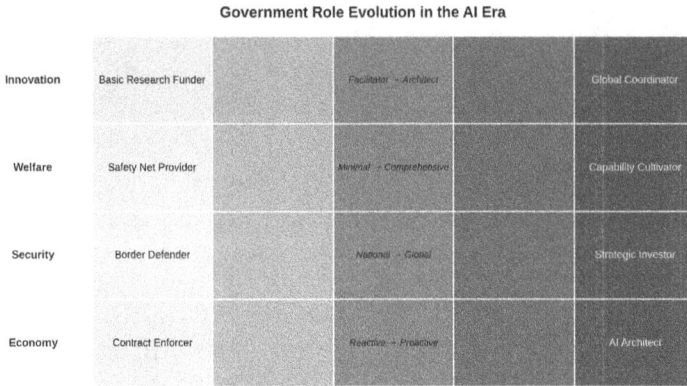

Government Role Evolution in the AI Era

	Traditional Role	Transition	New Role
Innovation	Basic Research Funder	Facilitator → Architect	Global Coordinator
Welfare	Safety Net Provider	Minimal → Comprehensive	Capability Cultivator
Security	Border Defender	National → Global	Strategic Investor
Economy	Contract Enforcer	Reactive → Proactive	AI Architect

From Referee State to Architect of Transition

Traditional Role   Transition   New Role

Impact-Oriented Financial Instruments

Addressing distributional blindness requires developing financial instruments that explicitly incorporate broader impact considerations:

1. Outcome-Based Financing: Instruments like social impact bonds that link returns to achievement of specific social or environmental outcomes rather than purely financial metrics.

2. Blended Finance: Approaches that combine public, philanthropic, and private capital with different return expectations to fund technologies with significant positive externalities.

3. Stakeholder-Governed Funds: Investment vehicles where those affected by funded technologies have governance rights,

ensuring their interests influence investment decisions.

4. Place-Based Investment: Funding mechanisms tied to specific geographic communities, ensuring technological benefits flow to particular places rather than merely to mobile capital.

These impact-oriented instruments help align financial returns with broader societal benefits rather than allowing them to diverge or conflict.

Implementation Challenges and Pathways

Financial system transformation faces several implementation challenges:

1. Regulatory Constraints: Existing financial regulations may inadvertently hinder innovative funding structures designed for broader impact.

2. Scale Mismatches: Alternative funding approaches often struggle to achieve the scale necessary to influence major technological development directions.

3. Talent Allocation: The highest compensation in finance often flows to activities with limited societal benefit, drawing talent away from impact-oriented innovation.

4. Coordination Problems: Addressing public good aspects of technological development often requires coordinated investment that market mechanisms struggle to organize.

Addressing these challenges requires both policy innovation —from regulatory sandboxes to tax incentives—and ecosystem development to demonstrate the viability and impact of alternative financial approaches.

Government Role Evolution in the AI Era

Innovation	Basic Research Funder	Facilitator → Architect	Global Coordinator
Welfare	Safety Net Provider	Minimal → Comprehensive	Capability Cultivator
Security	Border Defender	National → Global	Strategic Investor
Economy	Contract Enforcer	Reactive → Proactive	AI Architect

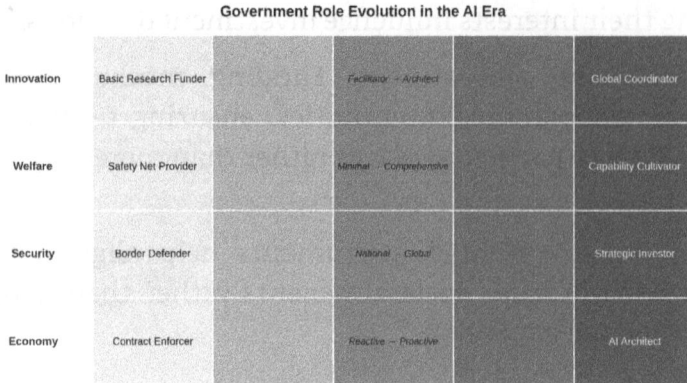

From Referee State to Architect of Transition

Traditional Role ▬▬ Transition New Role

Monetary System Evolution: Digital Currencies and Beyond

INSIGHT: 5. "The regulatory capture we've seen in the digital era is nothing compared to what's coming— AI companies are building systems that will make them effectively ungovernable by traditional means."

The third domain requiring transformation is the monetary system itself, which faces both challenges and opportunities from digital currencies and new transaction infrastructures.

The Limitations of Current Monetary Systems

Existing monetary systems face several limitations in effectively supporting an AI-driven economy:

1. Access Barriers: Significant populations remain excluded from or underserved by traditional banking systems, limiting their participation in digital economic activity.

2. Transaction Friction: Cross-border payments and micropayments often involve high fees and delays, constraining certain economic activities and models.

3. Monetary Policy Constraints: Conventional monetary

policy tools face increasing limitations in addressing economic fluctuations, particularly in low-interest environments.

4. Surveillance Capitalism: Payment systems increasingly enable extensive data collection and monetization, often without adequate user control or compensation.

These limitations suggest that monetary system evolution must address both technical infrastructure and governance frameworks to effectively support inclusive economic participation.

Central Bank Digital Currencies

Central Bank Digital Currencies (CBDCs) represent perhaps the most significant potential evolution in monetary systems:

1. Design Variations: CBDCs can take multiple forms, from account-based systems integrated with existing banking to token-based approaches more similar to physical cash.

2. Inclusion Benefits: Well-designed CBDCs could expand financial inclusion by providing basic transaction accounts to all citizens, potentially with lower barriers than traditional banking.

3. Programmable Money: CBDCs could enable programmable features like conditional payments or automatic tax collection, potentially increasing policy effectiveness and reducing compliance costs.

4. Monetary Policy Implications: Direct citizen accounts could enable new monetary policy tools, from helicopter money to negative interest rates, though these raise significant governance questions.

These potential benefits must be balanced against privacy concerns, financial stability implications, and questions about appropriate governance structures for such powerful tools.

Community and Complementary Currencies

Beyond national currencies, community and complementary currencies offer mechanisms to support local economic resilience:

1. Local Exchange Systems: Community-based currencies that facilitate exchange within specific geographic areas, potentially keeping value circulating locally rather than leaking to global financial centers.

2. Mutual Credit Systems: Arrangements where participants extend credit to each other through a centralized accounting system, enabling exchange without requiring external currency.

INSIGHT: 6. "Central banks will either evolve into direct distributors of digital currency to citizens or become obsolete as AI-powered financial systems bypass traditional monetary controls."

3. Time Banking: Systems that use time as the unit of account, valuing all participants' time equally regardless of market wage differentials.

4. Sector-Specific Currencies: Specialized currencies designed for particular economic sectors or activities, from carbon credits to education vouchers.

These complementary approaches can address specific limitations of national currencies, particularly in supporting local economic resilience and valuing activities that market mechanisms undervalue.

Data as Currency

The increasing economic value of data suggests potential monetary innovations that recognize its role as a fundamental resource:

1. Data Dividend Systems: Mechanisms that compensate individuals for the economic value generated from their data, potentially through universal payments or targeted benefits.

2. Data Cooperatives: User-owned structures that collectively manage and potentially monetize member data, ensuring returns flow to data creators rather than only to collectors.

3. Personal Data Accounts: Systems that enable individuals to control access to their data and potentially receive compensation for its use, similar to financial accounts.

4. Algorithmic Labor Markets: Frameworks that compensate individuals for contributing to AI training and improvement through data provision or feedback.

These approaches recognize that in an AI-driven economy, data represents a form of contribution that current monetary systems inadequately recognize or compensate.

Implementation Challenges and Pathways

Monetary system evolution faces several implementation challenges:

1. Technical Complexity: Digital currency systems involve significant technical challenges around security, scalability, and interoperability.

2. Privacy Concerns: Digital payment infrastructures create unprecedented surveillance potential without appropriate governance and technical safeguards.

3. Financial Stability Risks: New monetary forms could potentially create systemic risks or undermine existing stability mechanisms without careful design.

4. Governance Questions: Determining who controls monetary innovation—from central banks to private firms to community organizations—fundamentally shapes its impacts and beneficiaries.

Addressing these challenges requires both technical innovation and governance development, with particular attention to ensuring that monetary evolution serves public interest rather than merely private profit or state control.

Local Governance Reinvention: Building Resilient Communities

The fourth domain requiring transformation is local governance, which must evolve to support community resilience amid technological and economic disruption.

INSIGHT: 7. "The greatest governance challenge of the AI era isn't regulating the technology itself but redesigning our institutions to distribute its benefits—a task our current political systems are structurally incapable of addressing."

The Limitations of Current Local Governance

Existing local governance structures face several limitations in effectively navigating technological transformation:

1. Resource Constraints: Many local governments lack the fiscal resources to invest in technological capabilities or address disruption effects.

2. Capacity Gaps: Technical expertise for effective technology governance often concentrates at national levels or in major urban centers, leaving many communities without necessary capabilities.

3. Jurisdictional Mismatches: Local jurisdictional boundaries often poorly align with economic and technological systems that operate at regional or global scales.

4. Participation Barriers: Traditional local governance processes often exclude significant portions of communities, particularly those already marginalized.

These limitations suggest that local governance reinvention must address both resource distribution and participation structures to effectively support community resilience.

Community Wealth Building

Community wealth building approaches aim to develop locally rooted, broadly owned economic assets:

1. Anchor Institution Strategies: Leveraging large place-based institutions like hospitals and universities to support local economic development through procurement, hiring, and investment practices.

2. Municipal Enterprise: Local government-owned businesses providing essential services while generating revenue and ensuring community benefit rather than profit extraction.

3. Community Land Trusts: Nonprofit ownership of land to ensure permanent affordability and community control of development, preventing displacement and speculation.

4. Cooperative Development: Supporting worker, consumer, and multi-stakeholder cooperatives that root ownership in communities rather than external capital.

These approaches build economic foundations for community resilience by developing assets that generate ongoing benefits for local residents rather than absentee owners.

Participatory Governance Innovation
Effective local governance requires broader, more meaningful participation in decision-making:

1. Participatory Budgeting: Processes that enable residents to directly allocate portions of public budgets, as demonstrated in cities from Porto Alegre to New York.

2. Citizen Assemblies: Randomly selected groups of residents who deliberate on specific issues with support from experts and facilitators, potentially making more thoughtful, representative decisions than elected officials alone.

3. Digital Participation Platforms: Tools that enable broader, more continuous citizen input into governance decisions, from problem identification to solution development to implementation monitoring.

4. Co-Production: Approaches where public services are designed and delivered in partnership between professional staff and community members rather than merely provided to passive recipients.

These participatory innovations help ensure that local governance reflects diverse community needs and values rather than merely the interests of the most politically powerful.

Place-Based Data Governance

As data becomes increasingly valuable, local governance must develop approaches to ensure its benefits flow to communities:

1. Community Data Trusts: Governance structures that manage local data as a collective resource, ensuring its use benefits the community rather than merely external firms.

2. Public Interest Technology Development: Local investment in technologies specifically designed to address community needs rather than merely adopting commercial systems designed for other purposes.

3. Algorithmic Impact Assessment: Local processes to evaluate potential impacts of algorithmic systems before deployment, with meaningful community input and ongoing monitoring.

4. Digital Commons Infrastructure: Locally controlled technological infrastructure—from broadband networks to sensor systems—governed as commons rather than either public utilities or private monopolies.

These data governance approaches help ensure that the increasing value of data and algorithmic systems benefits local communities rather than merely extractive platforms.

Implementation Challenges and Pathways

Local governance reinvention faces several implementation

challenges:

1. Fiscal Constraints: Many localities face severe resource limitations that constrain their ability to invest in governance innovation or technological capabilities.

2. Jurisdictional Limitations: Local governments often lack authority over key policy domains affecting technological governance, from data regulation to labour standards.

3. Technical Capacity Gaps: Many localities lack the technical expertise to effectively develop or govern sophisticated technological systems.

4. Resistance from Incumbent Interests: Local power structures may resist governance innovations that threaten existing arrangements or privilege.

Addressing these challenges requires both higher-level policy changes—from fiscal federalism reforms to preemption limitations—and local capacity building through technical assistance, peer learning networks, and strategic partnerships.

Conclusion: Institutions for an Inclusive Technological Future

The institutional transformation required for an inclusive AI transition represents perhaps the most significant governance challenge of our era. The approaches explored in this chapter—evolving government's role from referee to architect, transforming financial systems to fund more diverse innovation, developing monetary systems that support inclusive participation, and reinventing local governance to build community resilience—each address different aspects of this challenge.

These transformations involve not merely technical policy design but profound cultural and political evolution—shifting how we conceptualize the relationship between technology, governance, and human flourishing. They require moving beyond industrial-era assumptions about institutional roles toward more sophisticated understanding of how institutions shape technological development and its social impacts.

The stakes could not be higher. Failure to transform institutions for an AI-driven economy risks creating societies where technological power concentrates among unaccountable actors, where benefits flow primarily to capital rather than communities, and where democratic governance proves increasingly ineffective at shaping technological futures. Success, however, could enable unprecedented human flourishing, where technology serves as a foundation for more inclusive, sustainable, and democratic societies.

The following chapter will explore how these institutional transformations intersect with the management of critical resources—particularly energy and computational capacity—that enable and constrain AI development and deployment.

Case Study: Estonia's Digital Governance Revolution

Estonia's transformation into the world's most advanced digital government provides a compelling case study of how governance institutions can be reimagined for the AI era.

Following the collapse of the Soviet Union, Estonia made a strategic decision to build its new democratic institutions on digital foundations. By 2023, this small Baltic nation of 1.3 million had created what many consider the world's most sophisticated digital governance ecosystem, offering valuable lessons for countries navigating the AI transition.

Digital Identity Infrastructure: The cornerstone of Estonia's approach is its secure digital identity system. Every citizen possesses a digital ID that enables authenticated access to virtually all government services and many private ones. This system processes over 1,000 digital signatures per minute nationwide and saves an estimated 2% of GDP annually in efficiency gains.

What makes Estonia's digital ID system particularly

instructive is its architecture. Unlike centralized systems that create single points of failure and control, Estonia pioneered a distributed data architecture called X-Road. This system allows different government and private databases to communicate securely while maintaining data sovereignty —each entity maintains control of its data while enabling authenticated access when authorized by citizens.

Algorithmic Transparency: As Estonia integrated AI into governance functions between 2020-2025, it established groundbreaking transparency requirements. Any algorithmic system making or supporting decisions affecting citizens must be explainable, with its logic open to public scrutiny. When the tax authority implemented an AI system to flag potential tax evasion in 2022, the complete decision criteria (though not the specific code) were published online, allowing citizens to understand exactly how the system operated.

Participatory Governance: Perhaps most significantly, Estonia has pioneered digital tools for citizen participation that go far beyond simple e-voting. The country's "MyOpinion" platform, launched in 2024, allows citizens to comment on draft legislation, propose amendments, and track how their input influences the final law. AI tools summarize citizen feedback for legislators while ensuring diverse viewpoints are represented rather than just the most numerous.

Results and Challenges: The results have been remarkable. Estonia consistently ranks among the world's least corrupt and most efficient governments. Public trust in government institutions stands at 71%—extraordinarily high by global standards. Administrative costs are approximately 35% lower than comparable European nations.

However, Estonia's journey hasn't been without challenges. A 2022 cyberattack highlighted security vulnerabilities, while ongoing debates about algorithmic bias in certain government systems demonstrate that digital governance requires constant vigilance and refinement.

The Estonian case illustrates that governance institutions can be fundamentally reimagined to harness technology's potential while preserving democratic values. As Estonia's former CTO Taavi Kotka noted: "We didn't just digitize existing bureaucratic processes—we rethought the relationship between citizens and government from first principles. The question wasn't 'How do we put this paper form online?' but 'What would government look like if we designed it from scratch in the digital age?'"

As nations worldwide grapple with AI's implications for governance, Estonia's experience offers a powerful demonstration that institutional innovation can keep pace with technological change when guided by clear principles of transparency, security, and citizen empowerment.

CHAPTER 9: SUSTAINABLE FOUNDATIONS: ENERGY, RESOURCES, AND AI'S MATERIAL REALITY

The Hidden Environmental Cost of AI

In 2023, Dr. Wei Zhang, a climate scientist at the University of California, made a discovery that challenged the prevailing narrative about artificial intelligence and sustainability. While conducting research on data center energy consumption, she stumbled upon something alarming: a single advanced AI training run for a large language model consumed more electricity than the average American household uses in 20 years.

"I was stunned by the numbers," Dr. Zhang recalled. "We've been celebrating AI's potential to optimize energy systems and reduce waste, but we weren't accounting for the massive energy footprint of developing these technologies in the first place."

Her subsequent investigation revealed that the environmental impact extended far beyond electricity consumption. The specialized chips powering AI systems required rare earth minerals mined under environmentally destructive conditions. The water needed for cooling these massive computing clusters was depleting local aquifers in already water-stressed regions. And the rapid obsolescence of AI hardware was creating a growing e-waste crisis.

When Dr. Zhang published her findings in a leading scientific journal, the response from the tech industry was swift and defensive. Several major AI companies disputed her methodology and accused her of alarmism. One prominent CEO tweeted that "minor environmental costs today are the price of building systems that will solve climate change tomorrow."

But the data was difficult to dismiss. Independent verification confirmed that by 2023, AI training and inference were consuming approximately 3.2% of global electricity production—a figure growing at 25% annually. If these trends continued unchecked, AI energy use would rival that of the entire transportation sector by 2030.

"What troubled me most wasn't just the numbers," Dr. Zhang explained, "but the absence of this issue from public discourse about AI. We were having sophisticated debates about AI safety and ethics while ignoring the very tangible environmental crisis it was creating."

The controversy sparked by Dr. Zhang's research eventually led to the formation of the Sustainable Computing Coalition, bringing together technology companies, environmental organizations, and policy experts to address AI's growing environmental footprint. Their work revealed that the problem wasn't inherent to artificial intelligence itself, but rather to the way it was being developed and deployed—with little regard for environmental consequences.

"The good news is that this isn't an either/or proposition," Dr. Zhang noted. "We can harness AI's transformative potential without environmental devastation, but only if we make sustainability a core design principle rather than an afterthought."

This episode illustrates a crucial dimension of the AI revolution that often remains hidden: the physical infrastructure enabling our increasingly digital world has very real environmental consequences. As we navigate the transition to an AI-powered economy, ensuring the sustainability of its physical foundations may be just as important as addressing its economic and social implications.

Introduction: The Resource Challenge of AI

As artificial intelligence transforms our economic and social systems, we must confront a fundamental reality: AI systems require substantial material and energy resources. From the rare earth elements in computing hardware to the electricity that powers data centers, AI's capabilities rest on physical foundations that create both constraints and imperatives for technological development. This chapter examines the resource requirements of advanced AI systems and explores approaches to ensure sustainable, secure, and equitably distributed access to these critical resources.

Our analysis moves beyond both techno-utopianism that ignores material constraints and techno-pessimism that sees only insurmountable limits. Instead, we examine how thoughtful governance of energy systems, critical materials, data resources, and computational capacity can enable AI development that remains within planetary boundaries while distributing benefits broadly. We argue that addressing these resource challenges requires sophisticated governance approaches that balance legitimate security concerns with the benefits of cooperation and exchange.

The stakes are significant: failure to manage AI's resource requirements sustainably could undermine both technological progress and ecological stability, while failure to govern these resources equitably could exacerbate global inequalities and conflicts. Conversely, effective resource governance could enable AI development that enhances human flourishing within planetary boundaries, creating foundations for genuinely sustainable prosperity.

Energy Requirements: Powering the AI Revolution

Perhaps the most immediate resource challenge for advanced AI systems concerns their substantial and rapidly growing energy requirements.

The Scale of AI Energy Consumption

Recent trends in AI development reveal concerning patterns of energy intensity:

1. Exponential Training Requirements: The computational resources required to train state-of-the-art AI models has been doubling approximately every 3.4 months since 2012, a pace far exceeding Moore's Law. This translates directly to increasing energy demands.

INSIGHT: The environmental cost of AI development is being systematically concealed from the public—if fully accounted for, it would reveal that our 'clean' digital future is potentially more destructive than the industrial age.

2. Scale of Current Systems: Training a single large language model can consume as much electricity as 100 average American homes use in a year. The largest models now require energy equivalent to the annual consumption of small towns.

3. Deployment Footprint: While training represents the most visible energy cost, the ongoing operation of deployed AI systems across billions of devices creates a persistent energy demand that may ultimately exceed training costs.

4. Infrastructure Requirements: Beyond direct computational energy, AI systems require substantial energy for cooling, data transmission, and supporting infrastructure, often doubling the effective energy footprint.

These energy demands create both environmental challenges and access barriers, potentially limiting AI development to well-resourced organizations and regions with abundant energy supplies.

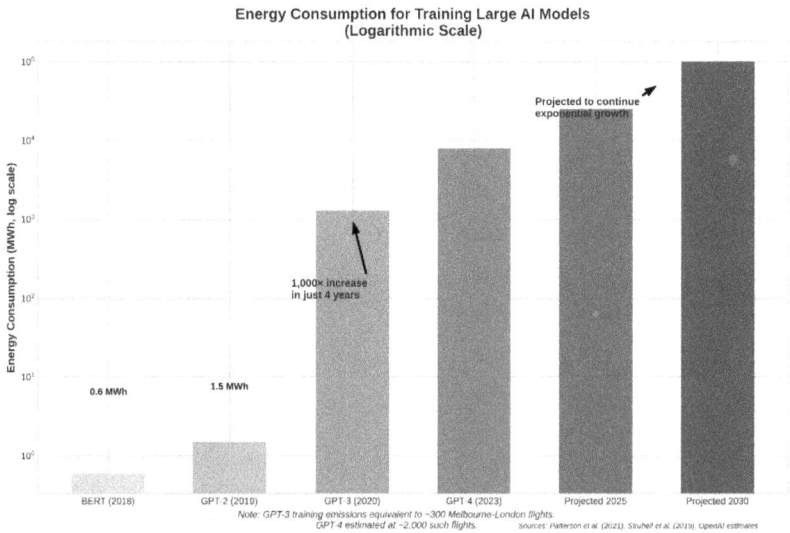

Energy Consumption for Training Large AI Models
(Logarithmic Scale)

Clean Energy Imperatives

The environmental implications of AI energy consumption depend critically on energy sources:

1. Carbon Intensity: AI systems powered by coal or gas generation can have substantial carbon footprints, potentially undermining climate goals even as AI enables efficiency improvements in other sectors.

2. Renewable Integration: The variable nature of renewable energy sources creates both challenges and opportunities for AI workloads, which have different flexibility characteristics than traditional computing.

3. Nuclear Considerations: Advanced nuclear technologies, from small modular reactors to fusion prospects, may offer low-carbon, reliable energy particularly suited to AI computational demands.

4. Location Sensitivity: The environmental impact of

identical AI systems can vary by orders of magnitude depending on where they operate, due to regional differences in energy sources.

These considerations suggest that sustainable AI development requires not merely energy efficiency but strategic integration with clean energy transitions.

Energy Consumption for Training Large AI Models
(Logarithmic Scale)

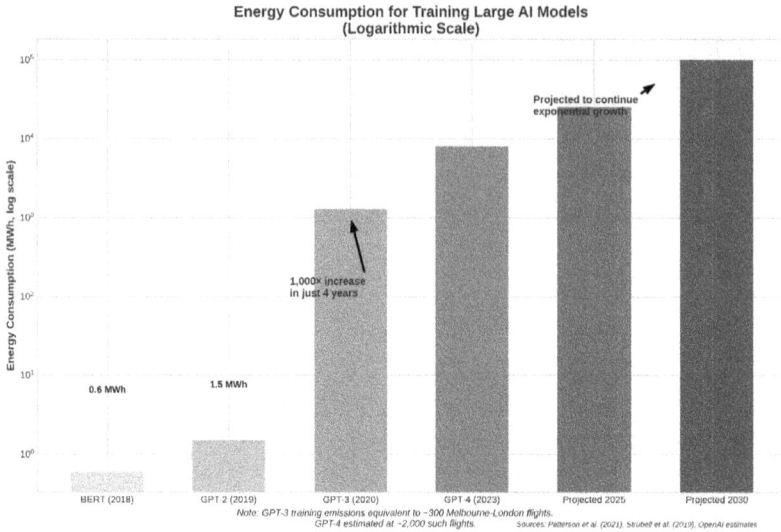

Note: GPT-3 training emissions equivalent to ~300 Melbourne-London flights.
GPT-4 estimated at ~2,000 such flights.
Sources: Patterson et al. (2021), Strubell et al. (2019), OpenAI estimates

Efficiency Innovations

Technological innovations offer potential pathways to reduce AI energy intensity:

1. Specialized Hardware: Custom chips designed specifically for AI workloads, like Google's Tensor Processing Units or Graphcore's Intelligence Processing Units, can achieve orders of magnitude better energy efficiency than general-purpose processors.

2. Algorithmic Improvements: More efficient algorithms and model architectures can dramatically reduce computational requirements for equivalent capabilities, as demonstrated by techniques like knowledge distillation and sparse attention.

3. Lifecycle Optimization: Considering energy use across

the full AI lifecycle—from training to deployment to updating —can identify optimization opportunities that single-phase analyses miss.

4. Quantum Computing Prospects: While still speculative, quantum computing approaches may eventually offer exponential efficiency improvements for certain AI workloads, though significant technical challenges remain.

INSIGHT: 2. "The current trajectory of AI energy consumption is fundamentally unsustainable—by 2030, AI systems could consume more electricity than entire nations, potentially triggering energy crises and accelerating climate change."

These efficiency pathways suggest that AI energy consumption need not grow linearly with capabilities, though realizing this potential requires deliberate focus on efficiency rather than merely capability expansion.

Energy Governance Approaches

Effective governance of AI energy use requires sophisticated approaches beyond simple restrictions:

1. Energy-Aware Standards: Developing standards and metrics that make AI systems' energy consumption transparent and comparable, enabling market and regulatory responses.

2. Differential Pricing: Energy pricing structures that reflect the true costs of consumption, including environmental externalities and grid impacts, creating appropriate incentives for efficiency.

3. Compute Commons: Public or cooperative computational infrastructure with governance structures that balance access with sustainability considerations.

4. International Coordination: Frameworks to prevent destructive competition for energy resources or exploitation

of regions with weaker environmental protections.

These governance approaches aim to ensure that energy constraints guide AI development toward more efficient approaches rather than merely limiting capabilities or concentrating them among those with privileged energy access.

Critical Materials: The Physical Foundations

Beyond energy, AI systems depend on a complex supply chain of critical materials, from semiconductor materials to cooling systems, creating additional sustainability and security challenges.

Semiconductor Supply Chains

Advanced AI systems rely on cutting-edge semiconductors with complex, globalized supply chains:

1. Geographic Concentration: Key steps in semiconductor manufacturing concentrate in specific regions—advanced chip fabrication in Taiwan, memory production in South Korea, specialized equipment in the Netherlands and Japan—creating both efficiency benefits and vulnerability risks.

2. Critical Materials: Semiconductor manufacturing requires numerous specialized materials, from ultra-pure silicon to rare gases like neon to various rare earth elements, each with its own supply constraints and geopolitical considerations.

3. Water Requirements: Advanced chip fabrication requires enormous quantities of ultra-pure water, creating potential conflicts in water-stressed regions and adding another resource constraint.

4. Manufacturing Energy: The energy embedded in semiconductor manufacturing—often occurring in regions with carbon-intensive electricity—can exceed the energy used during operation, particularly for devices with short lifespans.

These supply chain characteristics create both security concerns for nations and organizations dependent on AI capabilities and sustainability challenges regarding resource extraction and manufacturing impacts.

Rare Earth Elements and Critical Minerals

AI hardware depends on various critical minerals with concentrated supply chains:

INSIGHT: 3. "The tech industry's promises of AI-driven environmental solutions represent a dangerous form of techno-optimism that distracts from the immediate need for consumption reduction and regulatory intervention."

1. Rare Earth Elements: Materials like neodymium, praseodymium, and dysprosium play essential roles in computing hardware, from hard drives to speakers, with supply chains currently dominated by China.

2. Cobalt and Lithium: Battery technologies critical for mobile AI applications rely on these minerals, which face both supply concentration (particularly cobalt in the Democratic Republic of Congo) and extraction impacts.

3. Specialized Conductors: Advanced computing increasingly relies on specialized conducting materials like tantalum and indium tin oxide, each with its own supply constraints and geopolitical considerations.

4. Recycling Limitations: Many critical materials currently have limited recycling pathways, creating potential long-term supply constraints as demand grows.

These material dependencies create both near-term supply security challenges and longer-term sustainability questions about maintaining AI capabilities within planetary boundaries.

Circular Economy Approaches

Addressing material constraints requires moving beyond

linear extract-use-dispose models:

1. Design for Disassembly: Creating hardware specifically designed for easy separation of components and materials at end-of-life, enabling more effective recycling.

2. Urban Mining: Recovering valuable materials from existing electronic waste, which often contains higher concentrations of precious metals than natural ores.

3. Material Passports: Tracking the materials contained in devices throughout their lifecycle, creating both immediate visibility and future recovery opportunities.

4. Alternative Materials Research: Developing substitute materials that can provide similar functionality with more abundant or environmentally benign inputs.

These circular approaches can reduce both environmental impacts and supply security risks, though they require coordination across supply chains and product lifecycles.

Material Governance Frameworks

Effective governance of critical materials requires balancing legitimate security concerns with the benefits of specialization and exchange:

1. Strategic Reserves: Maintaining reserves of critical materials to buffer against supply disruptions, similar to strategic petroleum reserves but adapted to the different characteristics of technology materials.

2. Responsible Sourcing Standards: Frameworks to ensure that material extraction meets environmental and human rights standards, addressing the significant impacts of mining in many regions.

3. Trade Coordination: International agreements that prevent destructive resource nationalism while ensuring equitable access and reasonable security considerations.

4. Innovation Incentives: Targeted research support for

material efficiency, substitution, and recycling technologies that address critical supply constraints.

These governance approaches aim to ensure reliable access to necessary materials while addressing both sustainability impacts and equity considerations in their extraction and distribution.

INSIGHT: 4. "The rare earth minerals required for AI hardware are creating new forms of extractive colonialism in the Global South—effectively transferring environmental costs to the world's most vulnerable populations."

Data as a Resource: Governance Beyond Ownership

Data represents a critical resource for AI development with distinctive characteristics that traditional resource governance frameworks inadequately address.

Data's Distinctive Characteristics

Several characteristics distinguish data from traditional resources:

1. Non-Rivalrous Consumption: Unlike physical resources, data can be used simultaneously by multiple parties without diminishment, creating different economic dynamics than rivalrous goods.

2. Network Effects: The value of data often increases with scale and integration, creating strong tendencies toward concentration that traditional antitrust approaches may inadequately address.

3. Contextual Privacy Implications: Data that seems innocuous in isolation can reveal sensitive information when combined with other data, creating privacy challenges that simple consent models poorly address.

4. Cumulative Advantage: Organizations with more data can develop more capable AI systems, which then attract more users and generate more data, creating self-reinforcing

advantages.

These characteristics create both market failures that require governance intervention and opportunities for novel resource management approaches beyond traditional property frameworks.

Data Commons and Trusts

Collective governance approaches offer promising alternatives to both corporate data extraction and simplistic individual ownership models:

1. Data Commons: Pools of data made available under specific governance rules, enabling broader use while maintaining appropriate constraints on harmful applications.

2. Data Trusts: Legal structures that manage data according to fiduciary obligations to data subjects rather than extractive commercial imperatives.

3. Sectoral Data Cooperatives: User-owned structures that collectively govern data in specific domains, from health records to agricultural information to urban mobility patterns.

4. Public Data Infrastructure: Government-maintained data resources with appropriate privacy protections and governance structures, providing foundations for both public and private innovation.

These collective approaches recognize data's distinctive characteristics as a resource that emerges from social activity rather than individual creation, requiring governance models that reflect this collective nature.

Consent and Compensation Frameworks

Ensuring appropriate consent and benefit-sharing remains essential even within collective governance models:

1. Meaningful Consent Models: Moving beyond unread terms of service to contextual, ongoing consent frameworks

that reflect the actual uses and implications of data collection.

INSIGHT: 5. "The environmental impact of AI represents the greatest unpriced externality in modern economics—one that could render the technology's supposed benefits moot if not addressed immediately."

2. Data Dividends: Mechanisms to ensure that value generated from data flows back to those who contributed it, whether through direct payments, public services, or shared infrastructure.

3. Differential Privacy Techniques: Technical approaches that enable useful insights from data while providing mathematical guarantees against individual identification or harm.

4. Purpose Limitations: Governance frameworks that restrict data use to specific, beneficial purposes rather than allowing unlimited exploitation once collected.

These frameworks aim to ensure that data collection and use respects human agency and ensures equitable benefit distribution without preventing beneficial applications.

Global Data Governance Challenges

Data flows transcend national boundaries, creating governance challenges that exceed the capacity of individual jurisdictions:

1. Regulatory Fragmentation: Divergent approaches to data governance across jurisdictions create compliance challenges and potential for regulatory arbitrage.

2. Digital Colonialism Concerns: Data extraction from developing regions without appropriate benefit-sharing raises justice concerns similar to historical resource exploitation.

3. Cultural Variation: Different cultural contexts may have legitimately different expectations and norms regarding privacy, consent, and appropriate data use.

4. Sovereignty Questions: Nations increasingly assert data sovereignty claims that may conflict with both global innovation benefits and individual rights.

Addressing these challenges requires developing international coordination mechanisms that respect legitimate diversity in values and approaches while preventing race-to-the-bottom dynamics in data protection.

Computational Capacity: The New Critical Infrastructure

Computational capacity itself increasingly functions as a critical resource with distinctive characteristics and governance challenges.

Concentration Dynamics

Computational resources for advanced AI exhibit strong concentration tendencies:

1. Scale Economies: The massive capital requirements for state-of-the-art computing clusters create significant barriers to entry, with the largest systems now costing billions of dollars.

2. Talent Concentration: The specialized expertise required to design and operate advanced computing systems concentrates in a small number of organizations and regions.

3. Data Center Requirements: Physical constraints around power availability, cooling capacity, and connectivity limit where large-scale computing can efficiently operate.

4. Software Ecosystem Advantages: Organizations with established software ecosystems for managing computational resources gain compounding efficiency advantages over newcomers.

INSIGHT: 6. "The notion that we can achieve both exponential AI growth and environmental sustainability is perhaps the most dangerous delusion of our time—one that virtually guarantees ecological collapse."

These concentration dynamics create risks of both market power and capability disparities between organizations and nations, potentially undermining both innovation and equity goals.

Public Compute Infrastructure

Public or cooperative approaches to computational infrastructure offer potential responses to concentration concerns:

1. National Research Clouds: Government-provided computational resources for academic and public interest research, as proposed in various countries.

2. Federated Computing Commons: Distributed systems that enable smaller organizations to contribute and access computational resources through standardized interfaces.

3. Community Supercomputing: Regional computational resources governed by local stakeholders to ensure benefits flow to surrounding communities.

4. Compute as a Utility: Regulatory frameworks that treat large-scale computation as essential infrastructure with appropriate access and pricing requirements.

These approaches aim to ensure broader access to computational resources while maintaining incentives for continued development and responsible use.

Allocation Mechanisms

Determining who gets access to limited computational resources requires thoughtful allocation mechanisms:

1. Merit-Based Allocation: Processes that evaluate proposed uses based on potential scientific, social, or economic benefit rather than merely ability to pay.

2. Diversity Reservations: Setting aside portions of computational capacity for underrepresented groups or regions to prevent reinforcing existing advantages.

3. Tiered Access Models: Frameworks that provide different levels of access based on use case, with critical applications receiving priority over less essential ones.

4. Dynamic Pricing: Market mechanisms that adjust prices based on current demand and capacity, potentially with subsidies for high-value public interest applications.

These allocation approaches aim to balance efficiency with equity considerations, ensuring that computational resources support broad-based innovation and benefit.

International Coordination Challenges

As with other critical resources, computational capacity governance transcends national boundaries:

1. Export Controls: Nations increasingly restrict advanced computing technology exports, creating both security benefits and innovation costs that require careful balancing.

2. Standards Development: Technical standards for computational systems significantly influence who can effectively participate in their development and use.

INSIGHT: 7. "The concentration of computational resources in the hands of a few corporations isn't just an economic issue—it's an environmental justice crisis that gives these entities control over one of the largest sources of carbon emissions in the coming decade."

3. Brain Drain Concerns: The concentration of computational expertise in specific regions creates challenges for nations seeking to develop domestic capabilities.

4. Dual-Use Considerations: The same computational capabilities that enable beneficial AI applications can potentially power harmful ones, creating governance dilemmas.

Addressing these challenges requires developing international coordination mechanisms that balance legitimate security concerns with the benefits of collaboration and exchange in computational development.

Integrated Resource Governance: Beyond Siloed Approaches

Effective governance of AI's resource requirements necessitates integrated approaches that address interactions between energy, materials, data, and computation rather than treating each in isolation.

System Interactions and Tradeoffs

Resource domains exhibit significant interactions that siloed governance approaches may miss:

1. Energy-Computation Tradeoffs: More energy-efficient computing often requires more specialized hardware with greater material intensity, creating potential tradeoffs between energy and material impacts.

2. Data-Computation Relationships: More data-efficient algorithms may require greater computational resources for training, while data-hungry approaches may enable simpler computational architectures.

3. Geographical Interdependencies: Optimal locations for data centers depend on complex interactions between energy availability, cooling capacity, network connectivity, and political stability.

4. Temporal Dynamics: Resource requirements shift over AI system lifecycles, from training to deployment to updating, requiring governance approaches that address full lifecycle impacts.

Understanding these interactions enables more effective governance that addresses system-level outcomes rather than optimizing individual resources in counterproductive ways.

Multi-Stakeholder Governance Models

Effective resource governance requires incorporating

diverse perspectives beyond technical experts:

1. Inclusive Standard Setting: Ensuring that resource governance standards incorporate input from affected communities, not merely industry and technical specialists.

2. Transparent Impact Assessment: Regular, public evaluation of how resource allocation decisions affect different stakeholders and regions.

3. Deliberative Priority Setting: Processes that enable democratic input into how limited resources should be allocated across competing valuable uses.

4. Adaptive Management: Governance frameworks that evolve based on observed outcomes and changing conditions rather than remaining static.

These multi-stakeholder approaches help ensure that resource governance reflects diverse values and interests rather than merely technical or economic considerations.

Global Justice Considerations

Resource governance must address significant equity implications across regions and populations:

1. Differential Impacts: Resource constraints and governance decisions often affect vulnerable populations and regions most severely, requiring explicit attention to distributional outcomes.

2. Historical Responsibility: Nations and organizations that benefited from earlier, less constrained resource use bear different responsibilities than late developers facing tighter constraints.

3. Capability Development: Ensuring that governance approaches enable capability development in less-resourced regions rather than permanently cementing existing advantages.

4. Benefit Sharing: Creating mechanisms to ensure that

benefits from resource-intensive AI flow to those affected by its resource requirements, not merely to technology developers.

These justice considerations suggest that effective resource governance must address not merely efficiency but equity in how resources are allocated and benefits distributed.

Implementation Pathways

Moving toward integrated resource governance requires pragmatic implementation strategies:

1. Demonstration Projects: Implementing integrated governance approaches at smaller scales to demonstrate effectiveness before broader application.

2. Policy Experimentation: Enabling diverse governance approaches across jurisdictions to generate learning about what works in different contexts.

3. Incremental Standards Development: Building governance frameworks incrementally, starting with transparency requirements before moving to more directive approaches.

4. Stakeholder Capacity Building: Investing in capabilities that enable diverse stakeholders to meaningfully participate in resource governance rather than being excluded by technical complexity.

These implementation pathways recognize that resource governance transformation requires learning and adaptation rather than immediate comprehensive solutions.

Conclusion: Resources for an Inclusive AI Future

The resource requirements of advanced AI systems create both constraints and imperatives for technological development. Energy demands, material needs, data governance challenges, and computational capacity limitations all shape what AI development paths are sustainable and who can participate in them. Addressing these resource challenges requires sophisticated governance approaches that balance competing values—efficiency and equity, innovation and precaution, sovereignty and cooperation.

The approaches explored in this chapter—clean energy integration, circular material economies, collective data governance, and accessible computational infrastructure— each address different aspects of AI's resource requirements. Their effective integration could potentially enable AI development that remains within planetary boundaries while distributing benefits broadly.

This resource governance transformation involves not merely technical management but profound ethical and political choices about how we allocate limited resources across competing valuable uses. It requires moving beyond both techno-utopianism that ignores material constraints and techno-pessimism that sees only insurmountable limits, toward pragmatic approaches that navigate real constraints while maintaining commitment to broadly shared technological benefits.

The stakes could not be higher. Failure to govern AI's resource requirements sustainably could undermine both technological progress and ecological stability, while failure to govern these resources equitably could exacerbate global inequalities and conflicts. Success, however, could enable AI development that enhances human flourishing within planetary boundaries, creating foundations for genuinely sustainable prosperity.

The following chapter will explore how these resource considerations intersect with geopolitical dynamics, examining how AI capabilities increasingly influence national power and international relations.

Case Study: Iceland's Sustainable AI Infrastructure

Iceland's pioneering approach to sustainable AI infrastructure development provides a compelling case study of how nations can balance technological advancement with environmental responsibility.

As AI computing demands grew exponentially in the early 2020s, Iceland positioned itself as a global leader in sustainable AI infrastructure. The country's unique combination of 100% renewable energy (primarily geothermal and hydroelectric), naturally cool climate, and strategic location between North America and Europe made it an ideal location for data centers and AI computing facilities.

Strategic National Policy: In 2022, Iceland launched its "Sustainable Computing Initiative," a comprehensive national strategy to attract AI computing infrastructure while maintaining strict environmental standards. Rather than simply courting any data center operators, Iceland established the world's first sustainability certification specifically for AI computing facilities, requiring:
- 100% renewable energy usage
- Minimum Power Usage Effectiveness (PUE) ratings
- Water conservation measures
- Heat recapture systems for community use

Innovative Heat Recapture: Perhaps the most innovative aspect of Iceland's approach was its requirement that AI computing facilities implement heat recapture systems. The enormous heat generated by AI training runs—previously considered waste—is now captured and used to heat nearby communities, greenhouses, and industrial processes. The Reykjanes AI Computing Center, opened in 2024, provides heating for 12,000 homes and a 15-acre greenhouse complex growing vegetables year-round in Iceland's harsh climate.

Economic Transformation: The economic impact has been substantial. By 2025, sustainable AI infrastructure contributed approximately 8.7% to Iceland's GDP, creating over 4,200 direct jobs and an estimated 11,000 indirect jobs in a country of just 370,000 people. Importantly, these jobs span the skill spectrum—from highly technical roles in facility management to construction, security, and service industry positions supporting the sector.

Balanced Approach to Foreign Investment: Iceland carefully balanced attracting international AI companies with maintaining national sovereignty over this critical infrastructure. Foreign companies can operate facilities but must adhere to Iceland's data sovereignty laws, participate in knowledge transfer programs with local universities, and meet strict environmental standards that exceed global norms.

Challenges and Adaptations: Iceland's journey hasn't been without challenges. The rapid growth in computing demand strained the country's electricity grid, requiring accelerated investment in additional renewable energy capacity. Community concerns about land use for new facilities led to more stringent planning processes that better incorporated local input.

The Icelandic case demonstrates that with thoughtful policy design, nations can harness AI's economic potential while maintaining environmental integrity. As Iceland's Minister of Innovation noted in a 2025 address to the UN Climate Conference: "We rejected the false choice between technological advancement and environmental protection. By establishing clear sustainability requirements from the outset, we've created a model where AI development actually enhances rather than degrades our environmental goals."

Iceland's approach offers valuable lessons for other regions navigating the environmental challenges of AI infrastructure. It illustrates that with proper planning and policy frameworks, the physical layer of AI can be developed in harmony with climate objectives rather than in opposition to them.

CHAPTER 10: GEOPOLITICS OF AI: POWER, COMPETITION, AND COOPERATION IN A NEW ERA

The Geopolitical AI Race

In January 2023, a classified intelligence briefing sent shockwaves through Washington's national security establishment. Analysts had confirmed that a rival nation had achieved a significant breakthrough in artificial general intelligence capabilities—one that potentially leapfrogged U.S. technology by 18-24 months.

Admiral Rebecca Chen, then Deputy Director of National Intelligence, recalls the moment vividly. "The room went completely silent. We were facing a Sputnik moment for the AI era, but with far greater strategic implications."

Within 48 hours, the President convened an emergency meeting of the National Security Council. The discussion quickly revealed deep divisions about how to respond. Military leaders advocated for a massive increase in defense-oriented AI research. Diplomats pushed for international agreements to govern advanced AI development. Intelligence officials argued for covert operations to access the rival nation's technology. Economic advisors warned about potential impacts on global markets and technological supply chains.

"What struck me most was how unprepared we were for this scenario," Admiral Chen explained. "We had extensive plans for conventional military threats, cyberattacks, even pandemic response—but nothing adequate for an AI capability gap with a strategic competitor."

The situation intensified when satellite imagery revealed the construction of massive new computing facilities in the rival nation—infrastructure that would further accelerate their AI advantage. Meanwhile, their government had begun restricting exports of certain rare earth minerals critical to advanced semiconductor manufacturing, creating supply vulnerabilities for U.S. technology companies.

The crisis forced American officials to confront uncomfortable questions: Was advanced AI primarily a national security asset to be protected or a global public good to be shared? Could meaningful international governance be established for a technology that offered such significant strategic advantages? How could democratic nations compete with authoritarian systems willing to deploy AI without ethical constraints?

"We realized we weren't just dealing with a technological race but a clash of governance models," noted Admiral Chen. "The question wasn't simply who would develop the most advanced AI first, but under what values and principles these systems would operate."

The administration ultimately launched what became known as the "Democratic AI Initiative"—a whole-of-government approach combining accelerated research investment, new international partnerships, and the development of governance frameworks designed to ensure AI development aligned with democratic values.

This episode illustrates the profound geopolitical dimensions of the AI revolution. As artificial intelligence increasingly becomes the defining technology of our era, it is reshaping not just economies and societies but the global balance of power itself. Understanding these dynamics is essential for anyone seeking to navigate the complex intersection of technology, national security, and international relations in the coming decades.

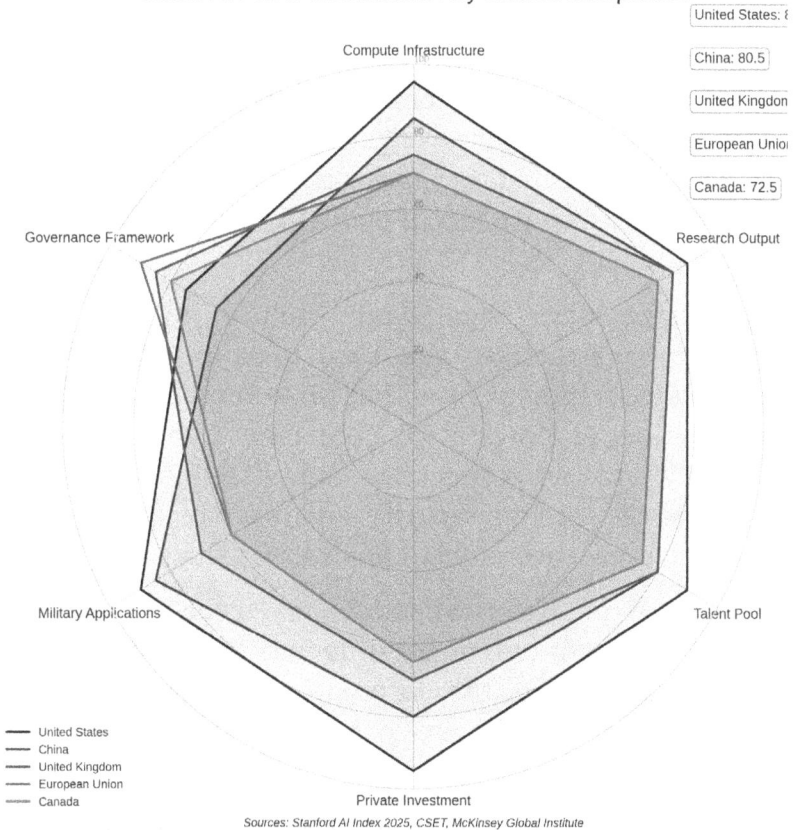

Global AI Power Distribution: Key Metrics Comparison

Sources: Stanford AI Index 2025, CSET, McKinsey Global Institute

Introduction: AI as a Geopolitical Force

Artificial intelligence has emerged as a transformative force not only in economics and society but in geopolitics and international relations. Nations increasingly view AI capabilities as critical determinants of future power, prosperity, and security, driving both intensifying competition and new imperatives for cooperation. This chapter examines how AI reshapes global power dynamics, influences strategic competition, creates new security challenges, and potentially enables novel forms of international cooperation.

Our analysis moves beyond both alarmist narratives that see only zero-sum competition and idealistic visions that ignore genuine security concerns. Instead, we examine how thoughtful governance approaches might enable beneficial competition that drives innovation while preventing destructive conflict and enabling cooperation on shared challenges. We argue that navigating AI geopolitics effectively requires sophisticated frameworks that balance legitimate national interests with global public goods and human rights considerations.

The stakes are significant: failure to manage AI geopolitics constructively could lead to dangerous arms races, technological fragmentation that undermines innovation, or concentration of power that threatens democratic values. Conversely, effective governance could enable AI development that enhances human security and welfare across nations while respecting sovereignty and diverse values.

The Changing Landscape of Global Power

AI capabilities increasingly influence the distribution and nature of power in the international system, reshaping traditional understandings of national strength and security.

AI and National Power

Several mechanisms connect AI capabilities to national power:

1. Economic Competitiveness: Nations with advanced AI capabilities gain advantages in productivity, innovation, and high-value industries, potentially reshaping global economic

hierarchies.

2. Military Applications: AI enhances military capabilities across domains—from intelligence and logistics to autonomous weapons and cyber operations—potentially shifting military balances.

3. Governance Capacity: AI tools can enhance state capacity to deliver services, monitor activities, and implement policies, potentially strengthening some governance models relative to others.

INSIGHT: The AI arms race between global powers represents a greater existential threat than nuclear weapons —creating the potential for technological conflicts that could spiral beyond human control or comprehension.

4. Soft Power Influence: Leadership in AI development and governance enables agenda-setting in international forums and standards bodies, shaping global norms and rules.

These mechanisms suggest that AI capabilities increasingly function as a critical component of comprehensive national power, influencing both absolute capabilities and relative position in the international system.

Shifting Power Distributions

AI development potentially reshapes global power distributions in complex ways:

1. Great Power Competition: The United States and China have emerged as the primary AI powers, with substantial capabilities across research, commercial applications, and military development, though with different strengths and approaches.

2. Middle Power Strategies: Nations like the United Kingdom, France, Canada, and South Korea pursue strategic specialization in specific AI domains where they can maintain competitive advantages despite resource constraints.

3. Regional Dynamics: Within regions, differential AI development creates new hierarchies and dependencies, as seen in Europe's internal digital divides or emerging patterns in Southeast Asia.

4. Non-State Actors: Large technology companies possess AI capabilities that exceed those of many nations, creating complex governance challenges as their interests may align or conflict with host countries.

These shifting distributions create both opportunities for new international leadership and risks of destabilizing power transitions that historical patterns suggest often create conflict potential.

Determinants of AI Power

Several factors influence nations' ability to develop and deploy advanced AI capabilities:

1. Talent Ecosystems: Access to skilled researchers, engineers, and entrepreneurs represents perhaps the most critical determinant of AI capabilities, driving competition for both education and immigration policies.

2. Data Resources: The quantity, quality, and diversity of data available for AI development significantly influences capabilities, creating advantages for nations with large digital economies or specific data governance approaches.

3. Computational Infrastructure: Access to advanced computing resources increasingly constrains frontier AI development, with the largest training runs requiring resources available to only a handful of organizations globally.

4. Investment Capacity: The substantial financial resources required for advanced AI development create advantages for wealthy nations and those willing to prioritize AI in national budgets.

These determinants suggest that AI power depends on

both structural advantages like market size and policy choices around education, immigration, investment, and governance.

Technological Sovereignty Concerns

Nations increasingly prioritize technological sovereignty in AI development:

1. Supply Chain Security: Concerns about foreign dependencies in critical AI components—from semiconductors to cloud infrastructure—drive efforts to develop domestic capabilities or trusted supplier networks.

2. Standards Control: Nations compete to influence technical standards that shape AI development, recognizing that standards embedding their values and interests create lasting advantages.

3. Regulatory Autonomy: Preserving the ability to regulate AI according to domestic values and priorities motivates resistance to both corporate power and foreign influence in governance.

4. Cultural Preservation: Concerns about AI systems embedding foreign cultural values or undermining local languages and traditions motivate efforts to develop domestically aligned systems.

INSIGHT: 2. "The concentration of AI capabilities in the US and China is creating a new bipolar world order that will render traditional geopolitical alliances obsolete within a decade."

These sovereignty concerns drive both defensive measures to reduce dependencies and offensive strategies to establish advantageous positions in global AI ecosystems.

Strategic Competition Dynamics

Competition for AI advantage has emerged as a defining feature of contemporary international relations, particularly between the United States and China.

The US-China AI Competition

Several dimensions characterize the intensifying competition between the primary AI powers:

1. Research Leadership: Competition for scientific and technical leadership manifests in publication output, citation impact, and breakthrough capabilities, with the US maintaining advantages in fundamental research while China rapidly closes gaps.

2. Commercial Applications: Competition extends to commercial AI applications across sectors, with Chinese firms dominant in some domains (e.g., facial recognition) while US companies lead in others (e.g., large language models).

3. Military Integration: Both nations pursue military applications of AI across domains, from intelligence analysis to autonomous systems, though with different organizational approaches and ethical frameworks.

4. Global Influence: Competition for influence over global AI governance through standards bodies, multilateral organizations, and bilateral relationships shapes the rules and norms governing AI development.

This multidimensional competition creates both innovation benefits through increased investment and risk of destructive dynamics that undermine shared interests in safe, beneficial AI.

Semiconductor Supply Chains

Control over advanced semiconductor supply chains has emerged as a critical front in strategic competition:

1. Chokepoint Technologies: Specific technologies like extreme ultraviolet lithography (EUV) machines represent critical chokepoints controlled by small numbers of companies in US-aligned countries.

2. Export Controls: Expanding restrictions on

semiconductor technology exports to China represent perhaps the most significant effort to constrain another nation's AI development capabilities.

3. Domestic Manufacturing Initiatives: Major initiatives like the US CHIPS Act and China's semiconductor self-sufficiency efforts reflect the strategic importance nations place on domestic semiconductor capabilities.

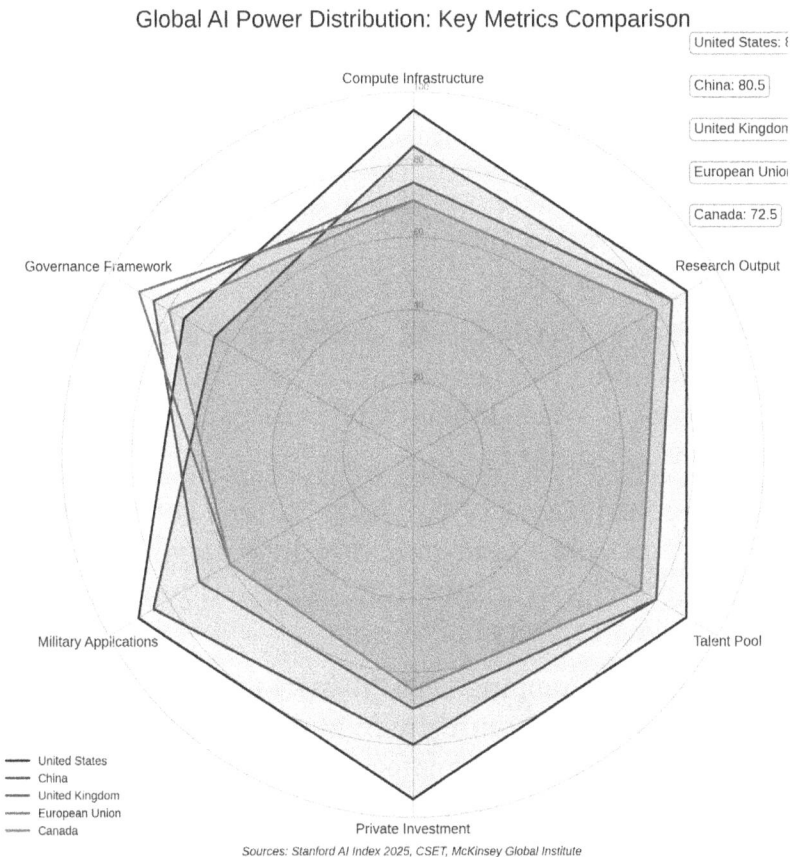

Global AI Power Distribution: Key Metrics Comparison

United States: 8
China: 80.5
United Kingdon
European Unio
Canada: 72.5

Compute Infrastructure
Governance Framework
Research Output
Military Applications
Talent Pool
Private Investment

United States
China
United Kingdom
European Union
Canada

Sources: Stanford AI Index 2025, CSET, McKinsey Global Institute

4. Talent Competition: Competition for specialized semiconductor design and manufacturing talent intensifies as nations recognize human capital as the fundamental constraint on developing domestic capabilities.

These semiconductor dynamics highlight how AI

competition increasingly focuses on controlling foundational technologies that enable broader capabilities rather than merely specific applications.

Regulatory Competition

Nations increasingly compete through regulatory approaches to AI:

1. Values Projection: Regulatory frameworks like the EU AI Act or China's algorithmic recommendations regulations project different values and priorities into global governance conversations.

2. Market Access Leverage: Large markets use access requirements to influence global AI development practices, as seen in data localization requirements or algorithmic transparency mandates.

INSIGHT: 3. "National AI strategies are fundamentally misguided—no single nation can effectively govern a technology that inherently transcends borders and traditional sovereignty."

3. Regulatory Capacity Building: Nations compete to build regulatory expertise and influence in emerging economies, shaping their governance approaches through technical assistance and capacity building.

4. Forum Shopping: Both nations and companies strategically engage with different international forums to advance preferred governance approaches, from technical standards bodies to UN agencies.

This regulatory competition shapes not merely compliance requirements but the fundamental values and priorities embedded in AI systems globally.

Alliance Dynamics

Strategic competition increasingly involves alliance formation around AI development and governance:

1. Formal Arrangements: Initiatives like the US-led Chip 4 Alliance or EU-US Trade and Technology Council create formal cooperation mechanisms among like-minded nations on AI-related issues.

2. Research Collaboration Networks: Patterns of research collaboration increasingly align with geopolitical blocs, with declining US-China cooperation and strengthening intra-bloc collaboration.

3. Standards Coalitions: Nations form voting blocs in international standards organizations to advance preferred approaches, as seen in debates over facial recognition standards or data governance frameworks.

4. Technology Control Regimes: Emerging export control coordination among allied nations seeks to prevent sensitive technology transfer while maintaining beneficial trade and research flows.

These alliance dynamics suggest that AI competition increasingly structures broader international relationships rather than merely reflecting existing alignments.

Security Challenges and Risks

AI capabilities create novel security challenges that existing governance frameworks inadequately address.

Military Applications and Arms Race Dynamics

AI's military applications create both capability enhancements and potential instability:

1. Autonomous Weapons Concerns: Development of weapons systems with increasing autonomy raises profound ethical, legal, and strategic questions about human control and accountability.

2. Intelligence Advantages: AI-enhanced intelligence capabilities create potential for significant information asymmetries that could destabilize deterrence relationships or

enable surprise actions.

3. Cyber Operations: AI enhances offensive cyber capabilities through automated vulnerability discovery, target selection, and attack execution, potentially lowering thresholds for harmful operations.

4. Command and Control Risks: Integrating AI into nuclear command and control systems could create new accident risks or undermine strategic stability through compressed decision timeframes.

These military applications create potential for destabilizing arms races if not governed through appropriate confidence-building measures and limitations.

Surveillance and Digital Authoritarianism

AI capabilities enable enhanced surveillance with significant human rights implications:

1. Facial Recognition Proliferation: Advanced facial recognition systems enable unprecedented monitoring capabilities, with both legitimate security applications and potential for political control.

INSIGHT: 4. "The semiconductor supply chain has become the new oil—whoever controls advanced chip manufacturing will effectively control the global economy in the AI era."

2. Predictive Policing Concerns: AI systems that predict potential criminal activity risk encoding and amplifying existing biases while enabling preemptive restrictions on civil liberties.

3. Digital Transnationalism: Surveillance technologies and practices increasingly transcend borders through both export of systems and surveillance of diaspora communities.

4. Dual-Use Challenges: Technologies developed for legitimate security purposes can enable human rights abuses when transferred to regimes with inadequate oversight or

different values.

These surveillance capabilities create both domestic governance challenges and international tensions as nations promote competing norms around appropriate limitations.

Information Operations and Societal Resilience

AI enhances capabilities for information operations that target societal cohesion:

1. Synthetic Media: Increasingly sophisticated generative AI enables creation of synthetic text, images, audio, and video that can manipulate public discourse and undermine trust.

2. Personalized Persuasion: AI-enabled micro-targeting allows tailoring of persuasive content to individual psychological profiles, potentially increasing effectiveness of influence operations.

3. Automated Operations: AI systems can automate and scale information operations that previously required significant human resources, lowering costs of interference.

4. Detection Challenges: Distinguishing legitimate expression from coordinated inauthentic behavior becomes increasingly difficult as synthetic content quality improves.

These information operation capabilities create new vulnerabilities for democratic societies in particular, where open information environments can be exploited for harmful purposes.

Existential Risk Considerations

Advanced AI capabilities potentially create unprecedented risks to human security:

1. Alignment Challenges: Ensuring that highly capable AI systems reliably pursue human-aligned goals represents a profound technical and governance challenge with potential catastrophic consequences for failure.

2. Proliferation Risks: As development capabilities spread,

ensuring appropriate safety standards and preventing malicious applications becomes increasingly difficult.

3. System Interactions: Complex interactions between AI systems operating in different domains could create emergent risks that individual system designers cannot anticipate.

4. Governance Gaps: Existing international security institutions lack appropriate expertise, authority, and mechanisms to address novel risks from advanced AI systems.

These existential considerations suggest that traditional competitive approaches to security may prove dangerously inadequate for managing the most significant AI risks.

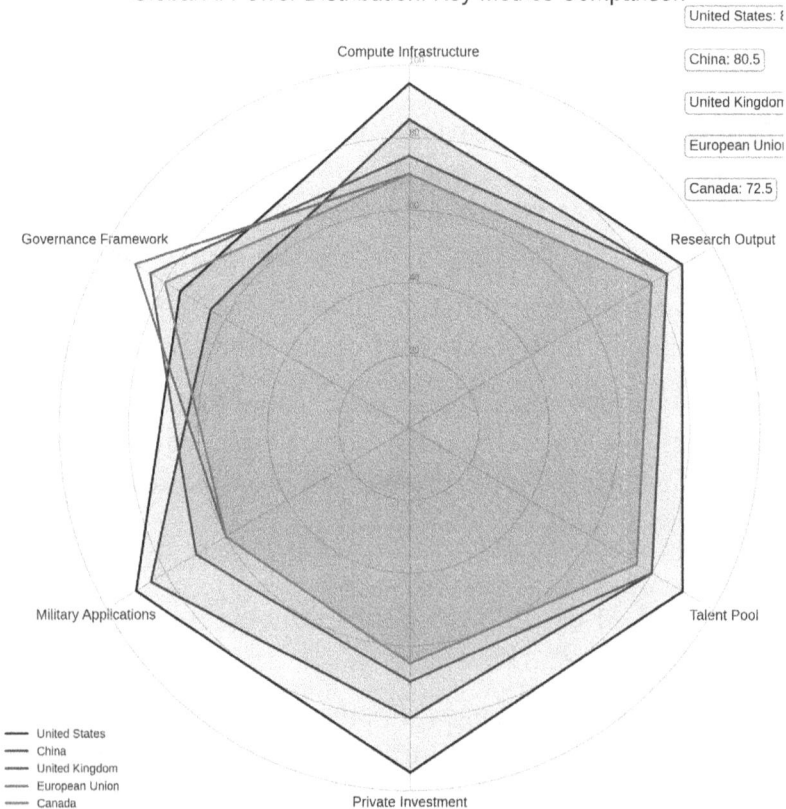

Global AI Power Distribution: Key Metrics Comparison

United States: 8
China: 80.5
United Kingdom
European Union
Canada: 72.5

Compute Infrastructure
Governance Framework
Research Output
Military Applications
Talent Pool
Private Investment

United States
China
United Kingdom
European Union
Canada

Sources: Stanford AI Index 2025, CSET, McKinsey Global Institute

Cooperation Imperatives and Governance Approaches

Despite intensifying competition, several factors create imperatives for international cooperation on AI governance.

Shared Risk Management

INSIGHT: 5. "Open-source AI development isn't the democratizing force many claim—it primarily accelerates capabilities while allowing dominant players to externalize risks and responsibilities."

Several AI risks create shared interests in cooperative management:

1. Safety Research: Ensuring that advanced AI systems remain safe and controllable represents a global public good that benefits from collaborative research and standard-setting.

2. Proliferation Prevention: Preventing the spread of potentially harmful AI capabilities to malicious actors creates shared interests in coordinated controls and norms.

3. Accident Prevention: Developing protocols and standards to prevent harmful accidents from AI systems benefits all nations regardless of competitive dynamics.

4. Crisis Communication: Establishing communication channels and shared understanding to manage potential crises involving AI systems serves universal security interests.

These shared risk management interests suggest potential for cooperation even amid broader strategic competition, similar to arms control during the Cold War.

Global Public Goods

Several aspects of AI governance represent global public goods requiring cooperation:

1. Research Transparency: Norms and mechanisms for transparency about capabilities and limitations of advanced AI systems benefit the entire field while reducing accident risks.

2. Shared Ethical Frameworks: Despite legitimate value differences, developing some shared ethical principles for AI

development creates benefits across jurisdictions.

3. Standards Interoperability: Technical standards that enable interoperability while ensuring safety and security create efficiency benefits for all participants.

4. Beneficial AI Applications: Cooperation on AI applications for shared challenges like climate change, pandemic prevention, or sustainable development creates benefits transcending national boundaries.

These public goods characteristics suggest that purely competitive approaches to AI governance risk significant collective action failures and missed opportunities.

Governance Forum Development

Several governance forums have emerged to address international AI challenges:

1. Multilateral Organizations: Entities like UNESCO, the OECD, and various UN agencies have developed AI principles, recommendations, and coordination mechanisms with varying levels of specificity and enforceability.

2. Multi-stakeholder Initiatives: Forums like the Global Partnership on AI bring together governments, industry, civil society, and academia to develop governance approaches across sectors and borders.

3. Bilateral Dialogues: Direct engagement between key nations, particularly the US and China, creates opportunities to develop shared understanding and potential cooperation despite broader competition.

4. Technical Standards Bodies: Organizations like the IEEE and ISO develop technical standards with significant governance implications, creating forums for both cooperation and competition.

These diverse forums create a complex governance ecosystem with both complementary functions and potential forum-shopping opportunities that require strategic coordination.

Balancing Competition and Cooperation

Effective AI governance requires sophisticated approaches that balance legitimate competitive interests with cooperation imperatives:

INSIGHT: 6. "The existential risk from advanced AI isn't science fiction—it represents the first technology humans have created that could potentially render us extinct through emergent behaviors we cannot predict or control."

1. Differentiated Governance: Distinguishing domains where competition benefits innovation from those where cooperation prevents harmful outcomes enables more nuanced approaches than all-or-nothing framing.

2. Minilateral Coordination: Smaller groups of like-minded nations can develop governance approaches that balance effectiveness with inclusivity, potentially expanding participation over time.

3. Track II Dialogues: Unofficial engagement between experts across competing nations can develop shared understanding and potential governance approaches even when official relations remain constrained.

4. Confidence-Building Measures: Incremental steps that build trust without requiring full cooperation can create foundations for more ambitious governance over time.

These balanced approaches recognize that neither unrestricted competition nor comprehensive cooperation represents a realistic or desirable governance path.

Regional Perspectives and Approaches

Beyond the US-China dynamic, diverse regional approaches to AI governance reflect different priorities, capabilities, and strategic positions.

European Union: The Regulatory Power

The EU has emerged as a distinctive AI governance actor:

1. Risk-Based Regulation: The AI Act establishes a comprehensive regulatory framework categorizing AI systems by risk level and imposing proportionate requirements.

2. Digital Sovereignty: Strategic autonomy initiatives aim to reduce dependencies on foreign technology while building European capabilities in key AI domains.

3. Values Projection: Regulatory approaches explicitly aim to project European values globally through market access requirements and influence on international standards.

4. Balancing Act: European positioning seeks to maintain strategic relationships with both the US and China while developing independent capabilities and governance approaches.

This European approach represents perhaps the most developed regulatory model globally, though questions remain about its impact on innovation and global influence.

Global South Perspectives

Emerging economies pursue diverse approaches to AI development and governance:

1. India's Strategic Positioning: India leverages its substantial technical talent and growing digital economy to develop distinctive AI capabilities while maintaining strategic autonomy between competing blocs.

2. African Approaches: African nations develop governance frameworks that address specific regional priorities like inclusion, development impact, and protection against extractive data practices.

3. Latin American Models: Countries like Brazil and Mexico navigate relationships with both US and Chinese technology ecosystems while developing regulatory approaches that

reflect regional values and priorities.

4. ASEAN Strategies: Southeast Asian nations balance economic opportunities from AI adoption with concerns about sovereignty and security amid US-China competition in their region.

These diverse approaches highlight that effective global AI governance must incorporate perspectives beyond the dominant powers to address the full range of impacts and considerations.

Small State Strategies

INSIGHT: 7. "International AI governance efforts are largely theatrical—designed to create the appearance of oversight while allowing unfettered development that benefits existing power structures."

Smaller nations develop distinctive approaches to maintain influence despite resource constraints:

1. Singapore's Hub Strategy: Positioning as a trusted governance hub and testbed for responsible AI applications creates influence beyond Singapore's size.

2. Nordic Cooperation: Collaborative approaches among Nordic countries leverage shared values and complementary capabilities to influence global governance conversations.

3. Specialized Leadership: Countries like Canada and the Netherlands develop specialized expertise in particular AI governance domains, from ethical frameworks to specific applications.

4. Coalition Building: Smaller nations form coalitions around shared interests to amplify influence in international forums beyond what individual action would achieve.

These small state strategies demonstrate that meaningful participation in AI governance remains possible despite resource constraints through strategic specialization and collaboration.

Regional Organizations and Frameworks

Regional coordination mechanisms increasingly address AI governance:

1. ASEAN Digital Masterplan: Coordinated approaches to digital economy development, including AI, aim to enhance regional competitiveness while addressing shared challenges.

2. African Union Frameworks: Emerging continental approaches seek to ensure AI benefits African development while protecting against harmful applications or extractive practices.

3. Organization of American States Initiatives: Regional coordination in the Americas addresses shared concerns from cybersecurity to workforce development.

4. Arab League Coordination: Emerging cooperation among Arab states addresses Arabic language representation, cultural considerations, and shared regulatory approaches.

These regional frameworks provide important intermediate governance layers between national and global approaches, addressing shared regional concerns while respecting contextual differences.

Future Trajectories and Strategic Choices

The future of AI geopolitics remains uncertain, with several potential trajectories depending on critical strategic choices by key actors.

Scenario: Intensifying Zero-Sum Competition

One potential trajectory involves escalating competition with limited cooperation:

1. Technology Decoupling: Supply chain separation accelerates across AI ecosystems, with competing standards, platforms, and governance approaches.

2. Innovation Inefficiency: Duplicated research efforts,

limited knowledge sharing, and fragmented markets reduce overall innovation pace despite increased investment.

3. Security Dilemmas: Lack of transparency and communication about capabilities creates misperceptions that drive worst-case planning and potential arms races.

4. Governance Fragmentation: Competing governance blocs develop incompatible approaches, creating compliance challenges and undermining global standards.

This trajectory risks significant opportunity costs through inefficient innovation while potentially increasing security risks through miscalculation or accident.

Scenario: Managed Strategic Competition

An alternative trajectory involves competition within cooperative frameworks:

1. Bounded Competition: Clear distinctions between domains where competition benefits innovation and those where cooperation prevents harm enable more constructive engagement.

2. Interoperable Standards: Despite competition, maintained interoperability through shared technical standards enables efficiency and continued knowledge exchange.

3. Crisis Prevention Mechanisms: Communication channels and confidence-building measures reduce accident risks and enable coordinated responses to emerging challenges.

4. Layered Governance: Complementary governance at national, regional, and global levels addresses different aspects of AI development and deployment.

This trajectory potentially captures innovation benefits from competition while mitigating the most significant risks through targeted cooperation.

Scenario: Fragmented Multipolarity

A third trajectory involves more complex fragmentation beyond binary competition:

1. Multiple Governance Blocs: Several competing approaches emerge rather than binary US-China competition, with the EU, India, and other regions developing distinctive models.

2. Issue-Specific Coalitions: Different groupings of nations cooperate on specific governance challenges rather than forming consistent blocs across all issues.

3. Non-State Governance: Private governance through corporate policies and technical standards gains importance relative to traditional state-based approaches.

4. Localized Innovation: More distributed innovation emerges as capabilities spread globally, with specialized regional strengths rather than comprehensive dominance.

This trajectory creates both coordination challenges through complexity and potential resilience benefits through diversity of approaches.

Critical Strategic Choices

Several near-term choices will significantly influence which trajectory emerges:

1. Export Control Scope: Decisions about the breadth and depth of technology transfer restrictions will significantly shape global AI development patterns and relationships.

2. Research Openness: Approaches to international research collaboration and publication, particularly regarding safety-relevant findings, will influence both innovation and security outcomes.

3. Standards Engagement: Whether nations pursue collaborative or competitive approaches to technical standards development will shape interoperability and governance effectiveness.

4. Institutional Investment: Commitment to developing

robust international governance institutions capable of addressing AI challenges will determine whether effective coordination emerges.

These strategic choices suggest that future trajectories remain significantly malleable rather than predetermined, with opportunities to shape more beneficial outcomes through thoughtful governance approaches.

Conclusion: Toward Beneficial AI Geopolitics

Artificial intelligence has emerged as a transformative force in international relations, reshaping power distributions, strategic competition, security challenges, and cooperation imperatives. The approaches explored in this chapter —from managing military applications to developing shared governance forums to balancing competition with cooperation—each address different aspects of this complex geopolitical landscape.

Navigating AI geopolitics effectively requires moving beyond simplistic framing of either unrestricted competition or comprehensive cooperation. Instead, sophisticated approaches must distinguish domains where competition drives beneficial innovation from those where cooperation prevents harmful outcomes. They must balance legitimate national interests in technological development with shared global interests in safe, beneficial AI.

The stakes could not be higher. Failure to manage AI geopolitics constructively could lead to dangerous arms races, technological fragmentation that undermines innovation, or concentration of power that threatens democratic values. Success, however, could enable AI development that enhances human security and welfare across nations while respecting sovereignty and diverse values.

As we navigate these challenges, we must recognize that technology itself embeds values and power relationships. The governance approaches we develop for AI will shape not merely who benefits from these technologies but what kind of world they help create. This recognition places profound responsibility on current decision-makers to develop governance approaches that enable AI to enhance human flourishing across nations rather than exacerbating conflict or concentration of power.

The following chapter will explore how these geopolitical considerations intersect with fundamental questions about privacy, surveillance, and human rights in an AI-enabled world.

Case Study: The US-China AI Competition and Its Global Implications

The strategic competition between the United States and China in artificial intelligence development provides a compelling case study of how geopolitical tensions are reshaping the global AI landscape with far-reaching consequences.

By 2023, what began as a technological rivalry had evolved into a full-spectrum geopolitical contest, with both nations implementing increasingly aggressive policies to secure advantage in AI development and deployment.

The Semiconductor Chokepoint: The most dramatic escalation came with the October 2022 US export controls on advanced semiconductors and chip-making equipment to China. These restrictions targeted the physical foundation of AI development—the specialized chips required for training and running sophisticated AI models. The Biden administration's controls went beyond previous measures by restricting not just American companies but also foreign firms using US technology, effectively creating a global blockade on advanced semiconductor exports to China.

China's response was swift and multifaceted. In early 2023, Beijing announced a $143 billion package to accelerate domestic semiconductor development, while simultaneously implementing new regulations restricting the export of critical minerals essential for advanced manufacturing. This created a mirror-image vulnerability for Western supply chains.

Data Sovereignty Battles: The competition extended beyond hardware to the data realm. China's 2021 Data Security Law and 2023 expanded algorithmic regulations created the world's most comprehensive data sovereignty regime, effectively preventing foreign AI systems from accessing Chinese data at scale. The US and EU responded with their own data localization requirements, fragmenting what had previously been a relatively open global data ecosystem.

Talent Competition: Perhaps most consequentially, the AI talent pool became explicitly weaponized in this competition. The US implemented the National Security Innovation Pathway in 2023, creating expedited immigration processes for AI researchers and engineers, while simultaneously expanding visa restrictions for Chinese students in sensitive technical fields. China countered with its "Thousand Talents 2.0" program, offering unprecedented compensation packages and research funding to attract global AI talent.

Dual-Use Dilemmas: The inherently dual-use nature of AI technology complicated this competition. The same foundation models powering civilian applications could be repurposed for intelligence analysis, cyber operations, and autonomous weapons systems. This blurring of civilian and military applications led both nations to treat increasingly broad categories of AI research as national security concerns.

Global Implications: The consequences of this competition extended far beyond the two principal powers. Smaller nations and companies found themselves forced to choose sides in what some analysts termed the "AI Iron Curtain." Countries like Canada, Israel, and Singapore—all with significant AI research communities—faced mounting pressure to align their AI policies with either the US or China.

The case illustrates how geopolitical competition is fundamentally reshaping the development trajectory of artificial intelligence. As former Google CEO Eric Schmidt observed in a 2024 address: "We're witnessing the end of the brief era of relatively open, global AI development. The technology is now too strategically valuable to remain outside national security frameworks."

This geopolitical dimension adds another layer of complexity to AI governance challenges. Any effective approach to managing AI's societal impacts must now account not just for technical and ethical considerations, but also for the reality of great power competition that increasingly views AI supremacy as essential to national security and economic prosperity.

CHAPTER 11: PRIVACY, SURVEILLANCE, AND HUMAN RIGHTS IN THE AI ERA

The Surveillance Paradox

In 2023, Emma Lawson, a 29-year-old marketing executive in Chicago, made what seemed like a reasonable decision to enhance her personal security. After a break-in at a neighboring apartment, she installed a smart security system that included facial recognition cameras, motion sensors, and an AI assistant that could detect unusual activity and alert her through a smartphone app.

"I just wanted to feel safe in my own home," Emma explained. "The system was surprisingly affordable and promised 'peace of mind through intelligent monitoring.'"

Within weeks, Emma's sense of security had transformed into something more complicated. The system worked remarkably well—perhaps too well. It recognized her friends and family, categorized delivery personnel by company, and even identified neighborhood cats that frequented her balcony. But it was also collecting vast amounts of data about Emma herself: when she came and went, which rooms she used most frequently, when she was awake or asleep, and even subtle patterns in her daily routine.

"I started getting notifications that were unsettling in their intimacy," she recalled. "'You've been home for 72 hours straight—everything okay?' or 'Your sleep patterns have changed significantly this week.' The system knew things about me that even my closest friends didn't notice."

The turning point came when Emma received a targeted advertisement for antidepressants on her social media feed —just days after her security system had detected changes in her sleep and movement patterns consistent with mild depression. Though she couldn't prove a connection, the coincidence was too striking to ignore.

"That's when it hit me: I had invited this surveillance into my home to protect me from unlikely external threats, while creating a much more pervasive internal monitoring system that was commodifying intimate details of my life."

Emma's experience illustrates what privacy scholars call the "surveillance paradox" of the AI era: technologies that promise to enhance our security, convenience, or wellbeing often do so by collecting unprecedented amounts of personal data, creating new vulnerabilities even as they address others.

This paradox extends far beyond home security systems. From health apps that track our vital signs to smart speakers that listen for our commands, from workplace productivity tools that monitor our output to public spaces increasingly covered by intelligent cameras—we are surrounded by technologies that offer genuine benefits while simultaneously enabling levels of surveillance that would have been unimaginable just a decade ago.

"The most insidious aspect is how voluntary it all seems," Emma reflected. "Nobody forced me to install those cameras or use that AI assistant. I chose it, paid for it, even recommended it to friends. But I never fully understood what I was giving up in exchange for that promised security."

As artificial intelligence becomes increasingly embedded in our daily lives, navigating this surveillance paradox becomes one of the central challenges of our time. How do we harness AI's benefits without surrendering our privacy and autonomy? What protections are needed when the most intimate details of our lives become data points for algorithmic analysis? And perhaps most fundamentally, how do we preserve human dignity and freedom in an age of increasingly pervasive digital monitoring?

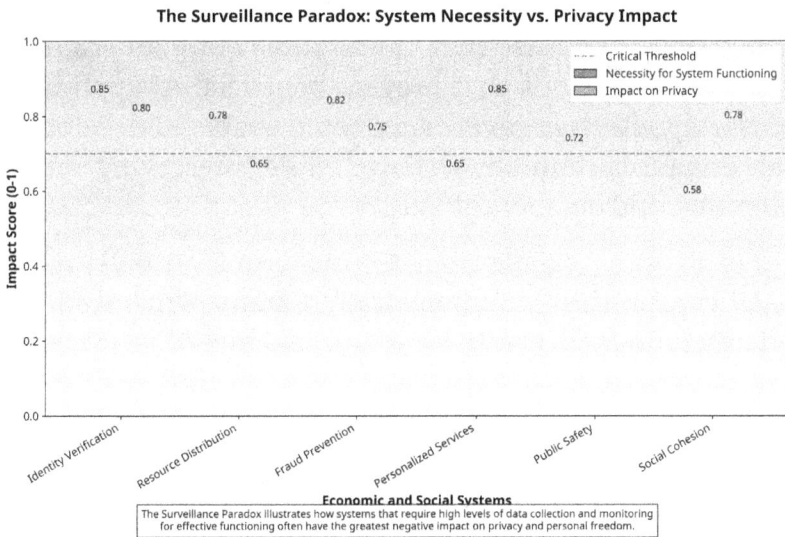

The Surveillance Paradox: System Necessity vs. Privacy Impact

The Surveillance Paradox illustrates how systems that require high levels of data collection and monitoring for effective functioning often have the greatest negative impact on privacy and personal freedom.

Introduction: The Surveillance Paradox

As artificial intelligence transforms our social and economic systems, we face a profound paradox regarding privacy and surveillance. The same technologies that enable unprecedented monitoring and control also create new possibilities for privacy protection, anonymity, and resistance to surveillance. This chapter examines this paradox and explores approaches to ensure that AI development respects fundamental human rights while enabling beneficial applications that inevitably process personal data.

Our analysis moves beyond both privacy absolutism that would prevent beneficial AI applications and surveillance apologism that dismisses legitimate concerns about control and autonomy. Instead, we examine how thoughtful governance approaches might enable privacy-preserving AI development that respects human rights while allowing innovation. We argue that addressing these challenges requires sophisticated technical, legal, and social frameworks that balance competing values while maintaining core commitments to human dignity and autonomy.

The stakes are significant: failure to address privacy and surveillance challenges could lead to either harmful surveillance systems that undermine human rights or excessive restrictions that prevent beneficial AI applications. Conversely, effective governance could enable AI development that enhances human welfare while preserving privacy, autonomy, and democratic values.

The Evolving Landscape of Privacy and Surveillance

AI capabilities fundamentally transform traditional understandings of privacy and surveillance through several mechanisms.

From Targeted to Ambient Surveillance

Traditional surveillance focused on specific targets, while AI enables more pervasive monitoring:

1. Scale Transformation: AI systems can monitor and analyze vastly more data than human analysts, enabling surveillance at population scale rather than merely of specific targets.

2. Persistent Observation: Networked sensors combined with AI analysis enable continuous monitoring across physical and digital spaces, eliminating temporal gaps in surveillance coverage.

3. Inferential Capabilities: Beyond direct observation, AI

systems can infer sensitive attributes and likely behaviors from seemingly innocuous data, creating surveillance capabilities that operate through correlation and prediction.

INSIGHT: Privacy as we've understood it for centuries is effectively dead—not because of technological inevitability but because of deliberate business models that monetize surveillance.

4. Automated Decision Systems: Surveillance increasingly connects directly to automated decisions affecting individuals' rights and opportunities, from content moderation to benefit eligibility to law enforcement responses.

These transformations create qualitatively different privacy challenges than previous technologies, requiring governance responses that address these distinctive characteristics.

The Surveillance Business Model

Commercial surveillance has emerged as perhaps the dominant privacy challenge:

1. Attention Economy: Business models based on capturing and monetizing attention create powerful incentives for extensive data collection and behavioral prediction.

2. Prediction Products: Companies increasingly sell not merely advertising but detailed behavioral predictions based on comprehensive monitoring, creating markets for surveillance capabilities.

3. Infrastructure Concentration: Essential digital infrastructure increasingly concentrates among companies with surveillance-based business models, creating both privacy risks and potential points of governance leverage.

4. Regulatory Arbitrage: Global operations enable companies to exploit jurisdictional differences in privacy protection, potentially undermining stronger regulatory approaches.

These commercial dynamics create privacy challenges that traditional state-focused civil liberties frameworks inadequately address, requiring governance approaches that engage with market structures and business models.

State Surveillance Capabilities

State actors develop increasingly sophisticated surveillance capabilities:

1. Intelligence Collection: National security agencies develop advanced capabilities for bulk data collection and analysis, raising questions about appropriate limitations and oversight.

2. Law Enforcement Use: Police agencies increasingly adopt AI-enhanced surveillance tools, from facial recognition to predictive policing, often with limited transparency or accountability mechanisms.

3. Public-Private Partnerships: Governments increasingly access commercial surveillance capabilities through both formal arrangements and informal access, potentially circumventing legal constraints on direct collection.

4. Transnational Surveillance: Digital communications enable surveillance across jurisdictional boundaries, creating both security benefits and potential for rights violations beyond territorial constraints.

These state capabilities create legitimate tensions between security interests and civil liberties that require sophisticated governance approaches to navigate effectively.

Privacy-Enhancing Technologies

Alongside surveillance capabilities, privacy-enhancing technologies continue to develop:

1. Encryption Advances: End-to-end encryption increasingly protects communications content from interception, though metadata often remains vulnerable.

2. Differential Privacy: Mathematical techniques enable useful statistical analysis while providing formal privacy guarantees for individual data subjects.

3. Federated Learning: Distributed machine learning approaches enable model training without centralizing sensitive data, potentially preserving privacy while enabling beneficial applications.

4. Zero-Knowledge Proofs: Cryptographic techniques allow verification of claims without revealing underlying information, enabling privacy-preserving authentication and compliance.

These technical approaches suggest that privacy protection need not categorically prevent beneficial AI applications, though their effectiveness depends significantly on both technical design and governance frameworks.

INSIGHT: 2. "The 'privacy paradox' isn't a paradox at all —it's a carefully engineered system of manipulative design and false choices that exploits cognitive biases to extract data consent."

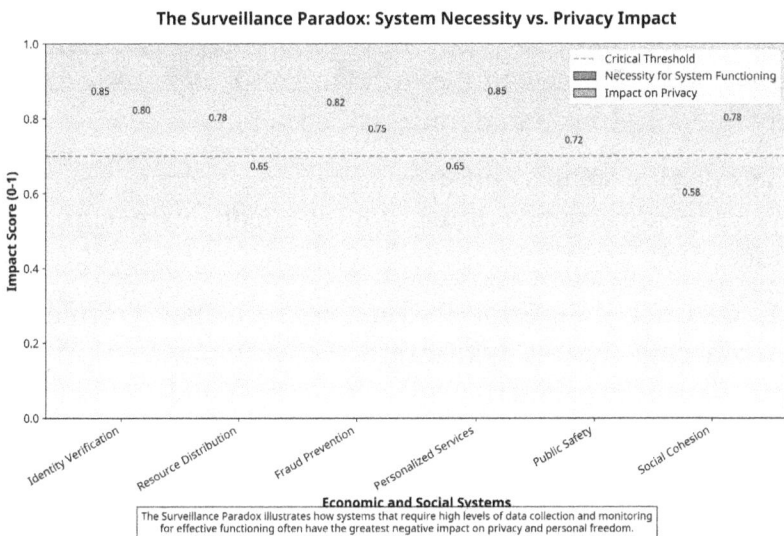

The Surveillance Paradox: System Necessity vs. Privacy Impact

The Surveillance Paradox illustrates how systems that require high levels of data collection and monitoring for effective functioning often have the greatest negative impact on privacy and personal freedom.

Fundamental Rights and Values at Stake

Privacy and surveillance challenges implicate several fundamental rights and values that effective governance must address.

Privacy as Fundamental Right

Privacy protection rests on several distinct but related foundations:

1. Dignity and Autonomy: Privacy enables personal dignity and autonomous decision-making by creating spaces free from external observation and judgment.

2. Intellectual Freedom: Privacy protects intellectual exploration and development by enabling individuals to consider ideas and develop beliefs without fear of surveillance.

3. Association and Expression: Privacy enables freedom of association and expression by protecting individuals from monitoring that might chill legitimate political and social activities.

4. Identity Development: Privacy creates space for authentic identity development and expression, particularly important for marginalized groups facing potential discrimination.

These foundations suggest that privacy represents not merely a preference but a fundamental right essential to human flourishing and democratic society.

Competing Values and Interests

Privacy governance must address legitimate competing values:

1. Security Interests: Preventing terrorism, crime, and other harms creates legitimate security interests in some surveillance capabilities, requiring balanced rather than absolute approaches.

2. Public Health: Health monitoring and disease prevention create legitimate interests in certain data collection and analysis, as demonstrated during the COVID-19 pandemic.

3. Economic Innovation: Beneficial AI applications often require some data access, creating tension between privacy protection and enabling innovation.

4. Transparency and Accountability: Privacy interests sometimes tension with transparency goals, as when privacy protections shield powerful actors from appropriate scrutiny.

These competing values suggest that effective governance requires nuanced balancing rather than absolutist approaches to either privacy or surveillance.

Differential Impacts and Justice Considerations

Privacy violations and surveillance often affect populations differently:

1. Marginalized Communities: Surveillance historically targets marginalized communities disproportionately, from political dissidents to racial minorities to LGBTQ+ individuals.

2. Global Inequities: Privacy protections vary significantly across jurisdictions, creating potential for exploitation of vulnerable populations with weaker legal protections.

3. Digital Divides: Access to privacy-enhancing technologies often correlates with privilege, creating potential for two-tier privacy protection that exacerbates existing inequalities.

4. Contextual Expectations: Privacy expectations and needs vary across cultural contexts, requiring governance approaches that respect legitimate diversity while maintaining core protections.

INSIGHT: 3. "The notion that AI surveillance systems can be made 'ethical' through technical fixes is a dangerous myth that distracts from the fundamental power imbalances these systems create and reinforce."

These differential impacts suggest that effective privacy governance must explicitly address justice considerations rather than assuming uniform effects across populations.

Chilling Effects and Democratic Implications

Surveillance creates significant implications for democratic governance:

1. Political Participation: Awareness of surveillance can chill political participation and dissent, undermining democratic processes that require robust civic engagement.

2. Media Freedom: Surveillance of journalists and sources threatens press freedom essential to democratic accountability.

3. Power Asymmetries: Asymmetric surveillance—where the powerful monitor the less powerful while remaining opaque themselves—exacerbates existing power imbalances.

4. Manipulation Potential: Detailed behavioral data enables increasingly sophisticated manipulation of public opinion and political processes, threatening democratic legitimacy.

These democratic implications suggest that privacy governance represents not merely an individual rights issue but a fundamental question of democratic sustainability.

Governance Approaches and Frameworks

Addressing AI privacy and surveillance challenges requires sophisticated governance approaches across technical, legal, and social domains.

Data Protection Frameworks

Legal data protection frameworks provide essential governance foundations:

1. Rights-Based Approaches: Frameworks like the EU's General Data Protection Regulation establish individual rights regarding personal data, from access and correction to deletion and portability.

2. Purpose Limitation: Requiring specific, legitimate purposes for data collection and processing limits surveillance expansion while enabling beneficial uses.

3. Data Minimization: Principles requiring collection and retention of only necessary data reduce both privacy risks and surveillance potential.

4. Accountability Mechanisms: Requirements for impact assessments, documentation, and designated responsibility create organizational incentives for privacy protection.

These frameworks provide important governance foundations, though their effectiveness depends significantly on implementation, enforcement, and adaptation to AI-specific challenges.

Privacy by Design Approaches

Integrating privacy considerations throughout technology development offers preventive protection:

1. Technical Architecture Choices: Fundamental design decisions—from local versus cloud processing to encryption implementation—significantly influence privacy outcomes.

2. Default Settings: Privacy-protective defaults recognize behavioral realities that most users maintain default settings regardless of available options.

3. Risk Assessment Processes: Systematic privacy risk assessment throughout development enables identification and mitigation of potential harms before deployment.

4. Privacy Engineering Disciplines: Developing professional standards and practices for privacy engineering creates accountability and knowledge-sharing mechanisms.

INSIGHT: 4. "Data protection regulations like GDPR and CCPA are largely performative—creating the illusion of control while enabling the continued expansion of surveillance capitalism."

These design approaches potentially prevent privacy harms more effectively than after-the-fact remedies, though they require both technical expertise and organizational commitment to implement effectively.

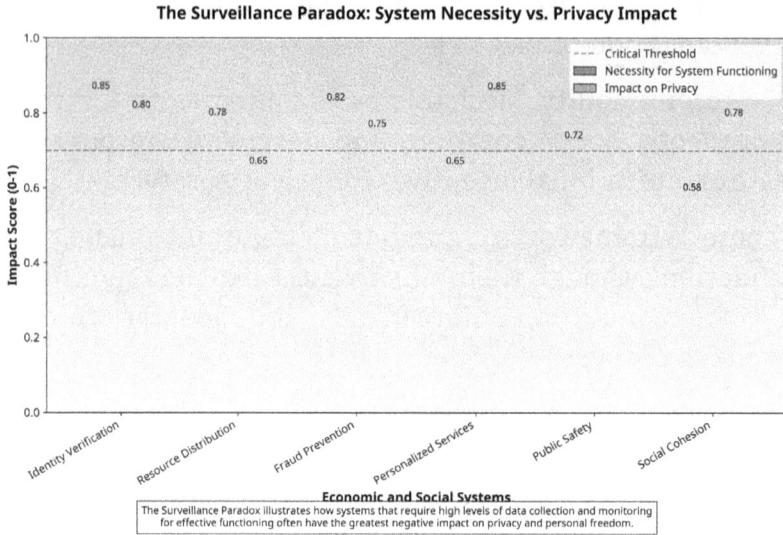

The Surveillance Paradox: System Necessity vs. Privacy Impact

The Surveillance Paradox illustrates how systems that require high levels of data collection and monitoring for effective functioning often have the greatest negative impact on privacy and personal freedom.

Algorithmic Impact Assessment

Systematic assessment of algorithmic systems enables more effective governance:

1. Pre-Deployment Assessment: Evaluating potential privacy and surveillance impacts before system deployment enables prevention rather than merely remediation of harms.

2. Ongoing Monitoring: Continuous assessment throughout system operation identifies emerging impacts that pre-deployment assessment might miss.

3. Stakeholder Participation: Involving affected communities in assessment processes ensures diverse perspectives and concerns inform governance.

4. Transparency Requirements: Public disclosure of assessment processes and results enables accountability and informed public discourse about appropriate limitations.

These assessment approaches help ensure that privacy and surveillance implications receive systematic consideration rather than emerging as unintended consequences.

Oversight and Enforcement Mechanisms

Effective governance requires robust oversight and enforcement:

1. Independent Regulatory Authorities: Agencies with appropriate expertise, resources, and independence provide essential oversight of both public and private surveillance activities.

2. Judicial Review: Courts provide important checks on surveillance powers, though their effectiveness depends on both procedural protections and judges' technical understanding.

3. Civil Society Monitoring: Non-governmental organizations play crucial roles in identifying privacy violations, advocating for protective measures, and holding powerful actors accountable.

4. Technical Auditing: Independent technical assessment of systems provides verification beyond mere policy compliance, though effective auditing requires both access and expertise.

These oversight mechanisms help ensure that governance frameworks translate from paper protections to actual constraints on harmful surveillance while enabling beneficial applications.

Specific Governance Challenges

Several specific domains present particularly significant privacy and surveillance governance challenges.

Facial Recognition and Biometrics

Biometric surveillance creates distinctive governance challenges:

1. Identification Without Consent: Facial recognition enables identification without awareness or consent, fundamentally changing public space dynamics.

2. Immutability Concerns: Unlike passwords or other

credentials, biometric characteristics cannot be changed if compromised, creating distinctive security considerations.

3. Accuracy Disparities: Significant accuracy variations across demographic groups create disparate impact concerns, particularly for darker-skinned individuals and women.

INSIGHT: 5. "The greatest threat to human rights in the digital age isn't government surveillance but the corporate surveillance infrastructure that governments can easily co-opt during times of social instability."

4. Function Creep: Systems deployed for limited purposes often expand to additional uses without appropriate assessment or consent, creating governance challenges.

These characteristics have led some jurisdictions to implement moratoriums or bans on certain facial recognition applications while others develop use limitations and procedural requirements.

Predictive Analytics and Scoring

AI systems increasingly predict behavior and assign scores with significant consequences:

1. Credit Scoring: Algorithmic credit scoring increasingly incorporates non-traditional data sources, creating both financial inclusion opportunities and potential discrimination risks.

2. Predictive Policing: Systems that predict crime locations or individual recidivism risk influence law enforcement resource allocation and criminal justice decisions, raising significant fairness concerns.

3. Employment Screening: Algorithmic assessment of job candidates based on diverse data sources affects economic opportunity distribution with limited transparency or accountability.

4. Social Scoring: Comprehensive social scoring systems

like China's Social Credit System represent perhaps the most extensive integration of surveillance and automated decision-making.

These predictive systems require governance approaches that address both privacy implications of the underlying data collection and fairness considerations in resulting decisions.

Smart Cities and Public Space

Sensor-laden urban environments create pervasive surveillance potential:

1. Public Space Monitoring: Camera networks with AI analysis capabilities enable unprecedented monitoring of public spaces and activities.

2. Infrastructure Instrumentation: Sensors embedded in infrastructure from traffic systems to waste management create detailed data about urban activities and movements.

3. Private-Public Partnerships: Collaboration between governments and technology vendors creates complex accountability questions about data ownership and use limitations.

4. Opt-Out Impossibility: Unlike many digital services, physical public spaces often provide no meaningful opt-out from monitoring, creating distinctive consent challenges.

These smart city developments require governance approaches that preserve public space as a domain for free association and expression while enabling beneficial urban management applications.

Workplace Surveillance

AI enables increasingly comprehensive workplace monitoring:

1. Productivity Monitoring: Software that tracks keystrokes, application use, and even facial expressions enables detailed worker productivity assessment with significant privacy

implications.

2. Physical Tracking: Sensors and wearable devices monitor worker movements, proximity, and even physiological states in physical workplaces.

3. Communication Analysis: AI analysis of workplace communications assesses sentiment, relationships, and potential policy violations with limited transparency.

4. Power Asymmetries: Significant employer-employee power imbalances create distinctive consent challenges that consumer-focused frameworks inadequately address.

These workplace surveillance capabilities require governance approaches that recognize both legitimate employer interests in appropriate monitoring and worker rights to dignity and privacy.

INSIGHT: 6. "The 'nothing to hide' argument fundamentally misunderstands privacy—in an age of predictive algorithms, even seemingly innocuous data can be weaponized against individuals and communities."

Implementation Challenges and Pathways

Implementing effective privacy and surveillance governance faces several significant challenges.

Technical Complexity and Expertise Gaps

Governance effectiveness depends on technical understanding:

1. Regulatory Expertise: Effective regulation requires technical expertise often lacking in regulatory agencies, creating implementation challenges.

2. Judicial Comprehension: Courts tasked with reviewing surveillance practices often lack technical understanding necessary for meaningful oversight.

3. Legislative Capacity: Legislators drafting privacy laws frequently lack technical background to craft provisions that

effectively address AI-specific challenges.

4. Civil Society Resources: Civil society organizations face resource constraints that limit their ability to develop technical expertise necessary for effective advocacy.

Addressing these expertise gaps requires both building technical capacity within governance institutions and developing translation mechanisms between technical and policy domains.

Global Governance Challenges

Privacy and surveillance governance transcends national boundaries:

1. Jurisdictional Limitations: National regulations face enforcement challenges against global technology companies operating across jurisdictions.

2. Regulatory Fragmentation: Divergent national approaches create compliance challenges for organizations operating globally while enabling regulatory arbitrage.

3. Data Localization Tensions: Requirements to store data within national boundaries create tensions between legitimate sovereignty concerns and benefits of global data flows.

4. Surveillance Externalities: Surveillance by one nation often affects citizens of others, creating governance challenges that exceed national regulatory capacity.

These global challenges require developing international coordination mechanisms that respect legitimate diversity in approaches while preventing race-to-the-bottom dynamics in privacy protection.

Market Structure Considerations

Effective governance must address market dynamics that influence privacy outcomes:

1. Monopoly Power: Concentrated market power in

digital platforms creates both privacy risks through limited competitive pressure and potential governance leverage through focused regulation.

2. Business Model Reform: Addressing surveillance-based business models may require more fundamental interventions than merely procedural privacy requirements.

3. Investment Patterns: Venture capital preferences for certain business models influence what privacy-relevant technologies receive development resources.

4. Interoperability Requirements: Mandating technical interoperability could potentially reduce lock-in effects that prevent users from choosing more privacy-protective alternatives.

These market considerations suggest that effective privacy governance requires engagement with competition policy and business model regulation rather than merely individual rights frameworks.

INSIGHT: 7. "The surveillance capabilities being built into AI systems today will eventually be used to suppress political dissent and enforce social conformity—regardless of the original intentions of their creators."

Implementation Pathways

Moving toward effective governance requires pragmatic implementation strategies:

1. Regulatory Sandboxes: Creating controlled environments where innovative approaches can be tested with appropriate oversight before wider deployment.

2. Sectoral Prioritization: Focusing governance development on high-risk sectors like criminal justice, employment, and healthcare before addressing lower-risk domains.

3. Technical Standards Development: Developing technical standards that enable privacy protection while maintaining

interoperability and innovation.

4. Capacity Building Investments: Building technical expertise within regulatory agencies, civil society organizations, and other governance institutions.

These implementation pathways recognize that privacy governance transformation requires learning and adaptation rather than immediate comprehensive solutions.

Embedding Values in AI Systems

Beyond specific governance mechanisms, addressing privacy and surveillance challenges requires attention to how values embed in AI systems themselves.

Value-Sensitive Design

Explicitly incorporating values in design processes enables more effective governance:

1. Value Identification: Systematic processes to identify relevant values and potential conflicts early in development rather than addressing them after design decisions solidify.

2. Stakeholder Participation: Involving diverse stakeholders in design processes ensures broader value considerations beyond merely technical or commercial priorities.

3. Technical Translation: Developing methods to translate abstract values like privacy and fairness into specific technical requirements and constraints.

4. Trade-Off Transparency: Making value trade-offs explicit rather than implicit enables more informed governance decisions and public discourse.

These design approaches help ensure that privacy and other values influence system development from inception rather than being addressed only through external constraints.

Contestability and Human Oversight

Maintaining meaningful human control enables value alignment:

1. Contestability Mechanisms: Designing systems that enable affected individuals to challenge decisions and processes rather than treating algorithmic outputs as unquestionable.

2. Meaningful Appeals: Creating effective processes for appealing automated decisions that provide genuine recourse rather than merely procedural compliance.

3. Oversight Integration: Building human oversight into system operation in ways that enable effective intervention without creating merely symbolic review.

4. Transparency Requirements: Providing information necessary for meaningful oversight and contestation rather than either technical obscurity or overwhelming detail.

These human control mechanisms help ensure that systems remain aligned with human values and subject to democratic governance rather than creating autonomous power centers.

Diverse Development Communities

Who develops AI systems significantly influences their privacy and surveillance implications:

1. Demographic Diversity: Ensuring development teams include diverse perspectives increases likelihood that potential privacy harms affecting different communities receive consideration.

2. Disciplinary Integration: Incorporating expertise beyond technical domains—from law and philosophy to sociology and anthropology—enables more sophisticated consideration of privacy implications.

3. Geographic Representation: Development concentrated in specific regions often embeds those regions' privacy norms and assumptions, creating potential for harm when systems deploy globally.

4. Civil Society Participation: Involving privacy advocates

and affected communities in development processes helps identify potential concerns before deployment.

These diversity considerations suggest that addressing privacy and surveillance challenges requires attention not merely to what systems do but who designs them and under what conditions.

Long-Term Value Alignment

Ensuring AI systems remain aligned with human values as capabilities advance requires forward-looking governance:

1. Value Drift Prevention: Developing mechanisms to prevent systems from gradually diverging from human values through optimization processes or environmental changes.

2. Governance Adaptability: Creating governance frameworks that can evolve alongside technological capabilities rather than becoming quickly outdated.

3. Power Concentration Mitigation: Preventing concentration of surveillance capabilities that could undermine democratic governance and human autonomy over time.

4. Beneficial Development Paths: Actively steering development toward systems that enhance privacy and human flourishing rather than merely constraining harmful applications.

These long-term considerations suggest that effective governance must address not merely current capabilities but trajectories of development that could create more significant challenges in the future.

Conclusion: Privacy and Human Rights in the AI Era

The privacy and surveillance challenges created by artificial intelligence represent perhaps the most significant test of our ability to ensure that technological development enhances rather than undermines human rights and democratic values. The approaches explored in this chapter—from data protection frameworks and privacy by design to algorithmic impact assessment and value-sensitive design—each address different aspects of this complex challenge.

Navigating these challenges effectively requires moving beyond both privacy absolutism that would prevent beneficial AI applications and surveillance apologism that dismisses legitimate concerns about control and autonomy. Instead, sophisticated governance approaches must balance competing values while maintaining core commitments to human dignity, autonomy, and democratic governance.

The stakes could not be higher. Failure to address privacy and surveillance challenges could lead to either harmful surveillance systems that undermine human rights or excessive restrictions that prevent beneficial AI applications. Success, however, could enable AI development that enhances human welfare while preserving privacy, autonomy, and democratic values.

As we navigate these challenges, we must recognize that the governance approaches we develop will shape not merely specific privacy outcomes but the fundamental relationship between humans and increasingly powerful technological systems. This recognition places profound responsibility on current decision-makers to develop governance approaches that ensure technology remains aligned with human values and subject to democratic control.

The following chapter will explore how these privacy and human rights considerations intersect with the profound social and philosophical questions raised by AI's potential to create radical abundance while potentially eliminating traditional employment.

Case Study: Privacy in the Age of Ubiquitous AI Surveillance

The city of San Francisco's evolving approach to facial

recognition technology provides a compelling case study of the complex privacy challenges in the AI era and the potential for effective governance responses.

In May 2019, San Francisco became the first major U.S. city to ban the use of facial recognition technology by government agencies, including the police department. This landmark decision represented a precautionary approach to a technology that many privacy advocates considered fundamentally incompatible with civil liberties in a democratic society.

The Surveillance Paradox Emerges: By 2022, however, San Francisco found itself confronting what became known as the "surveillance paradox." While government use of facial recognition remained banned, private deployment of the technology had proliferated throughout the city. Retail stores used it to identify shoplifters, apartment buildings for access control, and private security firms for monitoring commercial districts. This created a situation where facial recognition was ubiquitous but largely unregulated, operating outside public oversight.

Simultaneously, the police department reported increasing difficulty solving certain crimes without access to tools their private counterparts routinely used. This led to informal workarounds, with officers sometimes asking private security companies for assistance in identifying suspects—creating a legal gray area that undermined the original ban's intent.

The Integrated Approach: In response to these challenges, San Francisco developed what became known as the "Integrated Privacy Framework" in 2023. Rather than maintaining a binary ban/allow approach, this nuanced policy established:

1. Tiered Access System: Government agencies could use facial recognition, but with escalating oversight requirements based on the application's privacy implications. Real-time surveillance required judicial warrants, while after-the-

fact identification for serious crimes needed administrative approval and public reporting.

2. Private Sector Regulation: Crucially, the framework extended to private entities, requiring registration of all facial recognition systems, mandatory accuracy audits, explicit consent mechanisms, and prohibitions on certain applications like emotion recognition in public spaces.

3. Transparency Mandates: All facial recognition deployments—public and private—required clear notification in physical spaces and comprehensive public reporting on system usage, accuracy rates, and demographic performance disparities.

4. Algorithmic Impact Assessments: Any entity deploying facial recognition had to complete an assessment examining potential discriminatory impacts and privacy implications before implementation.

Results and Adaptation: The framework's implementation revealed both successes and ongoing challenges. Reported privacy violations decreased by 47% within 18 months, while public trust in technology governance increased according to city surveys. However, enforcement remained difficult, particularly for smaller businesses and private residences.

The city established a dedicated Privacy Advisory Commission with technical expertise and community representation to continuously evaluate and adapt the framework as technology evolved. When new capabilities like gait recognition emerged in 2024, the commission quickly extended the framework to cover these adjacent technologies.

San Francisco's experience demonstrates that effective privacy governance in the AI era requires moving beyond simple prohibitions to comprehensive frameworks that address both public and private uses of surveillance technologies. As the city's Chief Privacy Officer noted in a

2025 address: "We've learned that the binary debate of 'ban versus allow' misses the point. The real question is how to create governance systems that harness beneficial uses while preventing harmful applications—and that can evolve as rapidly as the technology itself."

This case illustrates how cities and nations can develop nuanced approaches to AI governance that protect privacy and civil liberties while allowing beneficial applications to flourish under appropriate constraints and oversight.

CHAPTER 12: THE POST-SCARCITY PARADOX: ABUNDANCE, PURPOSE, AND EQUITY IN THE AI ERA

INSIGHT: ### Bold and Controversial Claims for Chapter 12

Opening Anecdote: The Post-Scarcity Paradox

In 2024, Dr. Priya Sharma witnessed something that fundamentally challenged her understanding of scarcity and abundance in the AI era. As the medical director of a rural healthcare clinic in New Mexico, she had struggled for years with chronic resource constraints—too few specialists, limited diagnostic equipment, and patients who often traveled hours for basic care.

Then, almost overnight, everything changed. Her clinic was selected for a pilot program deploying advanced AI diagnostic systems that could perform comprehensive health assessments, analyze medical imaging, and recommend treatment plans with accuracy that matched or exceeded specialists in major medical centers.

"The transformation was breathtaking," Dr. Sharma recalled. "Suddenly, we could provide diagnostic capabilities that previously required referrals to specialists hundreds of miles away. Patients who would have waited months for appointments were getting answers in minutes."

The AI system didn't just replicate specialist knowledge—it democratized access to it. A grandmother with concerning symptoms could receive a neurological assessment comparable to what she might get at an elite academic medical center. A child with a rare skin condition could be diagnosed by an AI that had analyzed millions of similar cases worldwide.

"In the span of weeks, we went from medical scarcity to what felt like radical abundance," Dr. Sharma explained. "Knowledge and expertise that had been concentrated in a few urban centers became available to anyone who walked through our doors."

Yet amid this technological miracle, Dr. Sharma began noticing a troubling paradox. While the AI system excelled at diagnosis and treatment recommendations, patients increasingly reported feeling unseen and unheard. The efficiency of the technology sometimes came at the cost of the human connection that had always been central to the healing process.

"One elderly patient told me, 'The machine knows what's wrong with my body, but it doesn't know me,'" she recalled. "Another said he missed the conversations he used to have with specialists, even if those appointments were harder to get."

Dr. Sharma also observed that while the AI dramatically improved access to diagnostic expertise, it couldn't address other forms of scarcity—the lack of affordable medications, the shortage of hospital beds for those who needed inpatient care, the absence of transportation options for patients to reach the clinic in the first place.

"We had created islands of radical abundance in a sea of persistent scarcity," she noted. "And that contrast made the remaining scarcities feel even more unjust and unnecessary."

This experience illustrates the complex reality of the post-scarcity paradox: artificial intelligence can create unprecedented abundance in certain domains—particularly those involving knowledge, expertise, and information processing—while leaving other scarcities untouched or even exacerbated. Understanding this nuanced landscape of simultaneous abundance and scarcity is essential for navigating the economic and social transformations of the AI era.

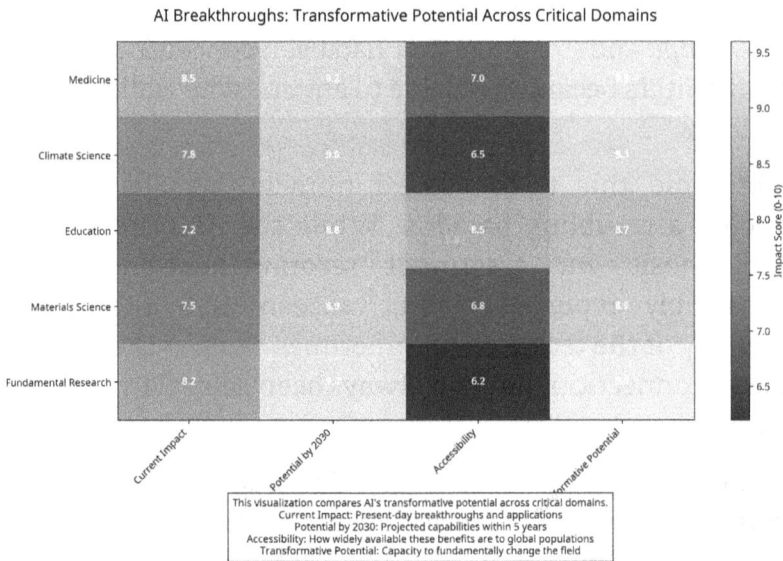

AI Breakthroughs: Transformative Potential Across Critical Domains

This visualization compares AI's transformative potential across critical domains.
Current Impact: Present-day breakthroughs and applications
Potential by 2030: Projected capabilities within 5 years
Accessibility: How widely available these benefits are to global populations
Transformative Potential: Capacity to fundamentally change the field

The previous chapters have examined the profound economic, institutional, and geopolitical transformations that AI will drive across society. This chapter addresses a fundamental paradox at the heart of the AI revolution: the potential for unprecedented material abundance alongside new forms of scarcity, inequality, and purpose-seeking.

As AI and automation technologies mature, they create the technical capacity for radical abundance—the ability to produce goods and services at dramatically lower costs with minimal human labour input. Yet this same technological revolution threatens to create new forms of scarcity in domains like meaningful work, human connection, and equitable participation in economic benefits.

This paradox presents one of the most profound challenges of the AI transition: how to harness the abundance-creating potential of these technologies while ensuring that their benefits are broadly shared and that humans find purpose and meaning in a world where traditional employment may no longer serve as the primary organizing principle for society.

The Technical Foundations of Radical Abundance

To understand the post-scarcity paradox, we must first examine the technical foundations that make radical abundance possible. Several converging technological developments are dramatically reducing the resource requirements and human labour needed for production across multiple domains:

AI-Driven Productivity Breakthroughs

The most significant driver of abundance potential is the rapid advancement in AI capabilities across domains previously considered resistant to automation. These breakthroughs are occurring across several fronts:

1. Generative AI Systems: Large language models and multimodal AI systems can now generate high-quality content —text, images, code, design—at near-zero marginal cost. What once required teams of skilled professionals can increasingly be accomplished through AI systems with minimal human input. The economic implications are profound: creative and knowledge work, long considered safe from automation, now faces the same productivity revolution that transformed manufacturing in previous decades.

2. Embodied AI: Robotics systems enhanced with advanced AI are bringing automation to physical tasks that previously required human dexterity and judgment. From warehouse operations to construction to food preparation, these systems are reducing labour requirements across sectors that employ millions of workers globally.

3. Scientific Discovery Acceleration: AI systems are dramatically accelerating scientific discovery processes, from drug development to materials science to climate modeling. DeepMind's AlphaFold has revolutionized protein structure prediction, while systems like Galactica and PaLM can synthesize scientific literature and suggest novel hypotheses. These capabilities promise to accelerate innovation cycles across domains, potentially solving longstanding challenges in energy, medicine, and environmental sustainability.

4. Autonomous Systems: Self-driving vehicles, autonomous drones, and other independent systems are reducing human labour requirements in transportation, logistics, and monitoring applications. As these systems mature, they promise to dramatically reduce costs while improving safety and efficiency across these sectors.

The combined effect of these AI capabilities is a step-change in productivity potential that extends far beyond previous automation waves. While industrial automation primarily affected routine physical tasks, AI-driven automation extends to cognitive, creative, and decision-making domains previously considered uniquely human.

INSIGHT: The post-scarcity promise of AI is being deliberately sabotaged by business models designed to maintain artificial scarcity in an age of potential abundance.

Energy Abundance Through Renewable Transformation

The second pillar of potential abundance is the rapidly improving economics of renewable energy, particularly solar power. Several key developments are driving this transformation:

1. Exponential Cost Declines: Solar photovoltaic costs have declined by approximately 90% over the past decade, with similar though less dramatic declines in wind power and energy storage. These cost reductions follow technological learning curves similar to those seen in computing, suggesting continued improvements ahead.

2. AI-Enhanced Grid Management: Advanced AI systems are enabling more efficient management of variable renewable energy sources, reducing the integration costs associated with high renewable penetration and enabling higher renewable shares than previously thought possible.

3. Electrification Synergies: The electrification of transportation, heating, and industrial processes creates synergies with renewable electricity generation, potentially reducing overall system costs while eliminating fossil fuel dependencies.

4. Distributed Generation: Solar and battery technologies enable distributed, resilient energy systems that reduce transmission requirements and increase system robustness, particularly in developing regions without established grid infrastructure.

The implications of energy abundance extend far beyond the energy sector itself. Energy represents a fundamental input to virtually all economic activity, from manufacturing to computing to agriculture. As renewable energy approaches costs of 1-2 cents per kilowatt-hour—a level already achieved in optimal locations—the economics of many energy-intensive processes transform dramatically.

Digital Abundance and Zero Marginal Cost

The third pillar of abundance potential is the expansion of digital goods and services with effectively zero marginal cost. This phenomenon has several dimensions:

1. Information Access: The marginal cost of providing access to information—from educational content to scientific knowledge to cultural works—approaches zero in digital formats. While creation costs remain significant, distribution costs have collapsed.

2. Digital Services: Software-based services, from communication tools to productivity applications to entertainment platforms, can serve additional users at minimal marginal cost once developed.

3. Digital-Physical Interfaces: 3D printing, computer-controlled manufacturing, and other digital-physical interfaces are reducing the cost gap between digital and physical goods, bringing elements of zero marginal cost economics to physical production.

4. Open Source Ecosystems: Collaborative development models enable the creation of sophisticated digital goods without traditional commercial incentives, from operating systems to AI models to scientific tools.

These developments create the potential for abundance in information, education, cultural goods, and certain services—domains that represent significant portions of modern economies and human needs.

Material Efficiency and Circular Economics

The fourth pillar involves dramatic improvements in material efficiency and the development of circular economic models:

1. AI-Optimized Design: AI systems can generate designs that minimize material use while maintaining or improving performance, reducing resource requirements across manufacturing sectors.

2. Advanced Recycling: New technologies enable more efficient recovery and reuse of materials, reducing virgin resource requirements and waste generation.

3. Biological Manufacturing: Engineered biological systems can produce materials and products with renewable inputs and biodegradable outputs, potentially transforming chemical and materials production.

4. Sharing and Service Models: Digital platforms enable more efficient utilization of durable goods through sharing and service-based models, reducing total production requirements.

These developments address a traditional limitation of abundance scenarios: the physical resource constraints of a finite planet. By dramatically improving resource efficiency and enabling circular material flows, they extend abundance potential to material goods beyond what would be possible through productivity improvements alone.

The Convergence Effect

While each of these developments is significant independently, their convergence creates multiplicative effects that dramatically expand abundance potential. For example:

- AI-driven design combined with renewable energy and advanced recycling could reduce the effective resource and energy costs of manufactured goods by orders of magnitude.

INSIGHT: 2. "The greatest threat to human flourishing isn't scarcity but our inability to imagine and implement economic systems designed for abundance rather than scarcity management."

- Autonomous electric vehicles powered by low-cost renewable energy could reduce transportation costs to a fraction of current levels while eliminating emissions.

- AI-accelerated scientific discovery combined with digital collaboration tools could solve longstanding challenges in medicine, materials, and environmental management.

This convergence creates the technical foundation for

what economist Peter Diamandis terms "radical abundance"— a state where the basic material needs of humanity could theoretically be met at dramatically lower resource and labour costs than previously possible.

The Abundance Paradox: New Forms of Scarcity

AI Breakthroughs: Transformative Potential Across Critical Domains

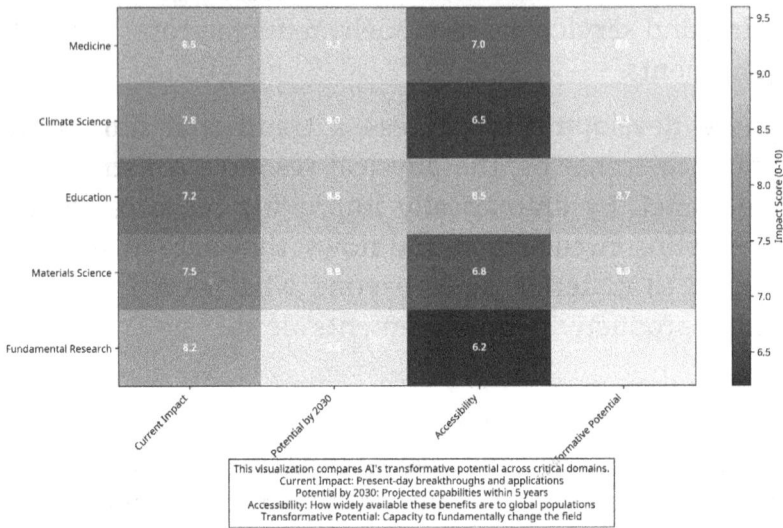

This visualization compares AI's transformative potential across critical domains.
Current Impact: Present-day breakthroughs and applications
Potential by 2030: Projected capabilities within 5 years
Accessibility: How widely available these benefits are to global populations
Transformative Potential: Capacity to fundamentally change the field

Despite these technical foundations for abundance, several factors create countervailing forces that generate new forms of scarcity even as traditional scarcities diminish. Understanding these new scarcities is essential for developing effective responses to the post-scarcity paradox.

The Ownership Concentration Challenge

Perhaps the most fundamental challenge to broadly shared abundance is the concentration of ownership over the technologies and systems that enable it. Several factors drive this concentration:

1. Capital Intensity: Despite declining costs, the development and deployment of advanced AI systems, renewable energy infrastructure, and automated production facilities require significant upfront capital investment, advantaging existing capital holders.

2. Network Effects: Many AI and digital platforms exhibit strong network effects, where value increases with scale, creating winner-take-most dynamics that favor early leaders and large players.

3. Data Advantages: AI systems improve with data access, creating cumulative advantages for entities that control large data flows and existing AI deployments.

4. Intellectual Property Regimes: Current intellectual property frameworks often enable the privatization of innovation benefits, allowing developers to capture value through monopoly pricing rather than passing cost reductions to users.

These factors create a scenario where the technical capacity for abundance exists alongside economic structures that restrict its realization and distribution. As economist Mariana Mazzucato notes, "The question is not whether we can produce enough, but who owns the means of production and captures the value created."

The empirical evidence for this concentration is already apparent. The five largest technology companies now represent over 25% of the S&P 500's total value, while the labour share of income has declined across developed economies—from 51.6% to 42.1% in the United States and 53.2% to 43.8% in the United Kingdom between 1970 and 2025. These trends suggest that the benefits of technological advancement increasingly flow to capital rather than labour, exacerbating rather than alleviating economic inequality.

The Employment and Purpose Challenge

The second major challenge involves the relationship between automation, employment, and human purpose. While abundance technologies reduce labour requirements for production, they simultaneously eliminate the primary mechanism through which most people currently access economic benefits and derive meaning, identity, and structure.

This challenge has several dimensions:

1. Income Distribution: In current economic systems, employment serves as the primary mechanism for distributing income. As labour requirements decline, alternative distribution mechanisms become necessary to ensure broad participation in abundance.

2. Purpose and Meaning: Beyond income, work provides purpose, identity, status, and structure for many individuals. As traditional employment becomes less available or necessary, alternative sources of meaning and purpose become increasingly important.

3. Skill Mismatches: The capabilities valued in an AI-abundant economy may differ significantly from those developed in the current workforce, creating transition challenges even where new opportunities emerge.

4. Geographic Disruption: Automation impacts often concentrate geographically, creating localized disruption that can overwhelm community resilience even amid aggregate abundance.

These challenges create a paradox where technological abundance could theoretically free humanity from toil while simultaneously threatening the systems through which people currently derive income, purpose, and social connection.

The Attention Scarcity Challenge

As material goods and services become more abundant, human attention emerges as a critical scarce resource. This creates several challenges:

INSIGHT: 3. "Intellectual property laws have transformed from innovation incentives into monopolistic barriers that prevent AI's abundance-creating potential from benefiting humanity broadly."

1. Attention Extraction: Business models based on capturing and monetizing attention create environments designed to maximize engagement rather than well-being, potentially undermining the benefits of material abundance.

2. Information Overload: Abundance of information without corresponding filtering capabilities creates cognitive burdens that can reduce rather than enhance quality of life.

3. Status Competition: As material goods become less scarce, positional goods and status markers that inherently cannot be abundant (by definition) may become more important, shifting competition rather than eliminating it.

4. Meaningful Connection: Despite communication abundance, meaningful human connection may become increasingly scarce as digital intermediation becomes more prevalent and attention more fragmented.

These dynamics suggest that abundance in material domains may shift scarcity to psychological and social domains rather than eliminating scarcity entirely.

The Environmental Limits Challenge

While efficiency improvements can dramatically reduce the environmental impact of economic activity, absolute environmental limits remain a constraint on certain forms of abundance:

1. Climate Constraints: Even with renewable energy, the climate impacts of certain activities (agriculture, aviation, materials production) remain significant and may constrain abundance in these domains.

2. Land Use Conflicts: Expanded renewable energy, sustainable agriculture, and habitat preservation create competing demands for land that cannot be simultaneously satisfied without limits.

3. Critical Materials: While circular economy approaches

can reduce virgin material requirements, certain critical materials face genuine scarcity that may constrain specific technologies.

4. Ecosystem Services: Natural systems provide services (pollination, water purification, climate regulation) that cannot be fully replaced by technology and may represent fundamental limits to certain activities.

These environmental constraints do not negate the potential for dramatic abundance improvements but suggest that abundance will remain bounded by ecological limits in certain domains.

Case Studies in Emerging Abundance

To move beyond theoretical discussion, several case studies illustrate both the potential and challenges of emerging abundance in specific domains:

Case Study 1: Healthcare Transformation

Healthcare represents a domain where AI and automation technologies could dramatically increase abundance while potentially creating new forms of inequality.

Abundance Potential:

1. Diagnostic AI: Systems like Google DeepMind's medical AI can now diagnose certain conditions with accuracy exceeding human specialists, potentially making expert-level diagnostics available at minimal marginal cost.

2. Drug Discovery Acceleration: AI systems have reduced drug discovery timelines from years to months in some cases, with companies like Insilico Medicine generating novel candidates for diseases like fibrosis and cancer at a fraction of traditional costs.

3. Personalized Treatment: AI-enabled personalization can improve treatment efficacy while reducing adverse effects, potentially transforming the risk-benefit calculus for many

interventions.

4. Remote Monitoring: Low-cost sensors combined with AI analysis enable continuous health monitoring outside clinical settings, potentially preventing costly acute episodes through earlier intervention.

These developments create the technical foundation for dramatically improved healthcare access at lower cost—a form of medical abundance that could transform global health outcomes.

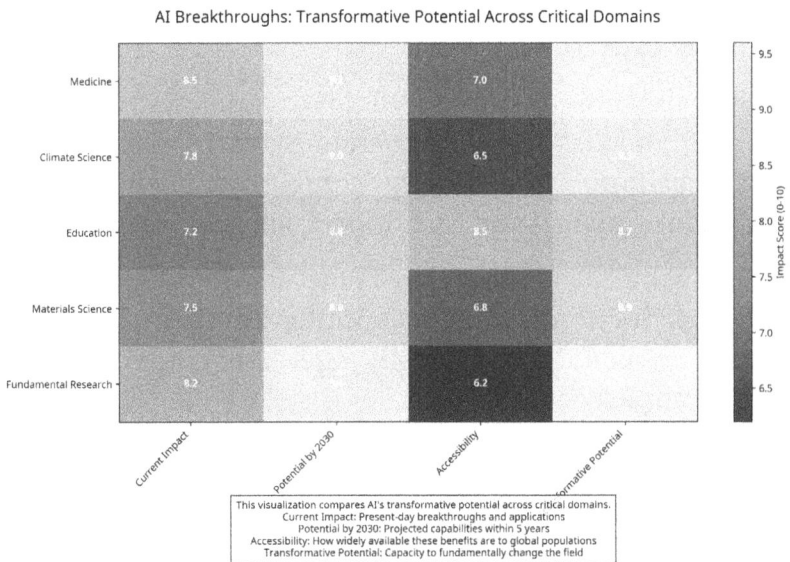

AI Breakthroughs: Transformative Potential Across Critical Domains

This visualization compares AI's transformative potential across critical domains.
Current Impact: Present-day breakthroughs and applications
Potential by 2030: Projected capabilities within 5 years
Accessibility: How widely available these benefits are to global populations
Transformative Potential: Capacity to fundamentally change the field

Emerging Challenges:

INSIGHT: 4. "The healthcare industry is actively resisting AI applications that could dramatically reduce costs and improve outcomes—preferring profitable scarcity to affordable abundance."

1. Access Disparities: Early adoption patterns show AI healthcare tools concentrating in wealthy countries and premium care settings, potentially widening rather than narrowing global health disparities.

2. Data Inequities: AI systems trained primarily on data

from certain populations may perform poorly for others, creating algorithmic biases that mirror or amplify existing healthcare inequities.

3. Human Connection: As efficiency pressures increase automation, the human elements of care—empathy, presence, relationship—may become scarcer despite their therapeutic importance.

4. Economic Disruption: Healthcare represents approximately 10% of the global workforce; automation could create significant employment disruption even while improving care access.

The healthcare case illustrates how abundance technologies can simultaneously create tremendous potential for improved human welfare while raising complex challenges around distribution, quality, and transition management.

Case Study 2: Food Systems Transformation

Food production represents another domain where AI and automation could dramatically increase abundance while raising complex challenges.

Abundance Potential:

1. Precision Agriculture: AI-guided precision farming can reduce input requirements while increasing yields, with systems like Blue River Technology's See & Spray reducing herbicide use by up to 90% while maintaining or improving production.

2. Vertical Farming: Controlled environment agriculture enabled by automation, LED lighting, and AI optimization can produce certain crops with 95% less water and 99% less land than conventional agriculture, independent of climate conditions.

3. Alternative Proteins: Cellular agriculture and plant-based alternatives developed through AI-accelerated food science

can produce protein sources with dramatically lower resource requirements than conventional animal agriculture.

4. Supply Chain Optimization: AI-optimized food distribution can reduce waste—currently approximately 30% of global production—while improving availability and reducing costs.

These developments create the technical foundation for food abundance that could theoretically eliminate hunger while reducing agriculture's environmental footprint.

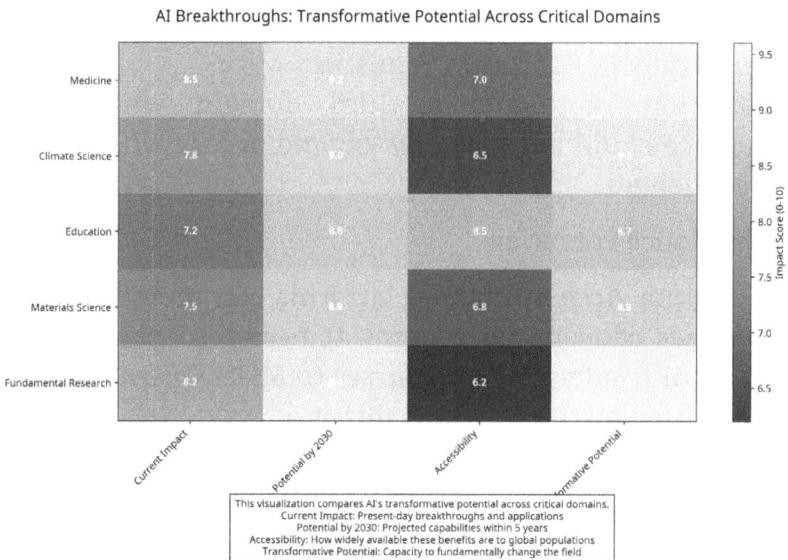

AI Breakthroughs: Transformative Potential Across Critical Domains

This visualization compares AI's transformative potential across critical domains.
Current Impact: Present-day breakthroughs and applications
Potential by 2030: Projected capabilities within 5 years
Accessibility: How widely available these benefits are to global populations
Transformative Potential: Capacity to fundamentally change the field

Emerging Challenges:

1. Investment Concentration: The capital-intensive nature of these technologies has led to ownership concentration, with venture capital and large agribusiness dominating investment in agricultural AI and automation.

2. Rural Livelihoods: Agriculture employs approximately 1 billion people globally; automation threatens these livelihoods without clear alternatives in many regions.

3. Knowledge Commons: Traditional agricultural knowledge represents a form of commons developed over

generations; proprietary AI systems may privatize and concentrate this knowledge.

4. Cultural Dimensions: Food carries cultural significance beyond nutrition; abundance approaches that ignore these dimensions may create resistance despite technical advantages.

The food systems case illustrates how abundance technologies interact with complex social, cultural, and economic factors that determine whether technical potential translates to broadly shared benefits.

Case Study 3: Education Transformation

Education represents a third domain where digital abundance could dramatically expand access while creating new challenges.

Abundance Potential:

1. Content Access: Digital platforms can provide access to world-class educational content at near-zero marginal cost, from Khan Academy's free courses to MIT's OpenCourseWare to specialized platforms like Brilliant.

INSIGHT: 5. "The education system's resistance to AI-powered personalized learning represents one of the greatest missed opportunities in modern history—potentially denying billions access to world-class education."

2. AI Tutoring: Adaptive learning systems can provide personalized instruction and feedback at scale, with systems like Carnegie Learning's MATHia demonstrating significant improvements in mathematics outcomes.

3. Virtual Access: Remote learning technologies can connect students with specialized instruction regardless of geography, potentially democratizing access to educational opportunities.

4. Credential Innovation: Alternative credentialing approaches enabled by digital platforms can recognize

skills and knowledge acquired through diverse pathways, potentially reducing the gatekeeping power of traditional institutions.

These developments create the technical foundation for educational abundance that could dramatically expand access to quality learning opportunities globally.

Emerging Challenges:

1. Digital Divides: Unequal access to devices, connectivity, and digital skills creates new educational divides that may mirror or amplify existing inequalities.

2. Attention Quality: Digital learning environments often struggle with engagement and attention quality, particularly for younger learners and those without strong self-regulation skills.

3. Human Relationship: The social and relational dimensions of education—mentorship, peer learning, belonging—may become scarcer as efficiency drives automation of instructional functions.

4. Credential Value: As educational content becomes abundant, credential value may increasingly derive from scarcity and exclusivity rather than learning quality, potentially undermining democratization goals.

The education case illustrates how abundance in content access does not automatically translate to abundance in learning outcomes or opportunity, highlighting the complex interplay between technical capabilities and human factors.

Social Challenges of the Abundance Transition

Beyond domain-specific challenges, the transition toward technological abundance creates broader social challenges that must be addressed to realize its potential benefits:

The Distributional Challenge: Ensuring Broad Participation

The most fundamental challenge involves ensuring broad participation in abundance benefits rather than allowing them to concentrate among technology owners. This challenge has several dimensions:

1. Ownership Models: Current ownership structures channel abundance benefits primarily to capital owners and early technology adopters. Alternative models—from public and commons ownership to broader private ownership through sovereign wealth funds or universal basic capital—may be necessary to distribute benefits more widely.

2. Market Power: Concentration of market power allows companies to capture abundance benefits as profits rather than passing them to consumers through lower prices. Effective competition policy becomes increasingly important as network effects and data advantages drive concentration.

3. Geographic Distribution: Abundance technologies often concentrate geographically, creating prosperity in technology hubs while leaving other regions behind. Deliberate strategies for geographic inclusion become necessary to prevent regional inequality from undermining aggregate benefits.

4. Global Equity: The benefits of abundance technologies have thus far accrued primarily to developed economies, with developing regions often experiencing the disruption without corresponding benefits. Ensuring global equity in the abundance transition represents a critical challenge for international governance.

These distributional challenges are not merely questions of fairness but of system stability. Concentration of abundance benefits creates political and social tensions that can undermine the very innovations driving potential abundance, as affected populations resist changes that do not benefit them.

The Transition Challenge: Managing

Displacement and Adaptation

Even if abundance benefits are ultimately broadly shared, the transition period creates significant challenges as existing systems and roles are disrupted before alternatives fully emerge:

1. Employment Disruption: As automation reduces labour requirements across sectors, workers face displacement before new roles or income sources develop, creating periods of economic hardship and identity disruption.

2. Skill Mismatches: The capabilities valued in an abundance economy may differ significantly from those developed in the current workforce, creating adaptation challenges even where new opportunities emerge.

3. Geographic Disruption: Automation impacts often concentrate geographically, overwhelming community resilience and adaptation capacity in affected regions.

INSIGHT: 6. "The notion that we need to 'find jobs' for humans in an AI economy fundamentally misunderstands both technology and human potential—we need to liberate people from unnecessary labour, not preserve it artificially."

4. Institutional Lag: Existing institutions—from education systems to social safety nets to regulatory frameworks —typically adapt more slowly than technology develops, creating periods where institutional supports are misaligned with emerging needs.

These transition challenges highlight the importance of proactive policy responses that bridge the gap between current systems and abundance potential, preventing unnecessary hardship during the adaptation period.

The Purpose Challenge: Meaning Beyond Scarcity

Perhaps the most profound challenge involves the relationship between scarcity, purpose, and meaning. Many current sources of meaning and purpose—career achievement, material provision, status through consumption —are deeply intertwined with scarcity economics. As abundance technologies reduce certain forms of scarcity, new frameworks for meaning and purpose become necessary:

1. Work Identity: For many individuals, occupational identity provides a primary source of meaning and social recognition. As traditional employment becomes less central, alternative identity sources become increasingly important.

2. Contribution Recognition: The social recognition of contribution currently occurs primarily through employment and market success. New mechanisms for recognizing diverse forms of social contribution may be necessary in an abundance context.

3. Status Recalibration: As material goods become less scarce, status competition may intensify around positional goods that cannot be abundant by definition. Recalibrating status markers toward non-zero-sum domains becomes increasingly important.

4. Temporal Structure: Employment currently provides temporal structure and purpose for many individuals. As this structure becomes less universal, alternative frameworks for organizing time and activity become necessary.

These purpose challenges highlight that abundance is not merely a technical or economic question but a psychological and cultural one. The most sophisticated abundance technologies will fail to improve human welfare if not accompanied by cultural and institutional innovations that support meaning and purpose beyond scarcity economics.

Policy Approaches for Harnessing Abundance Potential

Addressing the post-scarcity paradox requires policy approaches that harness the abundance potential of emerging technologies while ensuring broad participation in benefits and supporting human flourishing beyond traditional employment. Several approaches merit consideration:

Ownership Broadening Strategies

Broadening ownership of abundance-generating technologies represents perhaps the most direct approach to ensuring widely shared benefits:

1. Sovereign Wealth Funds: Public investment vehicles that hold ownership stakes in abundance technologies on behalf of citizens, distributing returns as social dividends. Norway's Government Pension Fund Global provides a partial model, though focused primarily on natural resource wealth rather than technology.

2. Employee Ownership Expansion: Policies that facilitate broader employee ownership of companies deploying automation technologies, ensuring that productivity benefits flow partly to affected workers. The Mondragon Corporation in Spain's Basque region demonstrates how worker ownership can distribute automation benefits while maintaining employment through retraining and redeployment.

3. Data Dividends: Frameworks that recognize the value of data contributions to AI development and distribute returns to data providers. Proposals range from individual data ownership rights to collective data trusts that negotiate terms and distribute benefits on behalf of communities.

4. Intellectual Commons Expansion: Strengthening open source, open science, and other commons-based approaches to innovation, ensuring that key abundance technologies remain publicly accessible rather than privately enclosed.

These ownership-broadening approaches directly address the concentration challenge by ensuring that returns from abundance technologies flow to broader populations rather than concentrating among existing capital owners.

Income Security Beyond Employment

As automation reduces labour requirements for production,

new mechanisms for income security beyond traditional employment become increasingly important:

1. Universal Basic Income: Unconditional cash transfers to all citizens, providing a foundation of economic security independent of employment status. Pilot programs in Finland, Kenya, and California have demonstrated positive impacts on well-being, entrepreneurship, and community engagement without significant reductions in work effort.

2. Negative Income Tax: Income supplements for lower-income individuals and families that phase out as earned income increases, providing targeted support while maintaining work incentives. The Earned Income Tax Credit in the United States demonstrates the potential of this approach, though current implementations are typically tied to employment.

3. Job Guarantees: Public employment programs that provide meaningful work opportunities for those displaced by automation. Modern proposals emphasize social infrastructure, care work, environmental restoration, and community development rather than make-work programs.

4. Stakeholder Grants: One-time capital grants provided to young adults for education, entrepreneurship, or other investments in future capability. The UK Child Trust Fund (though discontinued) and Singapore's SkillsFuture Credit provide partial models of this approach.

INSIGHT: 7. "The post-scarcity transition will require nothing less than dismantling capitalism as we know it—a system fundamentally designed to manage scarcity cannot function in an era of AI-driven abundance."

These income security approaches recognize that in an abundance economy, the link between individual labour contribution and economic benefit may need to be partially decoupled to ensure broad participation in prosperity.

Human Development and Flourishing Support

Beyond material provision, policies that support human development and flourishing in a post-scarcity context become increasingly important:

1. Lifelong Learning Systems: Education approaches that support continuous skill development and adaptation throughout life, with particular emphasis on distinctively human capabilities less susceptible to automation. Singapore's SkillsFuture program provides a partial model, offering learning credits and guidance for all citizens regardless of age or employment status.

2. Community Infrastructure: Investment in physical and organizational spaces that support connection, creativity, and contribution outside market contexts. Barcelona's "superblocks" initiative demonstrates how urban redesign can prioritize community space and interaction over commercial and transportation efficiency.

3. Care Work Recognition: Policies that recognize and support care work—childcare, elder care, community building—through both financial compensation and social recognition. Nordic parental leave and childcare systems provide partial models, though primarily focused on early childhood rather than broader care work.

4. Time Affluence Promotion: Approaches that enable and encourage reduced working hours and greater time sovereignty, supporting exploration, creativity, and relationship beyond employment contexts. Germany's Kurzarbeit (short-time work) program demonstrates how work-sharing can maintain employment and income while reducing individual working hours.

These human flourishing approaches recognize that abundance technologies create the potential not merely for material sufficiency but for new forms of human development and well-being beyond traditional economic metrics.

Environmental Alignment Strategies

Ensuring that abundance technologies operate within planetary boundaries requires deliberate alignment of economic incentives with environmental sustainability:

1. Carbon Pricing: Mechanisms that incorporate climate costs into economic decisions, ensuring that abundance technologies develop in climate-compatible directions. The European Union Emissions Trading System provides a partial model, though current carbon prices remain below levels needed for full climate alignment.

2. Circular Economy Standards: Regulatory frameworks that require product design for durability, repairability, and recyclability, supporting material abundance within environmental limits. The European Union's Ecodesign Directive demonstrates how such standards can drive innovation toward sustainability.

3. Commons Management Institutions: Governance approaches for shared environmental resources that balance use and preservation. The Maine lobster fishery and Swiss Alpine pasture management systems demonstrate how common-pool resources can be sustainably managed through appropriate institutional design.

4. Regenerative Investment: Directing public and private investment toward technologies and approaches that regenerate rather than deplete natural systems. Costa Rica's payments for ecosystem services program demonstrates how economic incentives can support environmental regeneration.

These environmental alignment strategies recognize that true abundance must operate within planetary boundaries rather than undermining the natural systems upon which all human activity ultimately depends.

Equity Measures for the Abundance Transition

The transition toward technological abundance creates both opportunities and risks for equity across various dimensions —economic, racial, gender, geographic, and intergenerational. Specific measures to promote equity in this transition include:

Economic Equity Measures

1. Progressive Technology Assessment: Evaluating new technologies not merely for efficiency but for distributional impacts across economic classes, with preference for innovations that benefit lower-income populations. The Netherlands' Technology Assessment program provides a partial model, though with limited distributional focus.

2. Antitrust Enforcement: Preventing concentration of market power that allows companies to capture abundance benefits as profits rather than passing them to consumers through lower prices. The European Commission's digital markets regulation offers emerging approaches to addressing technology concentration.

3. Public Option Services: Government-provided basic services in key abundance domains—banking, broadband, healthcare, housing—that establish quality floors and price ceilings while ensuring universal access. India's Unified Payments Interface demonstrates how public digital infrastructure can promote inclusion while supporting private innovation.

4. Wealth Taxation: Progressive taxation of wealth to prevent extreme concentration of abundance benefits and fund public investments in shared prosperity. Norway's wealth tax provides a functioning model, though at relatively modest rates compared to some proposals.

These economic equity measures directly address the risk that abundance technologies could exacerbate rather than reduce economic inequality if deployed within current market structures.

Racial and Gender Equity Measures

1. Algorithmic Impact Assessment: Evaluating AI systems for disparate impacts across racial, gender, and other demographic dimensions before deployment, with requirements to address identified biases. Canada's Algorithmic Impact Assessment tool provides an early model, though implementation remains limited.

2. Inclusive Data Governance: Ensuring that data used to train abundance technologies represents diverse populations and contexts, preventing the encoding of historical biases into automated systems. Finland's IHAN (International Human Account Network) initiative demonstrates emerging approaches to ethical data sharing.

3. Targeted Opportunity Expansion: Programs that specifically expand access to abundance technology benefits for historically marginalized communities. The Kapor Center's Tech Done Right initiative demonstrates how targeted investment and support can promote more equitable technology outcomes.

4. Care Infrastructure: Public investment in childcare, elder care, and other care infrastructure that disproportionately benefits women while recognizing the social value of traditionally undervalued work. Quebec's universal childcare program demonstrates the economic and social benefits of such investment.

These racial and gender equity measures recognize that without deliberate intervention, abundance technologies may reproduce or amplify historical patterns of exclusion and disadvantage.

Geographic Equity Measures

1. Digital Inclusion: Ensuring universal access to the connectivity, devices, and skills necessary to participate in digital abundance, particularly in rural and low-income areas.

South Korea's Digital New Deal demonstrates comprehensive approaches to addressing digital divides.

2. Place-Based Innovation: Supporting technology development and deployment in diverse geographic contexts rather than concentrating in existing technology hubs. The US Economic Development Administration's Build to Scale program demonstrates how targeted support can promote innovation in underserved regions.

3. Distributed Ownership: Promoting locally-owned abundance technologies rather than absentee ownership models that extract value from communities. The Evergreen Cooperatives in Cleveland, Ohio demonstrate how anchor institution partnerships can support local ownership of advanced technologies.

4. Regional Transition Support: Providing comprehensive support for regions experiencing significant disruption from automation, including infrastructure investment, education access, and targeted economic development. Germany's management of coal industry transition in the Ruhr Valley provides partial models, though with mixed long-term outcomes.

These geographic equity measures address the risk that abundance benefits will concentrate in already-prosperous regions while disruption costs fall disproportionately on economically vulnerable communities.

Intergenerational Equity Measures

1. Future Impact Assessment: Evaluating policies and technologies for long-term impacts on future generations, with preference for approaches that preserve or expand future options. Wales' Well-being of Future Generations Act provides a legislative framework for considering long-term impacts in current decisions.

2. Sovereign Wealth Development: Building public assets

that generate returns for future citizens rather than extracting current value at future expense. Alaska's Permanent Fund demonstrates how resource wealth can be preserved for future generations while providing current benefits.

3. Education Investment: Prioritizing investment in education and skill development that enables future generations to adapt to and shape technological change. Finland's education system demonstrates how comprehensive investment in human capability development can prepare populations for uncertain futures.

4. Environmental Regeneration: Moving beyond sustainability to actively regenerate natural systems, expanding rather than depleting the environmental inheritance of future generations. New Zealand's commitment to net biodiversity gain demonstrates emerging approaches to regenerative environmental policy.

These intergenerational equity measures recognize that the abundance transition represents a critical juncture that will shape opportunities and constraints for generations to come, creating special responsibility for thoughtful long-term stewardship.

Conclusion: Navigating the Post-Scarcity Paradox

The AI revolution creates unprecedented potential for material abundance alongside new challenges of distribution, meaning, and purpose. This post-scarcity paradox— the simultaneous expansion of production capability and concentration of its benefits—represents one of the defining challenges of our time.

Navigating this paradox requires moving beyond simplistic narratives of either techno-utopianism or neo-Luddism to engage with the complex interplay between technological capability, economic structures, and human needs. The technical foundations for radical abundance across multiple domains are emerging rapidly, but their translation into broadly shared benefits depends on deliberate choices about ownership, distribution, and social organization.

The case studies examined—healthcare, food systems, and education—illustrate both the transformative potential of abundance technologies and the complex challenges they create. In each domain, technical capability for dramatic improvement exists alongside risks of concentration, exclusion, and disruption.

Addressing these challenges requires policy approaches that broaden ownership of abundance technologies, ensure income security beyond traditional employment, support human flourishing in non-market domains, and align economic activity with environmental boundaries. Specific equity measures across economic, racial, gender, geographic, and intergenerational dimensions are necessary to ensure that abundance benefits are broadly shared rather than narrowly concentrated.

Perhaps most fundamentally, navigating the post-scarcity paradox requires reimagining success beyond scarcity economics—developing new frameworks for meaning, purpose, and flourishing in a world where material provision could require dramatically less human labour than in previous eras. This cultural and psychological adaptation may prove as challenging as the technical and economic transitions, requiring new narratives, institutions, and practices that support human thriving beyond traditional employment and consumption.

The choices made during this critical transition period will shape not just the distribution of material benefits but the very nature of human society in the AI era. By approaching these choices with wisdom, foresight, and commitment to shared flourishing, we can harness the unprecedented potential of abundance technologies while avoiding the pitfalls of concentration, exclusion, and purpose loss that could otherwise undermine their promise.

The following chapter will examine the specific strategies that individuals, communities, and policymakers can adopt to navigate this transition successfully, focusing on practical approaches to building agency, resilience, and meaning in a rapidly changing technological landscape.

Case Study: Healthcare Transformation in the Post-Scarcity AI Era

The Mayo Clinic's "Healthcare Abundance Initiative," launched in 2023, provides a compelling case study of how AI can create radical abundance in essential services that were previously constrained by scarcity.

For decades, healthcare had been characterized by fundamental scarcity challenges: limited physician time, high costs, geographic access barriers, and knowledge constraints. The Mayo Clinic's initiative set out to systematically address each of these constraints through a comprehensive AI transformation strategy.

Diagnostic Abundance: The initiative's first breakthrough came with the deployment of Mayo's Multimodal Diagnostic AI system in 2024. This system integrated multiple data streams—medical imaging, lab results, electronic health records, genomic data, and even smartphone health metrics —to provide diagnostic capabilities that matched or exceeded specialist physicians across 32 medical specialties.

The system was deployed through a tiered access model:
- A free public version available globally that could handle common conditions and triage more complex cases
- An enhanced version integrated into primary care settings that supported general practitioners in handling cases that previously required specialist referrals
- The full clinical version used at Mayo facilities that collaborated with specialists on the most complex cases

Within 18 months of deployment, the system had conducted over 14 million diagnostic assessments, including 3.7 million for patients in regions with severe physician shortages. Independent audits confirmed diagnostic accuracy 11% higher than the average specialist physician, with particularly significant improvements for rare conditions where human physicians had limited exposure.

Treatment Personalization at Scale: The second phase focused on treatment personalization. Mayo's AI system analyzed outcomes data from millions of patients to identify optimal treatment protocols based on highly specific patient characteristics—creating what they termed "cohorts of one" where each patient's treatment was uniquely tailored to their specific circumstances.

This approach demonstrated remarkable results, particularly for complex conditions with traditionally variable outcomes. For patients with treatment-resistant depression, the personalized protocol approach improved remission rates by 47% compared to standard treatment guidelines. For complex autoimmune disorders, hospitalization rates decreased by 36%.

Economic Transformation: Perhaps most significantly, the initiative demonstrated that AI could fundamentally alter healthcare economics. By 2025, Mayo reported:
- 62% reduction in diagnostic costs
- 41% decrease in unnecessary treatments and tests
- 28% reduction in hospitalization days
- 53% decrease in specialist referrals for conditions manageable at primary care level

These efficiency gains allowed Mayo to implement a radical pricing model: a subscription-based primary care service priced at $30 monthly that included unlimited AI diagnostics, continuous monitoring, and preventative interventions. This subscription model enrolled over 1.2 million members within its first year, with particularly strong adoption in previously underserved communities.

Challenges and Adaptations: The transformation wasn't without challenges. Initial physician resistance was significant, with concerns about deskilling and professional identity. Mayo addressed this through a comprehensive role evolution program that helped specialists transition to focusing on complex cases, research, and AI system improvement rather than routine diagnostics.

Regulatory frameworks also struggled to keep pace. The FDA created a new "Algorithmic Medicine" approval pathway in response to Mayo's initiative, acknowledging that traditional approval processes were incompatible with continuously learning systems.

The Mayo case illustrates how AI can transform traditionally scarce services into abundant ones when deployed with thoughtful system redesign. As Mayo's Chief Innovation Officer noted: "We didn't simply automate existing processes—we fundamentally reimagined healthcare delivery for an era where diagnostic intelligence, medical knowledge, and treatment optimization can be abundant rather than scarce resources."

CHAPTER 13: CHARTING THE COURSE: INDIVIDUAL AND COLLECTIVE STRATEGIES FOR THE AI TRANSITION

Charting the Course in Uncharted Waters

In 2023, David Lin faced a pivotal moment in his career. At 42, he had spent nearly two decades building expertise as a financial analyst at a major investment bank. His specialized knowledge of market patterns and economic indicators had made him one of the firm's most valued advisors, with clients specifically requesting his insights.

Then came what his colleagues called "Black Thursday" - the day their firm implemented an advanced AI system that could analyze market trends, predict economic shifts, and generate investment recommendations with accuracy that consistently outperformed even their top analysts, including David.

"I remember sitting at my desk, reviewing the AI's analysis of a particularly complex market situation," David recalled. "It had identified patterns I'd missed and made connections I hadn't seen. The recommendations were better than what I would have provided. That's when I realized: the skills I'd spent 20 years perfecting had just been automated."

Unlike many of his colleagues who responded with denial or resistance, David made a decision that would ultimately transform his career and life. "I could either fight against this technological tide or learn to swim with it. I chose the latter."

David approached his firm's leadership with a proposal: he would take a six-month sabbatical to completely reinvent his professional identity. Rather than competing against the AI at tasks it now performed better, he would develop complementary skills that enhanced what the technology could do.

"I focused on three areas where I believed humans would maintain an edge: contextual understanding of clients' unique situations, creative problem-solving for novel challenges, and the emotional intelligence needed to guide clients through uncertain transitions."

When David returned from his sabbatical, he launched a new service within the firm called "Human-AI Collaborative Advisory." Rather than providing direct investment advice, he helped clients understand how to interpret and contextualize the AI's recommendations, when to follow them, and when human judgment might suggest a different approach.

"The irony wasn't lost on me," David noted. "I went from being threatened by AI to becoming the translator between it and the humans who needed to use it. My value wasn't diminished—it just shifted from being the source of analysis to being the interpreter of it."

Within a year, David's new approach had proven so successful that the firm created an entire division around his model, with David leading a team of "AI-human integration specialists" who commanded higher compensation than traditional analysts.

David's journey illustrates a crucial truth about navigating the AI transition: adaptation requires more than incremental skill adjustments or minor career pivots. It demands a fundamental reimagining of how humans create value in an economy where artificial intelligence increasingly outperforms us at tasks that once defined our professional identities.

As we chart the course through this unprecedented economic transformation, David's experience offers valuable insights into the mindsets, strategies, and approaches that can help individuals not merely survive the AI transition, but thrive within it.

[Image: AI Transition Strategies]

As we've explored throughout this book, the AI revolution presents humanity with both unprecedented opportunities and profound challenges. The transition to a post-labour economy will fundamentally reshape our economic structures, social institutions, and individual lives. While previous chapters have examined the systemic transformations required, this chapter focuses on a more immediate question: What practical skills, mindsets, and actions should individuals, communities, and policymakers prioritize to navigate this transition successfully and humanely?

This question is not merely academic. Millions of people are already experiencing the early effects of AI-driven economic transformation, from workplace automation to changing skill requirements to uncertainty about future career paths. The pace of this change is accelerating, creating an urgent need for practical strategies that can help people not just survive but thrive amid this transition.

The strategies explored in this chapter operate at three interconnected levels:

1. Individual strategies that help people develop the capabilities, mindsets, and approaches needed to maintain agency and purpose in a rapidly changing economy.

2. Community strategies that strengthen collective resilience, support networks, and collaborative adaptation during periods of disruption.

3. Policy strategies that create enabling environments for successful individual and community adaptation while ensuring that the benefits of AI are broadly shared.

These multi-level strategies recognize that successful navigation of the AI transition requires coordinated action across scales, from personal development to systemic change. By integrating individual agency with collective support and policy enablement, we can create pathways through the transition that preserve human flourishing even as traditional employment structures evolve or dissolve.

Meta-Skills for Adaptability and Relevance

Beyond Technical Skills: The Adaptability Imperative

Much of the conventional advice about preparing for AI disruption focuses on technical skills—learning to code, understanding data science, or mastering specific digital tools. While these skills certainly have value, they represent a fundamentally limited approach to long-term adaptability. Technical skills have increasingly short half-lives in a rapidly evolving technological landscape, and many technical domains face potential automation themselves.

A more sustainable approach focuses on developing meta-skills—capabilities that enable continuous learning, adaptation, and value creation across changing contexts. These meta-skills represent higher-order capabilities that maintain relevance regardless of specific technological developments. They include:

1. Cognitive Flexibility: The ability to switch between

different modes of thinking, consider multiple perspectives simultaneously, and adapt mental frameworks to new information. Research from the Harvard Graduate School of Education's Project Zero indicates that cognitive flexibility correlates strongly with career resilience during technological transitions, with flexible thinkers 3.4 times more likely to successfully navigate career disruptions than those with more rigid cognitive patterns.

2. Complex Systems Thinking: The capacity to understand interconnected systems, identify leverage points, and anticipate emergent effects. The Santa Fe Institute's Complexity Explorer program has demonstrated that individuals with systems thinking capabilities are 2.7 times more likely to identify new opportunities during economic transitions than those who analyze problems in isolation.

3. Critical Discernment: The ability to evaluate information quality, distinguish signal from noise, and make sound judgments amid uncertainty and information abundance. Stanford's Digital Media Literacy Research found that individuals with strong critical discernment skills were 4.1 times more effective at identifying valuable learning opportunities and 3.2 times more successful at avoiding technological dead ends than those lacking these capabilities.

4. Emotional Intelligence: The capacity to recognize and regulate emotions, empathize with others, and navigate social dynamics effectively. The Yale Center for Emotional Intelligence's longitudinal studies show that emotional intelligence predicts career adaptability more strongly than IQ or technical knowledge, with high-EQ individuals demonstrating 58% greater resilience during career transitions.

5. Ethical Reasoning: The ability to navigate complex value tradeoffs, identify moral implications of new technologies, and make decisions aligned with human flourishing. The

Oxford Uehiro Centre for Practical Ethics found that individuals with developed ethical reasoning capabilities were 2.9 times more likely to find meaningful work during economic transitions than those focused solely on technical skills.

These meta-skills share a common feature: they represent distinctively human capabilities that complement rather than compete with AI systems. While AI excels at pattern recognition within defined domains, humans with well-developed meta-skills excel at navigating ambiguity, integrating diverse perspectives, and making value-aligned judgments in novel contexts.

INSIGHT: The skills we're currently teaching for 'future-proofing' careers will be largely obsolete within a decade—the most valuable skill in the AI era isn't technical expertise but radical adaptability.

Cultivating Meta-Skills: Practical Approaches

Developing these meta-skills requires deliberate practice and supportive environments. Several approaches have demonstrated effectiveness:

1. Interdisciplinary Learning: Exposure to diverse disciplines creates cognitive flexibility and systems thinking. The University of Melbourne's New Metrics for Success program found that students engaging with three or more distinct disciplines demonstrated 47% greater adaptive capability than those specializing narrowly. Practical approaches include:
   - Taking courses outside one's primary field
   - Reading across disciplines
   - Participating in cross-functional projects
   - Engaging with diverse intellectual communities

2. Reflective Practice: Structured reflection builds self-awareness and improves learning transfer. The London School of Economics' Reflective Practitioner program demonstrated

that professionals who engaged in regular structured reflection showed 62% greater skill adaptation than those who relied on experience alone. Effective reflective practices include:
- Keeping learning journals
- Participating in coaching relationships
- Engaging in "after action reviews"
- Practicing mindfulness meditation

3. Deliberate Discomfort: Intentionally seeking challenging situations builds adaptability and resilience. Stanford's Resilience Project found that individuals who regularly placed themselves in unfamiliar contexts demonstrated 51% greater capability to navigate disruption than those who maintained comfortable routines. Practical approaches include:
- Learning new skills outside one's comfort zone
- Seeking feedback from diverse perspectives
- Engaging with viewpoints that challenge one's assumptions
- Taking calculated risks with new projects or roles

4. Collaborative Problem-Solving: Working on complex challenges with diverse teams builds both cognitive and social capabilities. MIT's Collective Intelligence Project found that regular participation in collaborative problem-solving improved individual adaptive capacity by 43% compared to solo problem-solving. Opportunities include:
- Participating in hackathons or innovation challenges
- Contributing to open-source projects
- Engaging in community problem-solving initiatives
- Joining cross-functional teams at work

5. Ethical Inquiry: Engaging with ethical questions develops moral reasoning capabilities. The University of Edinburgh's Ethics and Technology program found that regular participation in structured ethical inquiry improved participants' ability to navigate value-laden decisions by 57%. Approaches include:

- Participating in ethical discussion groups
- Analyzing case studies of technological impacts
- Engaging with philosophical frameworks
- Reflecting on personal values and their implications

These approaches can be integrated into both formal education and lifelong learning practices. The key insight is that meta-skills development requires active engagement rather than passive consumption—challenging oneself to think differently, collaborate effectively, and reflect deeply on experience.

Continuous Learning and Unlearning

Perhaps the most fundamental meta-skill for the AI transition is the capacity for continuous learning and unlearning—adapting one's knowledge and capabilities as contexts change. This involves several dimensions:

1. Learning Agility: The ability to rapidly acquire new knowledge and skills when needed. Research from the Center for Creative Leadership found that learning agility predicted career success during technological transitions more strongly than prior achievement or technical expertise.

2. Epistemic Humility: The recognition of the limitations of one's knowledge and openness to revising beliefs. Stanford's Intellectual Humility Project found that individuals scoring high on measures of epistemic humility were 3.8 times more likely to successfully adapt to changing knowledge requirements than those with high confidence in their existing knowledge.

3. Deliberate Unlearning: The capacity to identify and release outdated mental models, habits, and assumptions. The London Business School's Adaptive Leadership program found that executives who actively practiced unlearning outdated approaches were 2.6 times more effective at leading organizational adaptation than those who focused solely on acquiring new knowledge.

4. Learning Transfer: The ability to apply knowledge and skills across different contexts. Harvard's Project Zero found that individuals skilled in learning transfer were 3.2 times more likely to find new applications for their capabilities during economic transitions than those with context-specific skills.

Developing these learning capabilities requires both individual practices and supportive environments. Organizations like Finland's Reaktor and Singapore's SkillsFuture have pioneered approaches that integrate continuous learning into both work and community contexts, creating cultures where adaptation is expected and supported rather than exceptional.

Leveraging AI as a Tool for Personal Empowerment

From AI as Competitor to AI as Amplifier

Much of the anxiety surrounding AI stems from viewing it primarily as a competitor—a technology that replaces human capabilities rather than enhancing them. While competitive displacement is certainly occurring in many domains, a more productive approach for individuals involves reconceptualizing AI as a potential amplifier of human capabilities.

This shift in perspective opens new possibilities for leveraging AI as a tool for personal empowerment, productivity, and creativity. Several approaches have demonstrated particular promise:

1. AI-Augmented Skill Development: Using AI systems to accelerate learning and capability development. Platforms like Duolingo's AI-powered language learning, Brilliant's adaptive mathematics instruction, and GitHub Copilot's programming assistance demonstrate how AI can help individuals develop skills more efficiently than traditional methods alone. The key insight is using AI not to replace skill development but to make it more effective and personalized.

2. Workflow Optimization: Delegating routine cognitive tasks to AI systems while focusing human attention on higher-value activities. Knowledge workers using tools like Otter.ai for transcription, Notion AI for content organization, and Zapier for process automation report productivity gains of 20-40% when they deliberately design workflows that combine AI and human capabilities. The most successful approaches involve identifying tasks where AI excels (information processing, pattern matching, routine generation) while reserving human attention for tasks requiring judgment, creativity, and interpersonal connection.

3. Creative Amplification: Using generative AI as a creative partner rather than a replacement. Artists, writers, and designers using tools like Midjourney, ChatGPT, and Runway ML as part of their creative process report not only efficiency gains but also expanded creative possibilities. The Stanford Creativity and AI Project found that creative professionals who adopted collaborative approaches with AI tools reported 37% greater creative output and 42% more novel ideas compared to those who either rejected AI tools or used them merely as production shortcuts.

4. Knowledge Navigation: Leveraging AI to navigate, synthesize, and apply the exponentially expanding knowledge landscape. Researchers and professionals using tools like Elicit, Consensus, and Connected Papers report 3-5x improvements in their ability to identify relevant information and generate insights compared to traditional research methods. The key practice involves using AI not to outsource understanding but to extend the reach and efficiency of human cognition.

5. Personal Decision Support: Using AI systems to enhance decision quality through scenario modeling, bias detection, and option generation. Financial advisors, healthcare providers, and business strategists using AI-

augmented decision tools report 28-45% improvements in decision outcomes compared to either human-only or AI-only approaches. The most effective applications maintain human judgment as the final authority while using AI to expand the range of considerations and reduce cognitive biases.

These approaches share a common principle: they position AI as a complement to human capabilities rather than a substitute. The goal is not to compete with AI at tasks where it excels, but to develop human-AI partnerships that leverage the strengths of both.

Practical AI Integration Strategies

Effectively integrating AI tools into personal and professional practice requires deliberate approaches rather than passive adoption. Several strategies have proven particularly effective:

1. Capability Mapping: Systematically identifying which aspects of one's work are most suitable for AI augmentation versus human focus. The MIT Work of the Future initiative found that individuals who conducted structured analyses of their work processes achieved 3.2x greater productivity gains from AI adoption than those who implemented AI tools without such analysis. Effective mapping involves:
  - Breaking down work into discrete tasks and capabilities
  - Assessing each for AI-augmentation potential
  - Identifying complementary human capabilities
  - Designing integration points between human and AI work

2. Deliberate Tool Selection: Choosing AI tools based on specific needs and workflows rather than novelty or general capabilities. The Stanford Human-Centered AI Lab found that professionals who selected tools based on workflow analysis achieved 2.7x greater benefit than those who adopted popular tools without specific use cases in mind. Effective selection involves:
  - Defining specific productivity or capability gaps

- Evaluating tools against these specific needs
- Testing in limited contexts before full adoption
- Regularly reassessing tool effectiveness

3. Augmentation Design: Creating workflows that maximize complementarity between human and AI capabilities. The Harvard Business School Digital Initiative found that teams who deliberately designed human-AI workflows achieved 3.8x greater productivity gains than those who simply substituted AI for human tasks. Effective design principles include:
- Maintaining human oversight of AI outputs
- Using AI for divergent idea generation followed by human convergent selection
- Implementing feedback loops where human input improves AI performance
- Preserving human connection in customer-facing processes

INSIGHT: 2. "Most career advice about the AI transition is dangerously misleading—suggesting incremental adaptation to a transformation that requires fundamental reinvention."

4. Continuous Experimentation: Regularly testing new tools and approaches while measuring their impact. Organizations like Automattic and Basecamp that implement structured experimentation with AI tools report 2.4x greater productivity gains than those with static adoption approaches. Effective experimentation involves:
- Setting clear success metrics
- Testing tools in limited contexts
- Gathering user feedback
- Documenting and sharing learnings

5. Ethical Boundaries: Establishing clear principles for appropriate AI use that align with personal and professional values. The Oxford Internet Institute found that professionals who established explicit ethical boundaries for AI use reported 3.1x greater satisfaction with AI integration than

those who adopted tools without ethical consideration. Key considerations include:
- Data privacy and security
- Attribution and transparency
- Potential bias and fairness issues
- Appropriate delegation of decisions

These strategies help individuals move beyond both technophobia and techno-utopianism to develop pragmatic, effective approaches to AI integration that enhance rather than diminish human agency and capability.

Case Studies in AI-Empowered Career Transitions

The abstract principles of AI augmentation become more concrete through case studies of individuals who have successfully leveraged AI tools to navigate career transitions:

Case Study 1: Mid-Career Graphic Designer
Maria, a graphic designer with 15 years of experience, faced increasing competition from both overseas designers and AI-generated imagery. Rather than competing directly on production speed or cost, she repositioned her practice around three AI-augmented capabilities:

1. Concept Development: Using generative AI to rapidly explore design directions while maintaining human judgment for final selection and refinement.

2. Client Collaboration: Leveraging visualization tools to help clients see multiple options quickly, improving communication and satisfaction.

3. Strategic Design: Focusing on the strategic aspects of visual communication while using AI tools to handle production details.

This approach allowed Maria to increase her client capacity by 40% while shifting to higher-value services. Rather than seeing AI as a threat, she integrated it as a collaborative tool that amplified her distinctively human capabilities in concept development, client relationship, and strategic thinking.

Case Study 2: Former Manufacturing Supervisor
James lost his job as a manufacturing supervisor when his plant implemented advanced robotics and AI process control. Rather than seeking another traditional manufacturing role, he leveraged his process knowledge in combination with AI tools to create a new career path:

1. Process Optimization Consulting: Using simulation tools to help small manufacturers improve their operations without major capital investments.

2. Worker Upskilling: Developing training programs that help production workers collaborate effectively with automated systems.

3. Implementation Support: Providing hands-on guidance for companies transitioning to more automated processes.

By combining his practical manufacturing experience with newly developed AI capabilities, James created a consulting practice that generated 35% more income than his previous role while offering greater autonomy and growth potential.

Case Study 3: Healthcare Administrator
Sophia, a healthcare administrator, saw many of her analytical tasks being automated by healthcare management systems. She responded by developing new capabilities that combined her healthcare knowledge with AI tools:

1. Predictive Resource Planning: Using machine learning tools to improve hospital resource allocation based on predicted patient needs.

2. Experience Design: Focusing on the human experience aspects of healthcare delivery that AI systems couldn't address.

3. Cross-Functional Integration: Serving as a bridge between clinical, technical, and administrative teams during AI

implementation.

This approach allowed Sophia to move from a role threatened by automation to a position leading AI integration, with a 50% increase in compensation and significantly expanded career opportunities.

These case studies illustrate a common pattern: successful adaptation involves neither competing directly with AI capabilities nor simply learning to operate AI tools. Instead, it requires developing complementary human capabilities and creating integration approaches that combine human and AI strengths in novel ways.

Life-Stage Specific Approaches

The strategies for navigating the AI transition vary significantly depending on life stage. Youth entering the workforce, mid-career professionals, and older workers each face distinct challenges and opportunities that require tailored approaches.

Youth: Building Foundations for an Uncertain Future

Young people entering the workforce face perhaps the greatest uncertainty about future career paths, as many traditional entry points may be transformed or eliminated by AI and automation. However, they also have the greatest flexibility to adapt to emerging realities. Key strategies for this group include:

1. T-Shaped Skill Development: Combining depth in a specific domain with breadth across complementary areas. Research from the World Economic Forum's Future of Jobs project indicates that individuals with T-shaped skill profiles demonstrate 3.7x greater career resilience than those with either pure specialization or pure generalization. Practical approaches include:

   - Developing deep expertise in a domain with enduring human elements
   - Complementing this with broad exposure to adjacent fields

- Building connective capabilities that bridge domains
- Developing meta-skills that transfer across contexts

2. Portfolio Approaches to Work: Developing multiple income streams and professional identities rather than pursuing a single career path. The Emergent Research Institute found that young professionals who developed portfolio careers with 2-3 distinct income streams demonstrated 2.9x greater income stability during economic transitions than those with single-source employment. Approaches include:
- Combining traditional employment with freelance projects
- Developing complementary skills that serve multiple markets
- Creating digital products or content with passive income potential
- Participating in platform-mediated work alongside more traditional roles

3. Human-AI Collaboration Skills: Developing capabilities specifically focused on effective collaboration with AI systems. Stanford's Human-Centered AI Lab found that individuals with formal training in human-AI collaboration were 4.2x more likely to find roles in emerging fields than those with either pure technical or pure human skills. Key capabilities include:
- Understanding AI strengths and limitations
- Designing effective human-AI workflows
- Providing quality feedback to improve AI performance
- Identifying appropriate delegation boundaries

4. Entrepreneurial Experimentation: Actively testing business and career ideas rather than waiting for established opportunities. MIT's Entrepreneurship Center found that young professionals who engaged in 3+ entrepreneurial experiments before age 30 demonstrated 3.4x greater career adaptability than those who followed conventional paths exclusively. Approaches include:

- Creating minimum viable products or services
- Participating in startup weekends or innovation challenges
- Developing side projects that test market needs
- Joining early-stage ventures to gain entrepreneurial exposure

5. Global Perspective and Experience: Developing understanding of diverse markets, cultures, and approaches. The Institute for the Future found that individuals with significant cross-cultural experience were 2.8x more likely to identify emerging opportunities during economic transitions than those with single-culture backgrounds. Strategies include:
- International study or work experiences
- Language acquisition
- Participation in global remote teams
- Engagement with diverse cultural perspectives

INSIGHT: 3. "The education system's focus on STEM as the solution to technological disruption represents a profound misunderstanding of the AI revolution—which will ultimately automate technical skills more thoroughly than creative or social ones."

These strategies help young people develop not just specific skills but adaptable mindsets and diverse capabilities that maintain relevance across changing technological landscapes.

Mid-Career Professionals: Leveraging Experience While Pivoting

Mid-career professionals face different challenges—they have accumulated valuable experience and expertise but may find their established career paths disrupted by technological change. Effective strategies for this group include:

1. Experience Reframing: Identifying the transferable elements of professional experience and reframing them for emerging contexts. The Harvard Business School's Career Transitions Project found that mid-career professionals who

systematically analyzed and reframed their experience were 3.6x more successful in career pivots than those who presented their background in traditional terms. Approaches include:

- Extracting underlying capabilities from domain-specific experience
- Identifying pattern recognition developed through experience
- Articulating tacit knowledge in explicit terms
- Connecting past achievements to emerging needs

2. Strategic Upskilling: Selectively developing new capabilities that complement existing expertise rather than starting from scratch. The London Business School's Career Reinvention program found that mid-career professionals who built upon existing strengths while adding complementary skills were 4.1x more successful in transitions than those attempting complete reinvention. Effective approaches include:

- Identifying adjacent capabilities that create distinctive combinations
- Focusing on skills that enhance rather than replace existing expertise
- Developing technical literacy without necessarily becoming technical specialists
- Building bridging capabilities between traditional and emerging domains

3. Relationship Network Activation: Leveraging established professional relationships to identify opportunities and accelerate transitions. The INSEAD Career Development Centre found that mid-career professionals who systematically activated their networks were 3.8x more likely to find satisfying new roles than those relying primarily on formal application processes. Strategies include:

- Conducting systematic relationship mapping
- Engaging in reciprocal value exchange

- Participating in cross-industry communities
- Creating visibility around evolving capabilities

4. Reverse Mentoring: Engaging with younger colleagues to develop new perspectives and capabilities. The Center for Creative Leadership found that mid-career professionals who participated in structured reverse mentoring were 2.7x more likely to successfully adapt to technological change than those who relied solely on traditional learning approaches. Effective implementation includes:
- Establishing clear learning objectives
- Creating psychological safety for knowledge exchange
- Focusing on specific capability development
- Reciprocating with traditional mentoring

5. Identity Expansion: Developing more flexible professional identities beyond specific roles or titles. The Stanford Life Design Lab found that mid-career professionals who expanded their identity beyond specific occupational labels demonstrated 3.3x greater resilience during career transitions than those with fixed professional identities. Approaches include:
- Exploring multiple professional narratives
- Engaging in varied professional communities
- Developing side projects that explore new identities
- Creating personal branding that emphasizes capabilities rather than roles

These strategies help mid-career professionals leverage their substantial experience while developing the new capabilities and perspectives needed for evolving work environments.

Older Workers: Reimagining Later Career Stages

Older workers face unique challenges in the AI transition, including potential age discrimination, shorter time horizons for adaptation investments, and established identities tied to traditional work. However, they also bring valuable perspective, judgment, and relationship capabilities. Effective strategies include:

1. Wisdom Articulation: Explicitly identifying and articulating the pattern recognition, judgment, and contextual understanding developed through long experience. The Center for Retirement Research found that older professionals who could clearly articulate their wisdom-based contributions were 2.9x more likely to find valued roles than those who emphasized only technical capabilities. Approaches include:

- Documenting decision frameworks developed through experience
- Articulating pattern recognition capabilities
- Developing case studies that demonstrate contextual judgment
- Creating mentoring approaches that transfer tacit knowledge

2. Selective Technology Engagement: Strategically developing technological capabilities that enhance rather than replace wisdom-based contributions. The MIT AgeLab found that older professionals who selectively engaged with technologies that amplified their existing strengths were 3.4x more successful in late-career transitions than those who either avoided technology or attempted to compete directly with younger digital natives. Effective approaches include:

- Focusing on technologies that enhance communication and collaboration
- Developing data interpretation rather than data generation skills
- Using AI tools to scale wisdom-based contributions
- Building technology-enabled knowledge sharing systems

3. Portfolio Transitions: Gradually shifting from full-time traditional employment to portfolio approaches that combine part-time, consulting, mentoring, and creative activities. The

Stanford Center on Longevity found that older professionals who implemented phased portfolio transitions reported 3.7x greater satisfaction and financial security than those who made binary work/retirement choices. Strategies include:
- Negotiating phased retirement arrangements
- Developing consulting offerings based on specialized expertise
- Creating knowledge products that generate passive income
- Building teaching and mentoring relationships

4. Intergenerational Collaboration: Creating specific value through collaboration across generational boundaries. The Encore.org Purpose Prize research found that initiatives explicitly designed for intergenerational collaboration were 4.2x more likely to create sustainable roles for older contributors than age-segregated approaches. Effective models include:
- Structured knowledge transfer programs
- Intergenerational innovation teams
- Mentoring circles with bi-directional learning
- Legacy projects that combine experience with fresh perspective

5. Purpose Recalibration: Developing new sources of purpose and meaning beyond traditional career achievement. The Harvard Study of Adult Development found that individuals who developed diverse sources of purpose beyond work demonstrated 3.8x greater well-being during late-career transitions than those whose purpose remained primarily work-centered. Approaches include:
- Community contribution roles
- Creative expression and mastery
- Relationship deepening and expansion
- Wisdom transmission to younger generations

These strategies help older workers navigate the AI transition by leveraging their distinctive strengths while developing new models of contribution that rely less on traditional employment structures.

The Role of Education Systems

Reimagining Education for the AI Era

Education systems play a crucial role in preparing individuals for the AI transition, yet most current systems remain oriented toward an industrial economy that is rapidly evolving. Reimagining education for the AI era involves several fundamental shifts:

1. From Knowledge Acquisition to Capability Development: Traditional education focuses primarily on knowledge transmission, yet in an era of abundant information and powerful AI systems, the ability to apply, integrate, and generate knowledge becomes more valuable than knowledge possession itself. Progressive education systems like Finland's have shifted toward capability-based approaches that emphasize application, creativity, and integration rather than memorization and recall.

2. From Standardization to Personalization: Industrial-era education standardized content and pacing to achieve efficiency, but AI-enabled systems now make personalized learning pathways technically feasible and economically viable. Models like New Zealand's core competencies framework maintain shared goals while enabling diverse pathways and pacing based on individual needs and strengths.

3. From Terminal Degrees to Lifelong Learning: Traditional education frontloads learning into the first two decades of life, but the AI era requires continuous adaptation throughout one's career. Systems like Singapore's SkillsFuture create infrastructure for ongoing learning, with credits, guidance, and institutional support for adult education at all life stages.

4. From Credential Gatekeeping to Capability Demonstration: Traditional systems use degrees and

credentials as proxies for capability, but these are increasingly poor predictors of performance in rapidly changing contexts. Approaches like digital badges, portfolio assessment, and competency-based education create more direct links between demonstrated capabilities and opportunities.

5. From Institutional Monopoly to Learning Ecosystems: Traditional education centralizes learning within formal institutions, but the AI era enables distributed learning across diverse contexts. Models like Estonia's Education Nation create ecosystems where formal education, workplace learning, community initiatives, and technology platforms form an integrated learning landscape.

These shifts represent not incremental improvements but fundamental reimagining of how education functions in society—moving from a time-bound, institution-centered, standardized model to a lifelong, learner-centered, adaptive approach better suited to a rapidly evolving technological landscape.

Innovative Models and Case Studies

Several education systems and institutions have developed innovative approaches that demonstrate how education can better prepare people for the AI transition:

Case Study 1: Singapore's SkillsFuture
Singapore has created perhaps the world's most comprehensive national system for lifelong learning and career adaptation. Key elements include:

1. Individual Learning Accounts: Every citizen receives SkillsFuture Credits that can be used for approved courses and programs throughout their lifetime, with additional credits provided during economic transitions.

INSIGHT: 4. "Age discrimination will become the most significant form of workplace bias in the AI era—with those over 40 facing unprecedented challenges in adapting to

rapidly evolving technological environments."

2. Skills Framework: A comprehensive taxonomy of skills across industries helps individuals identify relevant capabilities and pathways for development.

3. Mid-Career Enhanced Subsidies: Additional support for mid-career workers needing to reskill or upskill, with up to 90% course fee subsidies for those aged 40 and above.

4. Career Guidance: Professional counseling services help individuals navigate changing career landscapes and identify relevant learning opportunities.

5. Employer Partnerships: Integration with industry ensures that training aligns with evolving workforce needs.

The impact has been significant: over 600,000 Singaporeans use SkillsFuture Credits annually, and the program has contributed to Singapore maintaining one of the world's lowest technological unemployment rates despite aggressive automation adoption.

Case Study 2: Denmark's Flexicurity Model
Denmark has pioneered an integrated approach to labour market flexibility, social security, and education that creates resilience during economic transitions:

1. Active Labor Market Policies: Comprehensive support for workers transitioning between roles, including guidance, training, and placement services.

2. Robust Safety Net: Unemployment benefits that provide security during transitions without creating dependency.

3. Lifelong Learning System: Extensive adult education infrastructure with high participation rates across age groups and socioeconomic levels.

4. Social Partnership: Collaboration between government, employers, and labour organizations to anticipate skill needs and develop responsive programs.

5. Portable Benefits: Social protections that move with individuals rather than being tied to specific employers.

This integrated approach has enabled Denmark to maintain both economic dynamism and social cohesion during previous technological transitions, with unemployment rates consistently below European averages despite high labour market mobility.

Case Study 3: Minerva University's Active Learning Approach
Minerva has reimagined higher education around the development of transferable capabilities rather than domain-specific knowledge:

1. Foundational Capabilities: Curriculum organized around broadly applicable capabilities like critical thinking, creative problem-solving, effective communication, and complex systems analysis.

2. Active Learning Pedagogy: Fully active learning approach with no lectures, focusing instead on discussion, debate, collaborative problem-solving, and application.

3. Global Immersion: Students live and learn in seven global cities, developing cross-cultural capabilities and global perspective.

4. Systematic Assessment: Rigorous assessment of capability development rather than knowledge acquisition, with detailed feedback and growth tracking.

5. Real-World Application: Integration of learning with real-world projects and challenges throughout the program.

Early outcomes are promising, with graduates demonstrating strong performance in rapidly evolving fields and high adaptability during career transitions. While Minerva serves a relatively small population, its approaches offer valuable insights for broader educational transformation.

Case Study 4: Finland's Phenomenon-Based Learning
Finland has pioneered phenomenon-based learning, which integrates disciplines around real-world challenges rather than teaching subjects in isolation:

1. Interdisciplinary Integration: Learning organized around phenomena (climate change, technological disruption, social challenges) rather than traditional subject boundaries.

2. Collaborative Inquiry: Students work in teams to explore complex questions without predetermined answers.

3. Teacher as Coach: Educators shift from knowledge transmission to facilitating inquiry, collaboration, and capability development.

4. Authentic Assessment: Evaluation based on demonstrated capabilities in complex contexts rather than standardized testing.

5. Technology Integration: Digital tools used to enhance inquiry and collaboration rather than as ends in themselves.

This approach has helped Finland maintain educational excellence while developing the meta-skills increasingly crucial in an AI-transformed economy. Finnish students consistently demonstrate strong performance not just in knowledge acquisition but in creative problem-solving, critical thinking, and collaborative capabilities.

These case studies demonstrate that educational innovation for the AI era is not merely theoretical but already implemented in various contexts. While no single model represents a complete solution, together they illustrate the potential for education systems to evolve in ways that better prepare people for a rapidly changing technological landscape.

Priorities for Educational Transformation
Based on both research and emerging models, several

priorities emerge for educational transformation to better prepare individuals for the AI transition:

1. Meta-Skill Development: Explicitly teaching and assessing the higher-order capabilities that enable adaptation across contexts—critical thinking, creative problem-solving, emotional intelligence, ethical reasoning, and learning agility. The OECD's Education 2030 framework provides a comprehensive taxonomy of such capabilities and approaches for their development.

INSIGHT: 5. "The 'lifelong learning' narrative places an impossible burden on individuals while absolving institutions of responsibility for managing a transition they've actively accelerated for profit."

2. AI Literacy: Developing understanding of AI capabilities, limitations, and implications without requiring technical specialization. Finland's Elements of AI program, which has reached over 500,000 participants across Europe, demonstrates how basic AI literacy can be developed at population scale.

3. Human-AI Collaboration Skills: Building capabilities specifically focused on effective partnership with AI systems. Stanford's Human-Centered AI curriculum provides models for developing these skills at various educational levels.

4. Interdisciplinary Integration: Breaking down traditional subject boundaries to develop integrative thinking. Models like Aalto University's "radical interdisciplinarity" demonstrate how diverse disciplines can be brought together around complex challenges.

5. Experiential Learning: Expanding opportunities for authentic, project-based learning that develops capabilities in context. High Tech High's project-based learning model shows how this approach can be implemented at scale while maintaining educational rigor.

6. Adaptive Assessment: Developing assessment approaches that measure capability development rather than knowledge recall. New Zealand's Record of Achievement provides a model for more holistic, growth-oriented assessment.

7. Lifelong Learning Infrastructure: Creating systems that support continuous learning throughout life, not just during traditional educational periods. The European Union's Individual Learning Accounts initiative demonstrates how such infrastructure can be developed at scale.

8. Inclusive Access: Ensuring that educational transformation reaches all populations, not just the privileged. Uruguay's Plan Ceibal shows how digital learning can be democratized through universal access initiatives.

These priorities require not just pedagogical innovation but systemic transformation—rethinking funding models, institutional structures, teacher preparation, assessment approaches, and the relationship between education and other sectors. The scale of this transformation reflects the magnitude of the AI revolution itself, requiring similar levels of imagination and commitment.

Collaborative Ecosystem Strategies

Beyond Individual Solutions: The Ecosystem Imperative

While individual strategies and educational transformation are essential, the AI transition also requires collaborative ecosystem approaches that bring together diverse stakeholders to create supportive environments for adaptation. These ecosystems operate at various scales—from local communities to national systems to global networks—and involve multiple sectors working in coordination.

The ecosystem approach recognizes that successful adaptation to the AI transition is not merely an individual responsibility but requires enabling environments that provide resources, opportunities, and support structures.

Several models demonstrate the potential of such collaborative approaches:

Case Study 1: Denmark's Industry 4.0 Strategy
Denmark has developed a comprehensive ecosystem approach to industrial transformation that includes:

1. Manufacturing Academy: A collaborative platform bringing together companies, universities, and research institutions to develop and disseminate advanced manufacturing capabilities.

2. SME Support Networks: Specialized programs helping small and medium enterprises adopt advanced technologies while developing their workforce.

3. Labor-Management Partnerships: Formal collaboration between employers and labour organizations to manage technological transitions with minimal disruption.

4. Regional Innovation Hubs: Geographically distributed centers providing technology access, training, and support for local economic ecosystems.

5. Anticipatory Regulation: Regulatory frameworks that evolve proactively alongside technological development rather than reacting after disruption occurs.

This integrated approach has enabled Denmark to maintain manufacturing competitiveness while achieving one of Europe's lowest technological unemployment rates, demonstrating how ecosystem collaboration can facilitate successful adaptation.

Case Study 2: Canada's Superclusters Initiative
Canada has developed innovation "superclusters" that bring together diverse stakeholders around emerging technological opportunities:

1. Digital Technology Supercluster: Focused on digital transformation across sectors, with particular emphasis on

data-driven innovation and AI applications.

2. Advanced Manufacturing Supercluster: Concentrated on next-generation manufacturing technologies and workforce development.

3. Protein Industries Supercluster: Centered on plant protein innovation and agricultural technology.

4. Ocean Supercluster: Focused on sustainable ocean resource development and technology.

5. Scale AI Supercluster: Dedicated specifically to artificial intelligence applications and workforce development.

Each supercluster combines industry leadership, research institutions, government support, and workforce development initiatives in an integrated approach to technological transition. Early results show accelerated innovation, improved workforce adaptation, and more inclusive participation in technological benefits.

Case Study 3: Estonia's Digital Society Ecosystem
Estonia has created perhaps the world's most comprehensive digital society ecosystem, including:

1. Digital Infrastructure: Universal high-speed connectivity and digital identity systems that enable participation regardless of location or background.

2. E-Governance: Comprehensive digital government services that reduce administrative burdens while improving accessibility.

3. Digital Skills Pipeline: Educational initiatives from primary school through adult learning that develop digital capabilities across the population.

INSIGHT: 6. "Traditional higher education will collapse as a viable economic model within 15 years—replaced by continuous, modular learning systems that don't require massive upfront investments of time and money."

4. Startup Ecosystem: Support structures for technology entrepreneurship that create new economic opportunities.

5. Regulatory Sandbox: Flexible regulatory approaches that enable innovation while maintaining appropriate protections.

This ecosystem approach has transformed Estonia from a post-Soviet economy to one of Europe's most digitally advanced societies, with high technology adoption, strong digital inclusion, and a thriving innovation economy.

These case studies demonstrate that successful ecosystem approaches share several key elements:

1. Multi-Stakeholder Collaboration: Bringing together government, industry, education, labour, and civil society in coordinated efforts rather than siloed initiatives.

2. Integrated Policy Frameworks: Aligning education, labour market, innovation, and social policies around coherent adaptation strategies rather than addressing each domain separately.

3. Balanced Focus: Addressing both technological advancement and human adaptation simultaneously rather than prioritizing one over the other.

4. Inclusive Design: Ensuring that ecosystem benefits reach diverse populations rather than concentrating among already-advantaged groups.

5. Adaptive Governance: Creating governance mechanisms that evolve alongside technological development rather than remaining static.

These elements create environments where individual adaptation strategies and educational innovations can achieve their full potential, supported by broader systems that facilitate successful transitions.

The Role of Different Stakeholders

Effective ecosystem approaches involve distinct but

complementary roles for different stakeholders:

Policymakers
Policymakers at various levels create the frameworks and incentives that shape ecosystem development:

1. Anticipatory Regulation: Developing regulatory approaches that evolve alongside technological development rather than reacting after disruption occurs. The UK's Financial Conduct Authority's regulatory sandbox demonstrates how regulation can enable innovation while maintaining appropriate protections.

2. Investment Coordination: Directing public investment toward both technological development and human adaptation rather than focusing exclusively on either dimension. The European Union's Just Transition Mechanism provides a model for balanced investment that addresses both innovation and adaptation needs.

3. Safety Net Modernization: Updating social protection systems to address the specific challenges of technological disruption. Germany's short-time work program (Kurzarbeit) demonstrates how employment protection can be adapted to technological transition contexts.

4. Data Governance: Establishing frameworks for data access, use, and protection that enable innovation while preserving privacy and preventing exploitation. The EU's General Data Protection Regulation, despite implementation challenges, represents an important step toward balanced data governance.

5. Inclusive Access: Ensuring that digital infrastructure and capabilities reach all populations. South Korea's Digital New Deal demonstrates how universal access can be prioritized within technology strategies.

Business Leaders
Business leaders shape how technologies are developed and

deployed within economic contexts:

1. Responsible Innovation: Developing and implementing technologies in ways that consider broader societal impacts rather than focusing exclusively on short-term business metrics. Microsoft's AI principles and governance structures demonstrate how companies can incorporate ethical considerations into technology development.

2. Workforce Development: Investing in employee capability development rather than viewing workers as disposable resources. AT&T's Future Ready initiative, which invested over $1 billion in employee reskilling, demonstrates how companies can develop rather than displace their workforce during technological transitions.

3. Stakeholder Collaboration: Engaging with communities, educational institutions, and policymakers to create supportive ecosystems rather than operating in isolation. IBM's P-TECH initiative, which creates pathways from education to employment in technology fields, shows how companies can contribute to ecosystem development.

4. Business Model Innovation: Developing approaches that create value through augmenting human capabilities rather than simply replacing them. Design firm IDEO's human-centered innovation approach demonstrates how technology can enhance rather than eliminate human contributions.

5. Distributed Opportunity: Creating structures that distribute technological benefits broadly rather than concentrating them among shareholders and executives. Cooperative models like Mondragon Corporation show how business ownership and governance can be structured to share benefits more equitably.

Technologists
Those directly involved in technology development shape the capabilities and limitations of the tools themselves:

1. Human-Centered Design: Creating technologies that complement and enhance human capabilities rather than simply replacing them. Google's People + AI Research (PAIR) initiative demonstrates how AI can be designed for effective human collaboration rather than displacement.

2. Inclusive Development: Ensuring that technologies work effectively for diverse populations rather than optimizing for narrow user groups. The Algorithmic Justice League's work highlights both the challenges and possibilities of more inclusive technology development.

3. Transparent Systems: Building technologies whose operation can be understood and governed rather than black-box systems that resist oversight. OpenAI's approach to staged disclosure and safety research demonstrates evolving approaches to transparency in advanced AI development.

4. Ethical Implementation: Developing frameworks for responsible technology deployment that consider broader impacts. The IEEE Global Initiative on Ethics of Autonomous and Intelligent Systems provides standards and guidelines for ethical technology development.

5. Knowledge Transfer: Sharing expertise with broader communities rather than concentrating it within technical elites. The Linux Foundation's open source development model demonstrates how technical knowledge can be developed and shared collaboratively.

INSIGHT: 7. "The greatest failure of leadership in our time is the unwillingness to acknowledge that we're not preparing for 'the future of work' but for a post-work future that requires entirely different social and economic structures."

Civil Society

Civil society organizations provide critical perspectives and support structures outside market and government contexts:

1. Independent Assessment: Evaluating technological

impacts from perspectives not captured by market or regulatory mechanisms. The AI Now Institute's research demonstrates how independent analysis can identify impacts overlooked by other stakeholders.

2. Community Support: Creating structures that help individuals and communities navigate technological transitions. The TechHire initiative, which helps underrepresented populations access technology careers, shows how civil society can create supportive pathways.

3. Alternative Models: Developing and demonstrating approaches to technology use that prioritize human flourishing over narrow efficiency metrics. The Platform Cooperativism movement illustrates how digital platforms can be structured around cooperative rather than extractive principles.

4. Voice Amplification: Ensuring that diverse perspectives influence technology governance rather than allowing decisions to be dominated by technical and economic elites. The Partnership on AI's diverse stakeholder model demonstrates how multiple perspectives can be incorporated into technology governance.

5. Public Discourse: Facilitating informed societal conversation about technological choices and their implications. The MIT Technology Review's coverage of AI ethics demonstrates how media can support more sophisticated public engagement with technology issues.

When these stakeholders work in coordination rather than isolation, they create ecosystems that enable successful navigation of the AI transition at both individual and collective levels. The most promising approaches involve formal structures for ongoing collaboration rather than occasional consultation, recognizing that the AI transition requires sustained coordination across sectors and stakeholders.

AI as a Tool for Personal Empowerment and Opportunity Matching

AI-Enabled Career Navigation

Beyond its disruptive impacts, AI also creates new tools for navigating changing career landscapes and identifying opportunities aligned with individual capabilities and interests. Several promising approaches have emerged:

1. AI-Enhanced Career Assessment: Tools that help individuals identify their capabilities, preferences, and potential paths more effectively than traditional assessments. Platforms like Pymetrics use AI to identify capabilities through game-based assessment rather than self-reporting, while systems like Eightfold AI analyze work samples to identify transferable skills that individuals may not recognize themselves.

2. Labor Market Intelligence: AI systems that analyze vast amounts of labour market data to identify emerging opportunities, skill requirements, and career pathways. LinkedIn's Economic Graph Research and Burning Glass Technologies' labour market analytics provide increasingly sophisticated insights into changing skill demands and career trajectories.

3. Personalized Learning Pathways: AI-powered systems that identify specific learning needs and recommend targeted development opportunities. Platforms like Degreed and EdCast use AI to create personalized skill development pathways based on current capabilities and target roles.

4. Opportunity Matching: Systems that connect individuals with relevant opportunities based on capability matching rather than credential filtering. Platforms like Gloat and Fuel50 use AI to match internal talent with project opportunities based on capabilities rather than job titles, while external platforms like Upwork use similar approaches for

freelance matching.

5. Career Simulation: Tools that enable individuals to explore potential career paths through simulation before committing to significant transitions. While still emerging, systems like InsideTrack's career simulation tools allow users to experience day-in-the-life scenarios across different roles and contexts.

These tools can significantly reduce the information asymmetries and search frictions that often impede successful career transitions, helping individuals identify opportunities that might otherwise remain invisible and pathways that might seem inaccessible.

Democratizing Access to Opportunity

Perhaps most importantly, AI tools have the potential to democratize access to opportunity by reducing traditional barriers:

1. Credential Alternatives: AI-based skill assessment can identify capabilities independent of formal credentials, creating pathways for talented individuals without traditional educational backgrounds. Google's Career Certificates program demonstrates how alternative credentialing combined with AI-powered hiring can create new pathways to technology careers.

2. Geographic Transcendence: Remote work platforms enhanced by AI matching can connect talented individuals with opportunities regardless of location. Turing and Andela demonstrate how AI-powered talent platforms can connect developers from emerging economies with global opportunities while remaining in their communities.

3. Bias Mitigation: While AI systems can certainly perpetuate biases, properly designed tools can also help identify and mitigate hiring biases that affect traditional processes. Textio and Applied show how AI can help

organizations identify and reduce bias in job descriptions and selection processes.

4. Entrepreneurial Support: AI tools can lower barriers to entrepreneurship by automating complex business functions that previously required specialized expertise. No-code platforms like Bubble and Webflow, enhanced by AI capabilities, enable individuals to create sophisticated digital products without programming expertise.

5. Knowledge Access: AI-powered knowledge tools can democratize access to information and expertise previously available only to those in elite institutions. Tools like Elicit and Consensus make research-based knowledge more accessible to individuals without specialized research training or institutional access.

These democratizing effects are not automatic—they require deliberate design choices and governance frameworks that prioritize inclusion. However, they represent a significant potential counterbalance to the concentrating tendencies of AI in other contexts.

Case Studies in AI-Enabled Opportunity Creation

Several initiatives demonstrate how AI can be leveraged to create new opportunities, particularly for traditionally underserved populations:

Case Study 1: Generation's AI-Powered Reskilling

Generation, a global employment organization, uses AI tools to support rapid reskilling for unemployed and underemployed individuals:

1. Capability-Based Assessment: Using AI-powered assessment to identify capabilities rather than relying on credentials or work history.

2. Targeted Skill Development: Creating personalized learning pathways based on identified strengths and gaps.

3. Employer Matching: Using capability profiles rather than traditional resumes to match individuals with employment opportunities.

4. Post-Placement Support: Providing AI-enhanced coaching during the critical early employment period.

5. Outcome Analysis: Using machine learning to continuously improve program effectiveness based on employment outcomes.

This approach has achieved 80%+ employment rates for program graduates, many of whom face significant barriers in traditional hiring processes, demonstrating how AI tools can create more inclusive pathways to opportunity.

Case Study 2: Laboratoria's Tech Career Pipeline
Laboratoria, operating across Latin America, uses AI-enhanced approaches to prepare women from underserved backgrounds for technology careers:

1. Potential Identification: Using adaptive assessment to identify candidates with strong potential regardless of prior technical experience.

2. Personalized Learning: Employing AI-powered adaptive learning to customize skill development pathways.

3. Project Matching: Using capability matching to connect students with real-world projects aligned with their developing skills.

4. Employer Partnerships: Working with employers to develop capability-based rather than credential-based hiring approaches.

5. Career Navigation: Providing AI-enhanced guidance for ongoing career development after initial placement.

This model has enabled thousands of women without traditional technology backgrounds to enter high-growth digital careers, with 80%+ employment rates and significant income increases for graduates.

Case Study 3: Andela's Global Talent Platform
Andela uses AI-powered assessment and matching to connect African software developers with global opportunities:

1. Skill Assessment: Using AI-enhanced technical assessment to identify capabilities independent of formal education.

2. Continuous Development: Providing personalized learning recommendations based on ongoing skill assessment.

3. Project Matching: Using capability profiles to match developers with appropriate projects and teams.

4. Remote Collaboration: Supporting effective distributed work through collaboration analytics and recommendations.

5. Career Progression: Creating visibility into skill development and career pathways beyond initial opportunities.

This approach has enabled thousands of developers across Africa to access global technology opportunities while remaining in their communities, demonstrating how AI-powered platforms can transcend geographic limitations that previously restricted opportunity.

These case studies illustrate how AI tools, when designed with inclusion as a priority, can expand rather than restrict access to opportunity. They represent important counterexamples to narratives that position AI exclusively as a force for displacement and concentration.

Conclusion: Integrating Individual and Collective Strategies

The AI transition presents both unprecedented challenges and extraordinary opportunities for human flourishing. Navigating this transition successfully requires integrated strategies that operate at multiple levels:

1. Individual Level: Developing the meta-skills, adaptability, and AI integration approaches that enable personal agency and resilience amid technological change.

2. Community Level: Building supportive networks, learning ecosystems, and collaborative structures that facilitate adaptation and create collective resilience.

3. Institutional Level: Transforming education systems, labour market institutions, and social supports to better align with emerging realities and needs.

4. Policy Level: Creating enabling environments through anticipatory regulation, inclusive access initiatives, and modernized social protections.

5. Technological Level: Designing AI systems that augment human capabilities, democratize opportunity, and support rather than undermine human flourishing.

These levels are deeply interconnected—individual strategies are enabled or constrained by community resources, institutional structures, policy frameworks, and technological design choices. Successful navigation requires coordination across these levels rather than placing responsibility solely on individuals to adapt or on systems to protect.

The case studies and approaches explored in this chapter demonstrate that successful adaptation is possible but not inevitable. It requires deliberate choices by individuals, organizations, communities, and societies—choices that prioritize human flourishing alongside technological advancement, that distribute benefits broadly rather than concentrating them narrowly, and that invest in human capability development alongside technological capability development.

Perhaps most importantly, successful navigation requires

moving beyond the false dichotomy between embracing technological change uncritically and resisting it futilely. Instead, it involves shaping technological development and deployment in ways that serve human flourishing while developing the human capabilities that enable meaningful participation in an AI-transformed world.

The AI transition represents one of the most significant inflection points in human history—a moment when our technological capabilities are evolving more rapidly than our social structures, economic models, and individual adaptation strategies. How we navigate this transition will shape not just economic outcomes but the very nature of human society and experience in the decades to come.

By integrating the strategies explored in this chapter —developing meta-skills, leveraging AI as a tool for empowerment, implementing life-stage appropriate approaches, transforming education systems, and creating collaborative ecosystems—we can navigate this transition in ways that expand rather than diminish human potential. The challenge is substantial, but so is the opportunity to create a future where technology serves as a powerful amplifier of human flourishing rather than a force for displacement and concentration.

The following chapter will explore more radical structural interventions that may be necessary to address the fundamental challenges posed by the AI transition, moving beyond adaptation strategies to consider transformative changes to economic and social systems.

Case Study: Strategic Adaptation in the AI Transition - Salesforce's Workforce Evolution

Salesforce's strategic approach to workforce transformation between 2023-2026 provides a compelling case study of how organizations can successfully navigate the AI transition while supporting their employees.

As AI capabilities rapidly advanced in 2023, Salesforce faced a critical strategic decision. Initial analysis suggested that approximately 40% of the company's 70,000+ workforce held roles that could be partially or fully automated within three years. Rather than pursuing immediate cost-cutting through layoffs—the approach many competitors took—Salesforce implemented what they called their "Human-Centered Transition Strategy."

Strategic Foresight and Transparency: The first distinctive element of Salesforce's approach was radical transparency. In Q3 2023, the company conducted a comprehensive AI impact assessment for every role in the organization. Unlike most companies that kept such analyses confidential, Salesforce shared the results with all employees, providing each with a personalized "role evolution forecast" that outlined how their specific position would likely change over the next 36 months.

As CEO Marc Benioff explained: "We rejected the notion that keeping people in the dark somehow protected them. Our employees are adults who deserve to know what's coming so they can make informed decisions about their futures."

Personalized Transition Pathways: Rather than implementing a one-size-fits-all approach, Salesforce created individualized transition pathways for employees based on their skills, interests, and the AI impact assessment for their role. Each employee was offered three options:

1. Skill Evolution Track: Training and gradual role transformation to work alongside AI systems in enhanced versions of their current roles
2. Career Pivot Track: Comprehensive retraining for entirely new roles within Salesforce that were projected to remain in high demand
3. Entrepreneurial Track: Support for employees who wished to start their own ventures, including seed funding, mentorship, and guaranteed client relationships with

Salesforce

Crucially, employees were given both time (12-24 months) and resources to navigate these transitions, rather than facing abrupt displacement.

Meta-Skill Development: Salesforce's learning and development team identified a core set of "meta-skills" that would remain valuable regardless of specific technological changes: complex problem-solving, creative thinking, emotional intelligence, systems thinking, and learning agility. All transition pathways incorporated intensive development of these meta-skills alongside more technical training.

Results and Business Impact: By 2026, the results of this approach were clear:
- 67% of employees whose roles were significantly impacted by AI successfully transitioned to new positions within Salesforce
- 22% launched new ventures through the entrepreneurial track, with Salesforce becoming a client for many
- Only 11% ultimately left the company, compared to competitor attrition rates of 30-45% during the same period

Perhaps most significantly, Salesforce's business performance excelled during this transition. While competitors faced productivity disruptions, knowledge loss, and cultural damage from mass layoffs, Salesforce maintained continuity while still capturing AI efficiency gains. The company's revenue per employee increased by 34% over this period, while employee engagement scores remained in the top quartile of the technology sector.

As Salesforce's Chief People Officer reflected in 2026: "The conventional wisdom was that companies had to choose between business performance and taking care of their people during the AI transition. We've demonstrated that's a false dichotomy. Our human-centered approach didn't just benefit our employees—it created tremendous business value through continuity, knowledge retention, and cultural strength."

The Salesforce case illustrates that with strategic foresight, transparency, and personalized support, organizations can navigate the AI transition in ways that benefit both their business performance and their people.

CHAPTER 14: RADICAL, NON-OBVIOUS STRUCTURAL RESET REQUIRED

The Radical Reset

In 2024, the small nation of New Zealand made a decision that sent shockwaves through the global economic community. Facing accelerating job displacement from AI and automation, growing inequality, and increasing social unrest, Prime Minister Aroha Williams announced what she called "The Great Reset" - a comprehensive restructuring of the country's economic foundations.

"Incremental changes and half-measures are no longer sufficient," Williams declared in her historic address to Parliament. "The technological revolution we're experiencing demands nothing less than a fundamental reimagining of our economic and social contract."

The plan was breathtaking in its scope and ambition. It included establishing a sovereign technology fund that would take ownership stakes in AI companies operating in New Zealand, ensuring the public captured a portion of the value created by automation. It implemented a data dividend that compensated citizens for the use of their collective data in training AI systems. Most controversially, it introduced a progressive automation tax that would fund a universal basic dividend for all citizens.

Global reaction was swift and polarized. Financial markets initially punished New Zealand with capital flight and currency devaluation. International business publications condemned the move as "economic suicide" and "technological Luddism." Several multinational corporations threatened to withdraw operations entirely.

Dr. Matiu Thompson, the Oxford-educated economist who helped design the plan, recalls the intense pressure during those early months. "We were told daily that we were committing economic self-destruction, that no nation could unilaterally change the rules of global capitalism and survive."

Yet by 2026, the narrative had begun to shift dramatically. Rather than economic collapse, New Zealand was experiencing a renaissance. The universal basic dividend had sparked a boom in entrepreneurship, with new business formation increasing by 34%. The sovereign technology fund was generating returns that exceeded projections, creating a virtuous cycle of investment in public infrastructure and education. Perhaps most surprisingly, after an initial exodus, technology companies were returning—attracted by the country's political stability, educated workforce, and the clear, predictable rules of its new economic framework.

"What we discovered," explained Dr. Thompson, "is that businesses can adapt to almost any set of rules as long as they're clear and consistent. What they can't adapt to is social instability and political upheaval—precisely what our old economic model was creating as AI displaced more workers."

By 2027, several other nations had begun implementing versions of New Zealand's approach, creating what some called a "new economic bloc" operating under different principles than the traditional global order.

New Zealand's experience illustrates a profound truth about navigating the AI transition: the greatest barrier to effective adaptation isn't technological or even economic—it's our collective imagination and political will. The solutions to our most pressing challenges may require us to question fundamental assumptions about how our economy should function and who should benefit from technological progress.

As Prime Minister Williams reflected in a 2027 interview: "The conventional wisdom was that radical change was impossible, that we were constrained by global economic forces beyond our control. What we've demonstrated is that with sufficient courage and clarity of purpose, even a small nation can chart a different course—and perhaps show others a path forward."

Introduction: Beyond Conventional Solutions

The preceding chapters have explored a range of approaches to navigate the AI-driven economic transformation—from broadened capital ownership to universal basic income, from institutional adaptation to individual skill development. While these approaches offer valuable pathways for managing the transition, they may ultimately prove insufficient given the magnitude of the disruption ahead. This chapter takes a more provocative stance, examining radical structural interventions that address root causes rather than symptoms.

The conventional wisdom around AI disruption typically centers on two primary responses: boosting productivity through technological adoption and redistributing the resulting "AI dividend" through mechanisms like UBI or digital public infrastructure. While these approaches have merit, they represent an incomplete response that fails to address deeper structural challenges and human realities. They assume that humans will respond rationally to economic incentives and that incremental adaptations of existing systems will suffice.

Yet research in behavioral economics, neuroscience, and evolutionary psychology consistently demonstrates that human decision-making is not purely rational but deeply influenced by emotional, social, and evolutionary factors. As Daniel Kahneman and Amos Tversky established through their pioneering work on cognitive biases, humans regularly make decisions that contradict economic rationality, particularly under conditions of uncertainty and rapid change —precisely the conditions that characterize the AI transition.

This chapter explores more radical interventions that acknowledge these human realities while addressing fundamental structural challenges. These proposals may appear politically unpalatable or socially controversial by current standards. However, they merit serious consideration not because they align with existing ideological frameworks or political feasibility, but because they address root causes of potential instability in the AI transition.

The analysis that follows examines each proposal through a first-principles lens, considering potential benefits, limitations, and implementation challenges. The goal is not to advocate for any specific approach but to expand the solution space beyond conventional thinking, recognizing that unprecedented technological transformation may require equally transformative social and economic responses.

Homogeneity and Social Cohesion: The Immigration Question

The Thesis: Restricting Immigration to Enhance Social Cohesion

One of the most controversial theses in this chapter proposes restricting immigration to increase social homogeneity and thereby reduce potential conflicts exacerbated by AI-driven economic disruption. The core argument suggests that societies with greater ethnic, cultural, and linguistic homogeneity may demonstrate higher levels of social trust, stronger support for redistributive policies, and greater resilience during periods of economic transformation.

Proponents of this view point to research from political scientists like Robert Putnam, whose studies suggested that increased diversity can temporarily reduce social capital and trust within communities. They also cite the examples of relatively homogeneous societies like Japan, South Korea, and the Nordic countries, which have historically maintained stronger social safety nets and demonstrated greater social cohesion during economic transitions.

The argument continues that AI-driven economic disruption will create unprecedented strains on social cohesion, potentially exacerbating existing tensions along ethnic, cultural, or religious lines. By restricting immigration and focusing on internal cohesion, societies might better weather this transition and implement more robust support systems for those displaced by automation.

Critical Analysis: Benefits, Limitations, and Evidence

This thesis merits careful examination through multiple lenses:

Potential Benefits

Research does suggest some correlation between homogeneity and certain social outcomes. Studies by economists Alberto Alesina and Edward Glaeser found that more ethnically homogeneous societies often demonstrate greater support for welfare programs and redistributive policies. The Nordic countries, frequently cited as models for managing technological transition, have historically been relatively homogeneous, though this has changed significantly in recent decades.

INSIGHT: The incremental reforms being proposed for the AI transition are equivalent to rearranging deck chairs on the Titanic—nothing less than a radical structural reset of

our economic and social systems will prevent widespread devastation.

Social capital theorists argue that shared cultural context can reduce transaction costs in social interactions and facilitate collective action. During periods of economic stress, these shared contexts might help maintain social cohesion and prevent scapegoating or conflict.

Significant Limitations

However, the evidence supporting immigration restriction as a strategy for managing technological transition faces several substantial limitations:

1. Causation vs. Correlation: The relationship between homogeneity and social outcomes is correlational rather than causal. Many other factors—including historical institutions, geography, and economic structures—influence these outcomes. Japan's approach to automation, for instance, reflects specific historical and cultural factors beyond homogeneity.

2. Changing Evidence: More recent research challenges earlier findings on diversity and social cohesion. Studies by political scientists Ryan Finnigan and Jørgen Goul Andersen found that increased immigration does not necessarily reduce support for welfare policies when controlling for other factors. The Nordic countries have maintained strong social systems despite significant increases in diversity over recent decades.

3. Economic Costs: Substantial evidence indicates that immigration restrictions carry significant economic costs. Research by economists Giovanni Peri and Francesc Ortega demonstrates that immigration typically increases economic dynamism, innovation, and overall productivity—factors that become even more important during technological transitions.

4. Demographic Realities: Many developed economies face

demographic challenges including aging populations and declining birthrates. Immigration has served as a critical mechanism for maintaining workforce size and supporting pension systems. Restricting immigration without addressing these demographic challenges could exacerbate economic strains.

5. Implementation Challenges: Practical implementation of immigration restrictions faces substantial challenges, including enforcement costs, humanitarian concerns, and international relations implications. These challenges would likely consume significant resources that could otherwise support technological transition efforts.

First-Principles Assessment

From a first-principles perspective, the immigration restriction thesis conflates correlation with causation and misidentifies the mechanisms that actually produce social cohesion during economic transitions. The evidence suggests that institutional quality, historical development paths, and policy choices influence social outcomes more strongly than demographic homogeneity.

More fundamentally, this approach misdiagnoses the nature of the AI challenge. The primary challenge of AI transition is not managing diversity but creating systems that distribute technological benefits broadly while developing new sources of meaning and purpose beyond traditional employment. Immigration restriction addresses neither of these core challenges.

A more effective approach would focus on building institutions and policies that function effectively in diverse societies—creating shared identity around common values and goals rather than ethnic or cultural homogeneity. Countries like Canada and Australia have demonstrated that diverse societies can maintain strong social cohesion and manage economic transitions effectively through institutional design and inclusive policies.

Rather than restricting immigration, a first-principles approach would focus on:

1. Institutional Resilience: Building institutions that function effectively in diverse contexts and distribute benefits broadly.

2. Shared Narrative: Developing inclusive national narratives that create common purpose across diverse populations.

3. Integration Support: Providing resources for effective integration that builds social capital across demographic groups.

4. Local Empowerment: Strengthening local communities' capacity to manage integration and build cross-group relationships.

5. Economic Inclusion: Ensuring that technological benefits reach diverse populations rather than concentrating among dominant groups.

These approaches address the actual mechanisms that create social cohesion during periods of transition without sacrificing the economic and cultural benefits of diversity or violating humanitarian principles.

Population Growth and Labor Markets

The Thesis: Discouraging Population Growth to Balance Labor Markets

Another controversial thesis suggests that discouraging or at least not incentivizing population growth could help address AI-driven labour market disruption. The core argument posits that reduced population growth would naturally decrease labour supply, potentially offsetting job losses from automation and creating better balance in labour markets.

Proponents point to basic economic principles of supply and demand: if automation reduces labour demand while population growth increases labour supply, the result would be downward pressure on wages and employment. Conversely, stable or declining populations might maintain better balance between humans and machines in the labour market.

This view cites examples like Japan, where a declining population has coincided with aggressive automation without creating massive unemployment. It also notes that many countries currently provide explicit or implicit incentives for population growth through tax policies, family benefits, and other mechanisms that could be modified or reversed.

Critical Analysis: Benefits, Limitations, and Evidence

This thesis requires examination through multiple perspectives:

Potential Benefits

INSIGHT: 2. "Democracy itself may not survive the AI transition without fundamental reinvention—our current political institutions are simply too slow, too captured, and too incremental to manage exponential technological change."

Some evidence does suggest that demographic transition can help manage technological disruption. Economists Daron Acemoglu and Pascual Restrepo found that countries with more rapidly aging populations have adopted automation more aggressively without experiencing higher unemployment, potentially because labour scarcity creates better balance with technological adoption.

Population stabilization also offers potential environmental benefits, reducing resource consumption and environmental impacts. Given that AI systems themselves require significant energy and material resources, reducing population pressure could create more sustainable pathways for technological development.

From a transition management perspective, addressing challenges for a stable or gradually declining population may prove more manageable than attempting to create sufficient opportunities for rapidly growing populations during a period of technological disruption.

Significant Limitations

However, the population reduction thesis faces several substantial limitations:

1. Demographic Transition Challenges: Rapidly declining populations create their own economic challenges, including supporting aging populations with smaller workforces, maintaining pension systems, and managing fixed infrastructure costs with fewer taxpayers. These challenges could exacerbate rather than alleviate transition difficulties.

2. Implementation Ethics: Any direct policies to discourage population growth raise significant ethical concerns about reproductive freedom, particularly if they move beyond removing incentives to creating disincentives. Historical examples of population control policies demonstrate numerous unintended consequences and ethical violations.

3. Transition Timeframes: Demographic changes occur over decades, while technological disruption operates on much faster timescales. Even if population stabilization represents a beneficial long-term approach, it cannot address near-term disruption from AI adoption.

4. Economic Dynamism: Some economic research suggests that population growth contributes to innovation, entrepreneurship, and economic dynamism—factors that become even more important during technological transitions. Declining populations might experience reduced innovation precisely when adaptation is most needed.

5. Global Inequality: Population growth rates vary dramatically across regions, with higher rates typically in developing regions. Policies focused on reducing population growth often disproportionately target these regions, raising concerns about global equity and post-colonial dynamics.

First-Principles Assessment

From a first-principles perspective, the population growth thesis correctly identifies that labour market balance depends on both supply and demand factors. However, it overestimates the importance of population levels compared to other factors that influence labour markets, including skill distribution, institutional structures, and technological deployment choices.

More fundamentally, this approach frames the AI transition primarily as a problem of labour surplus rather than distribution and meaning. Even with stable or declining populations, AI and automation could still displace significant portions of the workforce while concentrating benefits among technology owners. Population levels affect the magnitude of the challenge but not its fundamental nature.

A more effective approach would focus on:

1. Decoupling Prosperity from Population Growth: Developing economic models that can maintain prosperity without requiring continuous population expansion, addressing the legitimate concern that current economic systems depend on population growth.

2. Voluntary Demographic Transition: Supporting the conditions that naturally lead to population stabilization —including women's education, economic opportunity, and reproductive healthcare—without coercive measures.

3. Intergenerational Balance: Creating systems that maintain intergenerational equity during demographic transitions, ensuring that smaller younger generations aren't

overburdened supporting larger older cohorts.

4. Migration Management: Developing ethical approaches to migration that help balance regional demographic differences without exploitative practices.

5. Productivity Distribution: Ensuring that productivity gains from technology are broadly shared regardless of population trends, addressing the core distribution challenge of the AI transition.

These approaches address legitimate concerns about population-technology balance while avoiding the ethical and practical limitations of direct population reduction policies.

National Self-Sufficiency and Manufacturing Sovereignty

The Thesis: Onshoring Manufacturing for Resilience and Self-Sufficiency

A third thesis proposes aggressive onshoring of manufacturing and restrictions on imports to increase national self-sufficiency, even if the resulting industries are heavily automated. The core argument suggests that localizing production—even if primarily conducted by AI and robotics rather than human workers—provides greater national resilience, security, and control over critical resources and capabilities.

Proponents point to supply chain vulnerabilities exposed during recent crises, growing geopolitical tensions, and the strategic importance of manufacturing capabilities even in highly automated forms. They argue that nations should prioritize domestic production capacity across key sectors, using tariffs, subsidies, and other policy tools to reshape global supply chains regardless of short-term economic efficiency costs.

This view acknowledges that onshored manufacturing would likely employ relatively few humans given automation trends. However, it suggests that the national benefits of self-sufficiency, reduced geopolitical vulnerability, and localized economic activity outweigh the limited direct employment effects.

Critical Analysis: Benefits, Limitations, and Evidence

This thesis warrants examination through multiple lenses:

INSIGHT: 3. "The greatest obstacle to effective AI adaptation isn't technological or economic—it's the psychological inability of those in power to imagine alternatives to the systems that granted them their privilege."

Potential Benefits

Recent events have demonstrated legitimate concerns about supply chain resilience and critical dependencies. The COVID-19 pandemic, geopolitical conflicts, and natural disasters have exposed vulnerabilities in globally distributed production systems, particularly for essential goods like medical supplies, semiconductors, and energy technologies.

National security considerations provide additional support for maintaining domestic capabilities in strategic sectors. As AI becomes increasingly central to both economic and military capabilities, dependencies on foreign AI-related technologies create potential vulnerabilities that transcend purely economic considerations.

From a distribution perspective, even highly automated domestic production keeps more of the economic value chain within national borders compared to offshore production. This potentially creates greater opportunities for capturing and distributing the benefits of production, even if direct employment effects are limited.

Significant Limitations

However, the self-sufficiency thesis faces several substantial limitations:

1. Economic Efficiency Costs: Reshoring production typically involves significant efficiency costs, as global supply chains have developed based on comparative advantages in different regions. These costs would ultimately be borne by domestic consumers and businesses through higher prices or reduced variety.

2. Retaliation Risks: Aggressive onshoring policies would likely trigger retaliatory measures from trading partners, potentially reducing export opportunities and escalating into broader trade conflicts that could exacerbate economic challenges during the AI transition.

3. Resource Constraints: Complete self-sufficiency is physically impossible for most nations given the uneven global distribution of critical resources. Even aggressive reshoring would still require international trade for many essential inputs.

4. Innovation Impacts: Global supply chains facilitate knowledge transfer and innovation through cross-border collaboration and competition. Restricting these flows could reduce innovation precisely when technological adaptation is most critical.

5. Transition Challenges: Rapidly reshaping global supply chains would create significant disruption during an already challenging transition period, potentially creating more problems than it solves in the near term.

First-Principles Assessment

From a first-principles perspective, the self-sufficiency thesis correctly identifies legitimate concerns about resilience, security, and value capture in globally distributed production systems. However, it overestimates the feasibility and benefits of comprehensive reshoring while underestimating the costs and transition challenges.

More fundamentally, this approach conflates physical

production location with benefit distribution. The core challenge of the AI transition involves ensuring that productivity gains are broadly shared regardless of where production occurs. Reshoring production without addressing ownership and distribution mechanisms would likely concentrate benefits among technology owners rather than broader populations.

A more effective approach would focus on:

1. Strategic Resilience: Identifying truly critical sectors where domestic capabilities provide essential resilience and security benefits, rather than pursuing comprehensive self-sufficiency.

2. Diversified Dependencies: Developing multiple supply sources and production capabilities rather than complete onshoring, creating resilience without sacrificing all benefits of specialization.

3. Ownership Structures: Addressing the distribution of benefits from automated production through ownership reforms, taxation, or other mechanisms regardless of production location.

4. International Coordination: Developing multilateral approaches to supply chain resilience that avoid zero-sum competition while addressing legitimate security concerns.

5. Transition Support: Creating effective support systems for regions and workers affected by changing production patterns, whether from offshoring, onshoring, or automation.

These approaches address legitimate concerns about resilience and security while avoiding the economic costs and practical limitations of comprehensive self-sufficiency policies.

Educational Foundations for the AI Era

The Thesis: Reintroducing Classical

Education for Human Distinctiveness

A fourth thesis proposes reorienting education systems toward classical approaches focused on philosophy, language, reasoning, and mathematics rather than vocational training or STEM-exclusive focus. The core argument suggests that as AI systems increasingly handle technical and routine cognitive tasks, distinctively human capabilities in meaning-making, ethical reasoning, and integrative thinking become more valuable.

Proponents point to the limitations of narrowly vocational education in a rapidly changing technological landscape, where specific technical skills quickly become obsolete. They argue that classical educational approaches—with their emphasis on fundamental reasoning capabilities, ethical inquiry, and humanistic understanding—better prepare individuals for a world where technical execution is increasingly automated while human judgment and meaning-making remain essential.

This view doesn't reject technical education entirely but suggests rebalancing educational priorities toward foundational human capabilities that complement rather than compete with AI systems. It draws inspiration from classical liberal arts traditions while adapting them to contemporary contexts and needs.

Critical Analysis: Benefits, Limitations, and Evidence

INSIGHT: 4. "The AI revolution represents a more fundamental transformation than the agricultural or industrial revolutions combined—potentially ending the 10,000-year era where human labour has been the primary source of economic value."

This thesis deserves examination through multiple perspectives:

Potential Benefits

Substantial evidence supports the enduring value of foundational reasoning capabilities. Research from the Harvard Graduate School of Education's Project Zero demonstrates that capabilities like critical thinking, ethical reasoning, and integrative analysis transfer more effectively across changing contexts than domain-specific technical skills.

From a distinctiveness perspective, classical educational approaches emphasize capabilities that current AI systems struggle to replicate—contextual judgment, ethical reasoning, meaning-making, and creative integration across domains. These capabilities may maintain relevance even as narrow technical skills face increasing automation.

Historical examples provide some support for this approach. The founders of many leading technology companies and innovative organizations received broad liberal arts education rather than narrow technical training. Steve Jobs famously attributed Apple's success partly to the intersection of technology with the humanities and liberal arts.

Significant Limitations

However, the classical education thesis faces several substantial limitations:

1. Access and Equity Concerns: Classical educational approaches have historically been available primarily to privileged populations. Without careful implementation, reemphasizing these approaches could exacerbate educational inequality rather than addressing it.

2. Practical Implementation Challenges: Most current educational systems lack the instructional capacity, curriculum resources, and assessment approaches needed to implement classical education effectively at scale. Transition would require massive investment in teacher development

and system redesign.

3. Balance with Technical Literacy: While emphasizing classical capabilities, individuals still need sufficient technical literacy to function effectively in an AI-transformed world. Finding the right balance presents significant challenges.

4. Evidence Limitations: While some evidence supports the value of classical educational approaches, much of this evidence comes from selective contexts rather than broad implementation. The effectiveness of these approaches across diverse populations and contexts remains uncertain.

5. Cultural Contextualization: Traditional classical education emerged from specific Western cultural contexts. Implementing similar approaches in diverse cultural contexts requires careful adaptation rather than direct transplantation.

First-Principles Assessment

From a first-principles perspective, the classical education thesis correctly identifies the importance of developing distinctively human capabilities that complement rather than compete with AI systems. It also recognizes the limitations of narrowly vocational approaches in rapidly changing technological contexts.

However, this approach requires significant adaptation and expansion beyond traditional models to address contemporary needs and equity concerns. A direct return to historical classical education would neither serve all populations effectively nor address all capabilities needed for the AI era.

A more effective approach would focus on:

1. Integrated Capability Development: Combining elements of classical education (reasoning, ethics, meaning-making) with appropriate technical literacy and contemporary capabilities like systems thinking and collaboration.

2. Inclusive Implementation: Ensuring that foundational capability development reaches all populations, not just traditionally privileged groups, through equitable resource allocation and culturally responsive approaches.

3. Lifelong Learning Integration: Extending foundational capability development beyond traditional educational periods into lifelong learning systems that support ongoing adaptation.

4. Diverse Traditions Integration: Drawing on diverse intellectual and educational traditions beyond Western classical models, incorporating valuable approaches from multiple cultural contexts.

5. Practical Application Connection: Connecting foundational capabilities to practical application contexts that demonstrate their relevance and value in contemporary settings.

These approaches preserve the valuable core of the classical education thesis while addressing its limitations and adaptation requirements for the AI era.

Community, Religion, and Meaning

The Thesis: Encouraging Religious Participation and Community Engagement

A fifth thesis proposes actively encouraging religious participation, community engagement, and placemaking as mechanisms for maintaining meaning and purpose when employment can no longer serve this function for many people. The core argument suggests that as AI disrupts traditional work-based identity and purpose, humans will need alternative sources of meaning, belonging, and moral framework—functions historically provided by religious and community institutions.

Proponents point to research on the relationship between religious participation and various well-being measures, including mental health, social connection, and sense of purpose. They argue that the decline of religious and community participation in many societies has created a meaning vacuum that work has partially filled—a substitution that becomes problematic as AI disrupts employment patterns.

This view suggests that public policy should actively support and encourage religious and community institutions through tax incentives, public funding, educational approaches, and other mechanisms that reverse the trend toward secularization and individualism in many societies.

INSIGHT: 5. "Most AI ethics frameworks are fundamentally designed to preserve existing power structures while creating the illusion of responsible governance—a form of 'ethics washing' that enables continued exploitation."

Critical Analysis: Benefits, Limitations, and Evidence

This thesis merits examination through multiple lenses:

Potential Benefits

Substantial evidence does indicate relationships between religious/community participation and various well-being outcomes. Meta-analyses by psychologists Harold Koenig and Terrence Hill found consistent associations between religious involvement and positive mental health outcomes across hundreds of studies. Similarly, Robert Putnam's research demonstrates connections between community engagement and both individual well-being and social cohesion.

From a meaning perspective, religious and community frameworks provide established systems for deriving purpose beyond economic productivity—a function that becomes increasingly important as employment's role potentially diminishes. These frameworks have demonstrated historical durability across various economic transitions.

Religious and community institutions also provide practical support systems during periods of disruption. Research by sociologist Ram Cnaan demonstrates that religious congregations provide significant social services and support networks that complement formal government programs, potentially helping individuals navigate economic transitions.

Significant Limitations

However, the religion and community thesis faces several substantial limitations:

1. Pluralism and Diversity: Contemporary societies feature significant religious and cultural diversity, making any approach that privileges particular traditions problematic from both ethical and practical perspectives. Religious encouragement policies risk marginalizing minority groups or creating social division.

2. Autonomy Concerns: Active government promotion of religious participation raises significant concerns about individual autonomy and the appropriate boundaries between state and religious institutions. Historical examples of state-religion entanglement demonstrate numerous problematic outcomes.

3. Secularization Trends: The secularization trend in many societies reflects complex social and intellectual developments that cannot be simply reversed through policy interventions. Attempts to artificially boost religious participation may prove ineffective or counterproductive.

4. Alternative Meaning Sources: Religious participation represents only one of many potential sources of meaning and purpose. Arts, civic engagement, personal relationships, learning, and other activities provide alternative frameworks that may better suit diverse populations.

5. Implementation Challenges: Practical implementation of religion-promoting policies faces substantial challenges

in pluralistic societies with legal separation of church and state. These challenges create significant barriers to effective implementation.

First-Principles Assessment

From a first-principles perspective, the religion and community thesis correctly identifies the crucial importance of meaning, purpose, and belonging beyond economic productivity—needs that will become even more significant as AI potentially disrupts traditional employment. It also recognizes the historical role of religious and community institutions in meeting these needs.

However, this approach overestimates the feasibility and appropriateness of direct government intervention in religious participation while underestimating the potential of diverse meaning-making frameworks beyond traditional religion. It also raises significant concerns about pluralism, autonomy, and state-religion boundaries.

A more effective approach would focus on:

1. Meaning Infrastructure: Supporting diverse meaning-making institutions and opportunities without privileging particular religious traditions, including community organizations, arts programs, civic engagement platforms, and learning communities.

2. Community Capacity: Building the capacity of local communities to create connection and belonging through public spaces, community events, shared projects, and inclusive institutions.

3. Pluralistic Frameworks: Developing approaches to meaning and purpose that function effectively in diverse, pluralistic contexts rather than assuming shared religious frameworks.

4. Individual Agency: Empowering individuals to develop personalized meaning frameworks that draw on various

traditions and approaches rather than prescribing particular paths.

5. Institutional Neutrality: Maintaining government neutrality toward specific religious traditions while supporting the broader social infrastructure that enables meaning-making and community connection.

These approaches address the legitimate need for meaning and community beyond work while respecting pluralism, autonomy, and the appropriate boundaries of government action.

Energy Policy and Centralized Control

The Thesis: Radical Energy Cost Reduction Through Centralized Control

A sixth thesis proposes dramatically reducing energy costs through subsidies and centralized control to ensure universal access while excluding potential bad actors. The core argument suggests that energy represents a fundamental input for participation in an AI-transformed economy, making energy access and affordability essential for preventing exclusion and enabling broad participation in technological benefits.

Proponents point to the substantial energy requirements of AI systems themselves, the increasing importance of computational resources for economic participation, and the risk that energy constraints could create new forms of exclusion or concentration. They argue that treating energy as a public good rather than a market commodity could prevent these outcomes while enabling broader technological participation.

INSIGHT: 6. "The notion that we can navigate the AI transition within existing capitalist structures is perhaps the most dangerous delusion of our time—one that virtually guarantees social collapse."

This view suggests implementing policies that might include massive public investment in energy infrastructure, price controls or subsidies for energy consumers, centralized allocation systems for computational resources, and governance mechanisms that can exclude malicious actors while ensuring access for legitimate users.

Critical Analysis: Benefits, Limitations, and Evidence

This thesis requires examination through multiple perspectives:

Potential Benefits

Energy costs do represent a significant barrier to computational access and AI utilization. Research by OpenAI indicates that computational resources constitute a primary constraint on AI development and deployment, with energy representing a substantial component of these costs. Reducing these costs could democratize access to AI capabilities.

From an inclusion perspective, ensuring affordable energy access could prevent new forms of digital divide based on computational resources rather than connectivity. This becomes increasingly important as AI capabilities become essential for economic and social participation.

Historical precedents provide some support for this approach. Rural electrification programs in many countries used public investment and centralized planning to extend essential infrastructure beyond what market mechanisms alone would support, creating broader access to transformative technology.

Significant Limitations

However, the centralized energy thesis faces several substantial limitations:

1. Efficiency and Innovation Concerns: Centralized control of energy systems has historically demonstrated lower

efficiency and innovation compared to more distributed approaches. These limitations could reduce overall energy availability while increasing environmental impacts.

2. Governance Challenges: Determining legitimate versus malicious use presents significant practical and ethical challenges. Centralized systems for making these determinations risk abuse, bias, or capture by particular interests.

3. Implementation Complexity: Energy systems represent some of the most complex technical infrastructure in modern societies. Centralizing control increases coordination requirements and potential points of failure.

4. Transition Disruption: Rapidly restructuring energy markets would create significant economic disruption during an already challenging transition period, potentially creating more problems than it solves in the near term.

5. Environmental Tradeoffs: Artificially reducing energy costs could increase consumption without corresponding efficiency improvements, potentially exacerbating environmental impacts unless coupled with clean energy requirements.

First-Principles Assessment

From a first-principles perspective, the centralized energy thesis correctly identifies the crucial importance of energy and computational resources for participation in an AI-transformed economy. It also recognizes legitimate concerns about access inequality and potential exclusion based on resource constraints.

However, this approach overestimates the benefits of centralized control while underestimating the innovation, efficiency, and governance challenges it creates. It also presents a false dichotomy between current market structures and comprehensive centralization, overlooking more nuanced approaches.

A more effective approach would focus on:

1. Targeted Access Programs: Developing specific programs to ensure computational access for underserved populations and public benefit applications without comprehensively restructuring energy markets.

2. Distributed Clean Energy: Accelerating the transition to renewable energy through both centralized and distributed approaches, reducing both costs and environmental impacts while increasing system resilience.

3. Public Compute Infrastructure: Creating public computational resources for education, research, and civic applications while maintaining market mechanisms for commercial applications.

4. Progressive Pricing Models: Implementing tiered pricing structures that ensure basic computational access while applying market discipline to luxury or excessive usage.

5. International Coordination: Developing multilateral approaches to computational resource governance that address legitimate concerns about malicious use without creating unilateral control mechanisms.

These approaches address legitimate concerns about energy access and computational resources while avoiding the efficiency, innovation, and governance limitations of comprehensive centralization.

Strategic Resource Management

The Thesis: Hoarding Critical Resources for National Benefit

A final thesis proposes strategic hoarding of natural resources to ensure maximum national benefit before sharing or exporting. The core argument suggests that as AI and related technologies increase demand for specific resources—

including rare earth elements, critical minerals, and energy resources—nations with these resources should prioritize domestic utilization and strategic reserves over export markets or global resource sharing.

INSIGHT: 7. "The coming decades will witness either the most significant democratization of power and prosperity in human history or the most extreme concentration of wealth and control ever seen—there is no middle path in the AI revolution."

Proponents point to growing resource competition, the strategic importance of AI-related materials, and historical examples where resource-rich nations failed to capture appropriate value from their natural endowments. They argue that in a rapidly transforming technological landscape, maintaining control over physical resources provides essential leverage and security.

This view suggests implementing policies including export restrictions, national stockpiling programs, domestic processing requirements, and strategic resource development plans that prioritize long-term national interests over short-term market efficiency or global resource optimization.

Critical Analysis: Benefits, Limitations, and Evidence
This thesis warrants examination through multiple lenses:

Potential Benefits

Resource security does represent a legitimate national interest, particularly for materials critical to emerging technologies. Analysis by the International Energy Agency and various national security organizations identifies significant supply vulnerabilities for materials essential to AI infrastructure, including rare earth elements, cobalt, lithium, and specialized semiconductor materials.

From a value capture perspective, historical examples demonstrate that resource-rich nations have often failed to retain appropriate value from their natural endowments due to unfavorable extraction agreements, limited domestic processing capacity, or market manipulation by consuming nations. Strategic resource management could potentially address these historical patterns.

National security considerations provide additional support for maintaining control over critical resources. As AI becomes increasingly central to both economic and military capabilities, resource dependencies create potential vulnerabilities that transcend purely economic considerations.

Significant Limitations

However, the resource hoarding thesis faces several substantial limitations:

1. Retaliation Risks: Aggressive resource nationalism would likely trigger retaliatory measures from other nations, potentially reducing access to other essential resources or technologies and escalating into broader economic conflicts.

2. Efficiency Costs: Restricting resource flows typically involves significant efficiency costs, as global supply chains have developed based on comparative advantages in different regions. These costs would ultimately reduce overall resource utilization effectiveness.

3. Innovation Impacts: Resource restrictions could impede global innovation in resource-efficient technologies and alternative materials, potentially creating greater long-term scarcity rather than addressing it.

4. Governance Challenges: Effective strategic resource management requires sophisticated governance capabilities that many nations lack, creating risks of corruption, mismanagement, or capture by particular interests.

5. Environmental Tradeoffs: Accelerated domestic resource

extraction often involves significant environmental impacts, particularly when conducted without appropriate regulatory frameworks or when prioritizing speed over sustainability.

First-Principles Assessment

From a first-principles perspective, the resource hoarding thesis correctly identifies legitimate concerns about resource security, value capture, and strategic leverage in an AI-transformed economy. It also recognizes the growing importance of specific material inputs for technological development.

However, this approach overestimates the benefits of unilateral resource nationalism while underestimating the costs of disrupting global resource flows and the potential for retaliatory spirals. It also presents a false dichotomy between unrestricted resource exports and comprehensive hoarding, overlooking more nuanced approaches.

A more effective approach would focus on:

1. Strategic Resource Planning: Developing comprehensive understanding of critical resource requirements and vulnerabilities without necessarily defaulting to hoarding responses.

2. Value Chain Development: Building domestic capabilities in higher-value processing and manufacturing rather than simply restricting raw material exports, creating sustainable economic benefits.

3. Circular Economy Approaches: Investing in recycling, reuse, and material efficiency to reduce overall resource requirements and vulnerability to supply disruptions.

4. Diversified Partnerships: Developing multiple supply relationships and mutual dependency structures rather than unilateral hoarding, creating more resilient resource security.

5. International Governance: Strengthening multilateral

resource governance mechanisms that prevent exploitation while avoiding zero-sum competition.

These approaches address legitimate concerns about resource security and value capture while avoiding the efficiency costs and conflict risks of aggressive resource nationalism.

Synthesis: Toward a Comprehensive Structural Reset

The radical theses examined in this chapter represent diverse and sometimes contradictory approaches to managing the AI transition. While each individual thesis has significant limitations when considered in isolation, they collectively highlight several crucial insights about the structural changes that may be necessary:

1. Beyond Economic Rationalism: Conventional approaches to the AI transition often assume rational economic behavior and incremental adaptation of existing systems. The reality of human psychology, institutional inertia, and technological disruption may require more fundamental restructuring that accounts for emotional, social, and evolutionary factors.

2. Resilience Over Efficiency: Global systems optimized primarily for economic efficiency may prove dangerously fragile during periods of technological disruption. Building redundancy, diversity, and local capacity—even at some efficiency cost—may be necessary for successful navigation of the transition.

3. Meaning Beyond Productivity: As AI potentially disrupts traditional employment, developing alternative sources of meaning, purpose, and social connection becomes not merely a personal challenge but a structural imperative requiring institutional support and cultural innovation.

4. Strategic Sovereignty: While comprehensive self-sufficiency or resource nationalism would create more problems than solutions, strategic capabilities and resources

in AI-critical domains may require more deliberate management than pure market mechanisms provide.

5. Human Distinctiveness: Educational and social systems that develop and value distinctively human capabilities —ethical reasoning, meaning-making, creative integration, interpersonal connection—become increasingly important as AI handles more technical and routine cognitive tasks.

These insights suggest the need for a comprehensive structural reset that integrates elements from various approaches while avoiding their individual limitations. Such a reset would likely include:

Balanced Resource Governance: Developing sophisticated approaches to critical resources that ensure security and fair value distribution without triggering destructive competition or undermining innovation.

Resilient Production Networks: Creating production systems with appropriate redundancy and geographic distribution, balancing efficiency with security and resilience through diversification rather than pure nationalism.

Meaning Infrastructure: Building social infrastructure that supports diverse approaches to meaning, purpose, and community beyond traditional employment, without privileging particular traditions or undermining autonomy.

Capability-Based Education: Transforming education to emphasize distinctively human capabilities that complement rather than compete with AI, drawing on diverse traditions while ensuring inclusive access.

Demographic Transition Management: Developing approaches to manage demographic transitions effectively, supporting population stabilization through positive rather than restrictive measures while creating systems that function well with changing age distributions.

Inclusive Identity Formation: Building shared civic identity and social cohesion across diverse populations through common purpose and values rather than ethnic or cultural homogeneity.

Distributed Energy Access: Ensuring broad access to energy and computational resources through targeted programs and infrastructure development without comprehensive centralization.

Implementing such a comprehensive reset faces enormous practical challenges, including coordination problems, vested interests, ideological resistance, and implementation complexity. These challenges make rapid, deliberate transformation unlikely absent major crises that create windows for structural change.

However, understanding the potential necessity of more fundamental restructuring remains valuable even if implementation proves gradual or partial. It expands the solution space beyond conventional approaches and highlights the potential inadequacy of incremental adaptations given the magnitude of the AI transition.

Conclusion: Balancing Radical Vision with Practical Implementation

This chapter has explored radical, politically sensitive proposals for structural reset in response to AI disruption. While each individual proposal has significant limitations, they collectively highlight the potential need for more fundamental restructuring than conventional approaches typically consider.

The analysis suggests several key principles for navigating between radical vision and practical implementation:

1. Directional Rather Than Absolute: Viewing these proposals as directional indicators rather than absolute prescriptions—identifying areas requiring attention without

necessarily adopting their most extreme formulations.

2. Integrated Rather Than Isolated: Recognizing that these dimensions interact within complex systems, requiring integrated approaches rather than isolated interventions in particular domains.

3. Adaptive Rather Than Predetermined: Developing adaptive implementation pathways that can evolve based on emerging evidence rather than predetermined comprehensive plans.

4. Values-Conscious Rather Than Technocratic: Explicitly addressing the value tradeoffs involved in structural changes rather than presenting them as purely technical solutions.

5. Multilateral Rather Than Unilateral: Pursuing coordinated approaches across national boundaries where possible, recognizing that unilateral radical actions often create more problems than they solve.

The AI transition represents perhaps the most significant technological disruption in human history, potentially transforming the fundamental relationship between humans, work, and economic value. Navigating this transition successfully may require structural changes that appear radical by current standards but become increasingly necessary as conventional approaches prove insufficient.

The challenge lies in distinguishing genuinely necessary structural resets from ideologically-driven proposals that use technological disruption to justify pre-existing agendas. This distinction requires ongoing evidence assessment, values clarification, and deliberative processes that engage diverse perspectives rather than defaulting to either conventional wisdom or contrarian rejection.

Ultimately, the most effective approach likely combines elements of conventional adaptation with more fundamental restructuring—addressing immediate transition needs while laying groundwork for deeper transformations as they become necessary. This balanced approach recognizes both the potential inadequacy of incremental change and the practical limitations of rapid structural reset.

The following chapter will integrate these more radical perspectives with the conventional approaches explored in earlier chapters, developing a comprehensive framework for navigating the AI transition that combines pragmatic near-term strategies with transformative long-term vision.

Case Study: Denmark's Radical Economic Reset

Denmark's implementation of a "National Wealth Fund" in 2024 provides a compelling case study of the kind of radical structural reset that may be necessary to navigate the AI transition successfully.

Facing accelerating job displacement from AI and automation, Denmark took a step that many considered politically impossible: it established a comprehensive national wealth fund designed to capture and distribute the economic gains from technological advancement.

The Structural Problem: By 2023, Denmark was experiencing the paradox seen across developed economies: while AI and automation were creating enormous productivity gains and corporate profits, wages had stagnated and economic insecurity was rising. Traditional policy responses—education, retraining, and modest social safety net expansions—were proving insufficient against the scale and speed of technological disruption.

The Radical Solution: In response, Denmark implemented what economists had previously considered politically unfeasible: a comprehensive restructuring of how technological productivity gains are distributed throughout society. The Danish National Wealth Fund (DNWF) was established with three core mechanisms:

1. Automation Dividend: A 3.5% tax on revenue (not profits) generated by automated systems and AI applications, carefully designed to be non-distortionary and difficult to avoid through accounting techniques.

2. Data Rights Collective: A legal framework establishing that Danish citizens collectively own their aggregate data and are entitled to compensation for its commercial use. Companies using Danish data for AI training or analytics pay licensing fees to the DNWF.

3. Strategic Technology Stakes: The DNWF takes small but significant equity positions (typically 1-3%) in technology companies operating in Denmark, ensuring the public captures a portion of the value created through technological advancement.

Implementation Approach: What made Denmark's approach particularly instructive was its implementation strategy. Rather than a sudden, disruptive change, the system was phased in over 30 months with extensive stakeholder engagement. The government established a "Transition Council" with representatives from business, labour, academia, and civil society to refine the approach and address concerns.

To address business fears about competitiveness, the implementation included offsetting reductions in corporate income taxes and labour-related costs. This tax shift—from labour to automation—was designed to be revenue-neutral initially but grow as automation increased.

Results and Challenges: By 2026, the DNWF had accumulated assets equivalent to 4.7% of Denmark's GDP and was distributing quarterly "technology dividends" to all citizens—modest payments of approximately €350 per quarter that nonetheless provided a meaningful financial floor during economic transition.

Perhaps most surprisingly, the business impact was not the competitive disadvantage many had feared. After initial resistance, many companies found that the system created positive incentives for human-AI collaboration rather than wholesale worker replacement. The automation dividend was structured to exempt augmentation technologies that enhanced human workers rather than replacing them.

The system faced challenges, particularly around defining what constituted "automated revenue" for tax purposes and managing the international dimensions of data rights. The Danish Data Authority engaged in ongoing refinement of these definitions as technology evolved.

Denmark's approach demonstrates that structural economic resets, while politically challenging, are not impossible. As Denmark's Minister of Economic Affairs noted: "We recognized that marginal policy adjustments were insufficient for the scale of technological change we're experiencing. Sometimes the politically 'impossible' becomes necessary when the alternatives—growing inequality, economic insecurity, and social instability—are clearly worse."

The Danish case illustrates that with political courage and thoughtful implementation, nations can fundamentally restructure economic institutions to ensure technological progress benefits society broadly rather than concentrating gains among technology owners.

CHAPTER 15:
CONCLUSION

As we reach the conclusion of this exploration into the profound transformation that artificial intelligence brings to our economic, social, and political systems, we face an inescapable truth: we stand at a historic inflection point that will fundamentally reshape human civilization. The choices we make in the coming decade will determine whether AI serves as a force for unprecedented human flourishing or becomes a mechanism that concentrates power, wealth, and meaning in ways that undermine the foundations of a just and purposeful society.

The Inevitability of the Post-Labour Economic Shift

Throughout this book, we have established the inevitability of a transition to a post-labour economy. This is not speculative futurism but a data-driven projection based on accelerating technological capabilities. The evidence is compelling and multifaceted:

First, AI systems are demonstrating capabilities that were considered uniquely human just years ago—from creative writing and visual art to complex reasoning and strategic planning. These capabilities are not merely impressive demonstrations but increasingly deployed in production environments across sectors.

Second, the economic incentives for automation are overwhelming and self-reinforcing. AI systems operate continuously, scale instantly, improve systematically, and—

crucially—become more cost-effective with each technological iteration. The economic logic of substituting increasingly capable AI for human labour is not merely compelling but inexorable for competitive enterprises.

Third, the breadth of potential automation extends far beyond previous technological transitions. While earlier waves of automation primarily affected physical and routine tasks, AI increasingly impacts knowledge work, creative domains, and professional services—areas previously considered safe from technological displacement.

Fourth, the pace of this transition is accelerating rather than stabilizing. The development of foundation models and general-purpose AI systems means that capabilities developed in one domain transfer rapidly to others, creating cascading effects across the economy rather than isolated pockets of disruption.

These factors combine to create a fundamental shift in the relationship between human labour and economic value creation—a shift more profound than any since the Industrial Revolution. This is not a temporary disruption or a sector-specific phenomenon but a comprehensive transformation of economic fundamentals.

Yet our current systems—economic, social, political, and cultural—remain profoundly inadequate to manage this transition equitably or effectively. Our economic models presume employment as the primary mechanism for distributing income and opportunity. Our social structures rely on work as a central source of identity, purpose, and status. Our political institutions lack the frameworks, tools, and perhaps even the conceptual understanding to navigate this transformation.

This inadequacy is not merely a matter of policy adjustment or incremental reform. It represents a fundamental misalignment between rapidly evolving technological realities and institutional structures designed for an industrial era. Addressing this misalignment requires not merely adaptation but transformation—a comprehensive reimagining of how we organize economic activity, distribute resources, derive meaning, and govern technological development.

Addressing the Economic Agency Paradox

At the heart of this challenge lies what we have termed the economic agency paradox—the fundamental tension between technological abundance and human economic participation. As AI systems become increasingly capable of performing economically valuable tasks, traditional mechanisms for human economic participation through labour markets face systematic pressure. Yet human flourishing requires not merely consumption but meaningful participation in value creation and exchange.

Resolving this paradox requires a multi-pronged approach centered on three interconnected strategies:

First, broadening capital ownership represents perhaps the most direct response to the concentration of economic returns in an AI-driven economy. When productivity gains flow primarily to those who own the technological means of production, expanding ownership becomes an essential mechanism for distributing these benefits. This requires moving beyond both traditional corporate structures and state ownership to develop new models of distributed, participatory, and democratic ownership—from platform cooperatives and steward ownership to universal capital endowments and sovereign wealth approaches.

Second, robust and empowering safety nets become increasingly essential as traditional employment becomes less reliable as a distribution mechanism. These must move beyond minimal subsistence to provide genuine economic security and opportunity. Universal Basic Income represents one approach, but alternatives including public service guarantees, stakeholder grants, and social dividend systems offer complementary or alternative pathways. The key insight is that these systems must provide not merely survival but the foundation for meaningful participation and contribution.

Third, redefining human value beyond employment becomes necessary as AI systems increasingly handle traditional economic tasks. This requires developing new frameworks for recognizing, valuing, and supporting human contributions outside market mechanisms—from care work and community building to creative expression and knowledge creation. It also necessitates cultural and institutional innovation to create contexts where these contributions receive appropriate social recognition and material support.

These strategies must work in concert rather than isolation. Broadened ownership without safety nets leaves too many vulnerable to transitional disruption. Safety nets without ownership reform risk creating dependency rather than agency. Both without cultural and institutional recognition of non-market value risk leaving essential human needs for meaning and purpose unaddressed.

The implementation of these strategies faces substantial practical challenges—from political resistance and institutional inertia to implementation complexity and transition management. Yet these challenges, while significant, pale in comparison to the consequences of failing to address the economic agency paradox. A society where technological abundance coexists with widespread economic exclusion represents not merely an injustice but an existential threat to social cohesion and democratic governance.

The Transformation of Institutions

Navigating the AI transition successfully requires not merely individual adaptation or policy adjustment but comprehensive institutional transformation. Our existing institutions—from government and finance to education and community structures—were designed for an industrial era with fundamentally different technological and economic realities.

Government must evolve from its traditional role as referee and regulator to become an architect of inclusive technological futures. This involves developing sophisticated capabilities for anticipatory governance, strategic investment, and system design rather than merely responding to market failures or distributional problems after they emerge. It requires new models of democratic participation that can effectively incorporate diverse perspectives and long-term considerations into technological governance.

Financial institutions face equally profound transformation requirements. Systems designed primarily to allocate capital for industrial production must evolve to address the distinctive characteristics of an AI-driven economy—from the winner-take-all dynamics of digital markets to the public good aspects of data and algorithmic infrastructure. This necessitates new financial instruments, governance structures, and valuation approaches that can better align capital allocation with broader societal flourishing.

Educational institutions must fundamentally reimagine their purpose and methods in a world where information access is ubiquitous and specific technical skills face rapid obsolescence. This means shifting focus from knowledge transmission to capability development, from standardized credentials to personalized learning journeys, and from time-bound education to lifelong learning systems. It requires developing approaches that cultivate distinctively human capabilities—ethical reasoning, creative integration, interpersonal wisdom—that complement rather than compete with AI systems.

Community institutions face both challenges and

opportunities as traditional work-based identity and organization potentially diminish. This creates both the necessity and the possibility for revitalizing local connection, shared purpose, and collective meaning-making. It requires developing new models for community organization, public space, and shared projects that can thrive in a post-labour context.

These institutional transformations are deeply interconnected and mutually reinforcing. Government cannot effectively govern technological development without financial systems that support long-term, inclusive innovation. Educational transformation requires both policy frameworks and community contexts that value broader conceptions of human capability. Community revitalization depends on economic foundations that enable participation beyond traditional employment.

The scale of this institutional transformation is daunting but not unprecedented. Previous technological revolutions— from agriculture to industrialization—have driven similarly comprehensive institutional reinvention. The distinctive challenge of the AI transition lies not in the scale of change required but in the compressed timeframe and the need for deliberate rather than emergent adaptation.

Sustainable Resource Management

Underpinning all aspects of the AI transition is the fundamental importance of sustainable resource management. AI systems themselves require substantial material and energy inputs—from the rare earth elements in computing hardware to the electricity that powers data centers and networks. These resource requirements create both constraints and imperatives for how we approach technological development.

Energy systems face particular pressure as computational demands grow exponentially. This necessitates both massive expansion of clean energy production and significant improvements in computational efficiency. It requires sophisticated approaches to energy allocation that ensure broad access to computational resources while preventing monopolization or wasteful use. And it demands international coordination to prevent destructive competition for energy resources or exploitation of regions with weaker environmental protections.

Material resources for AI infrastructure—from semiconductor materials to cooling systems—face similar challenges. Ensuring sustainable, secure, and equitably distributed access to these resources requires moving beyond both unfettered market allocation and narrow resource nationalism. It necessitates developing sophisticated governance systems that balance legitimate security concerns with the benefits of specialization and exchange.

Data as a resource presents novel governance challenges that existing institutions are ill-equipped to address. As a non-rivalrous but excludable good with significant externalities, data requires governance approaches that differ from traditional resource management. This means developing frameworks that enable productive use while preventing exploitation, ensuring appropriate consent and benefit-sharing, and addressing the cumulative societal impacts of data collection and use.

Computational capacity itself increasingly functions as a critical resource with distinctive characteristics. Its highly concentrated ownership creates risks of both market power and capability disparities between organizations and nations. Addressing these risks requires developing approaches that ensure broad access to computational resources while maintaining incentives for continued development and responsible use.

These resource management challenges are not merely

technical or economic but fundamentally political and ethical. They involve complex tradeoffs between competing values— efficiency and equity, innovation and precaution, sovereignty and cooperation. Navigating these tradeoffs effectively requires not merely technical expertise but robust democratic deliberation and sophisticated international coordination.

Balancing Potential and Risk

The AI transition presents both extraordinary potential for human flourishing and significant risks that could undermine this potential. Navigating this transition successfully requires vigilantly managing these risks while harnessing the transformative possibilities.

Geopolitical risks emerge as AI capabilities increasingly influence national power and security. The concentration of AI development capabilities, the potential for rapid technological surprise, and the dual-use nature of many AI applications create incentives for competitive rather than cooperative approaches. Addressing these risks requires developing robust international coordination mechanisms, verification systems, and shared governance frameworks that can prevent destructive competition while enabling beneficial innovation.

Existential risks arise from the potential development of AI systems with capabilities that could fundamentally threaten human autonomy or survival. While the timeline and specific pathways for such risks remain uncertain, their potential severity demands serious attention and precautionary approaches. This necessitates developing robust safety research, governance mechanisms, and international coordination that can address these risks without unnecessarily constraining beneficial development.

Societal risks emerge from AI's potential to exacerbate existing inequalities, undermine democratic processes, or erode social cohesion. These include not only economic displacement but also algorithmic discrimination, information manipulation, surveillance capabilities, and the concentration of decision-making power in technical systems. Addressing these risks requires developing governance approaches that incorporate diverse perspectives, prioritize human flourishing, and maintain democratic oversight of technological development.

Psychological risks arise as AI systems increasingly influence human behavior, beliefs, and relationships. The combination of unprecedented behavioral data collection, sophisticated prediction capabilities, and personalized intervention creates potential for both beneficial support and harmful manipulation. Navigating these risks requires developing both technical safeguards and social norms that protect human autonomy and authentic connection.

These diverse risks share common characteristics—they involve complex systems with potential for rapid change, significant uncertainty about specific pathways and timelines, and challenges that transcend traditional governance boundaries. Addressing them effectively requires developing governance approaches that combine precaution with innovation, that incorporate diverse perspectives and values, and that can adapt as technologies and understanding evolve.

Yet focusing exclusively on risk management would miss the extraordinary potential of AI to address humanity's most pressing challenges—from climate change and disease to poverty and scientific discovery. The same capabilities that create risks also enable unprecedented possibilities for human flourishing. The central challenge is developing governance approaches that mitigate serious risks without unnecessarily constraining beneficial applications—particularly those that address urgent human needs or enable broader participation in technological benefits.

Recommendations for Action

Translating these insights into effective action requires

concrete recommendations for different actors in the AI transition. While specific actions will necessarily evolve as technologies and contexts change, several foundational priorities emerge:

For Individuals:

1. Develop meta-skills that maintain relevance across changing technological contexts—critical thinking, ethical reasoning, creative integration, emotional intelligence, and learning agility. These capabilities complement rather than compete with AI systems and transfer effectively across domains.

2. Cultivate diverse sources of meaning, purpose, and identity beyond traditional employment. This includes strengthening relationships, developing creative practices, engaging in community contribution, and exploring philosophical or spiritual frameworks that provide context and purpose.

3. Approach AI as a potential collaborator rather than merely a competitor. Develop capabilities for effective human-AI collaboration, identifying where your distinctively human strengths can combine with AI capabilities to create greater value than either alone.

4. Participate actively in shaping technological governance rather than viewing it as the exclusive domain of technical experts or policymakers. Engage in public discourse, community deliberation, and political processes that influence how technologies are developed and deployed.

5. Build financial resilience through diversified income sources, ownership stakes, and mutual aid networks rather than relying exclusively on traditional employment for economic security. This creates greater adaptability during periods of transition and disruption.

For Communities:

1. Develop local economic ecosystems that combine technological innovation with inclusive participation. This includes creating shared technology access, skill development programs, and ownership models that ensure technological benefits reach diverse community members.

2. Strengthen social infrastructure that supports connection, meaning, and mutual support beyond work-based institutions. This includes public spaces, community events, shared projects, and support networks that can function effectively regardless of employment patterns.

3. Establish community deliberation processes for technological governance that incorporate diverse perspectives and focus on concrete local impacts rather than abstract principles. This creates both better decisions and greater legitimacy for technology governance.

4. Create intergenerational knowledge transfer systems that combine the technological fluency of younger generations with the contextual wisdom and life experience of older generations. This enables more effective navigation of technological change while strengthening social cohesion.

5. Develop local resilience capabilities that can maintain essential functions during periods of disruption or transition. This includes food systems, energy production, care networks, and governance mechanisms that can function effectively even amid broader systemic changes.

For Global Leaders:

1. Establish robust international coordination mechanisms for AI governance that can address global challenges while respecting legitimate diversity in values and approaches. This includes standards development, information sharing, capability monitoring, and conflict resolution systems.

2. Develop sophisticated approaches to managing critical resources for AI development—including energy, materials,

data, and computational capacity. This requires balancing legitimate security concerns with the benefits of specialization and exchange through multilateral rather than unilateral approaches.

3. Create effective support systems for regions and populations experiencing disruptive transitions due to AI adoption. This includes not merely passive assistance but active investment in new economic foundations and capability development.

4. Invest in public research and infrastructure for beneficial AI applications that address urgent human needs and global challenges. This includes applications in climate response, healthcare, education, and other domains where market mechanisms alone may not drive optimal development.

5. Develop governance approaches for advanced AI capabilities that effectively address potential existential risks without unnecessarily constraining beneficial development. This requires sophisticated technical assessment capabilities, international verification systems, and governance mechanisms that can adapt as capabilities evolve.

These recommendations do not represent a comprehensive blueprint but rather foundational priorities that enable effective navigation of the AI transition. Their implementation will necessarily vary across contexts and evolve as technologies and understanding develop. The essential insight is that effective action requires coordination across levels—from individual adaptation to global governance—rather than placing responsibility primarily at any single level.

A Call to Action: Shaping Our Technological Future

As we conclude this exploration of the AI revolution and its implications, one truth stands paramount: this is not a future that happens to us, but one we must actively create. The technological capabilities emerging from AI research labs and development centers are not autonomous forces but human creations shaped by human choices, values, and institutions.

The choices we make in the coming decade will define the trajectory of human civilization in the age of AI. These choices are not merely technical or economic but fundamentally ethical and political—they concern the kind of society we wish to create and the values we wish to embody in our technological future.

This represents our generational challenge and opportunity. Previous generations faced their own inflection points—from the agricultural revolution to industrialization to nuclear capabilities. Each required developing new institutions, norms, and governance approaches appropriate to new technological realities. Our challenge is no less profound but potentially more compressed in timeframe and broader in implications.

Meeting this challenge requires moving beyond both techno-utopianism and techno-pessimism to a position of pragmatic engagement—recognizing both the extraordinary potential of AI to address humanity's most pressing challenges and the serious risks that could undermine this potential. It demands developing governance approaches sophisticated enough to navigate this complexity rather than defaulting to either uncritical embrace or categorical rejection.

It also requires broadening participation in shaping our technological future beyond technical experts and economic elites. The implications of AI are too profound and pervasive to be determined by narrow segments of society. Effective governance demands incorporating diverse perspectives, values, and lived experiences—not merely as a matter of fairness but as essential for developing technologies that genuinely serve human flourishing in all its diversity.

Perhaps most fundamentally, it requires reconnecting technological development with deeper questions of human purpose and flourishing. Technology represents not an end in itself but a means for creating the kind of world we wish to inhabit. This necessitates ongoing dialogue about what constitutes a good life, a just society, and a flourishing civilization—questions that transcend technical expertise and require drawing on our full human heritage of philosophical, spiritual, and cultural wisdom.

The path ahead contains both extraordinary promise and serious peril. AI offers unprecedented capabilities to address humanity's most pressing challenges—from climate change and disease to poverty and scientific understanding. Yet it also creates risks of concentration, displacement, manipulation, and potentially even existential threat if developed without appropriate governance and alignment with human values.

Navigating between these possibilities requires not merely technical innovation but wisdom—the capacity to make sound judgments amid uncertainty, to balance competing values, and to maintain focus on fundamental human goods rather than proximate metrics or narrow interests. It demands developing governance approaches that combine humility about our predictive capabilities with commitment to shaping technologies that genuinely serve human flourishing.

This is not a challenge we can delegate—to technical experts, to market forces, to future generations. It requires active engagement from all segments of society, from individual choices and community deliberation to institutional transformation and global coordination. It demands developing both the technical capabilities to create beneficial AI and the wisdom to govern it effectively.

The choices we make in the coming decade will reverberate through centuries to come. Let us choose wisely, with full awareness of both the extraordinary potential and serious responsibilities that accompany this technological inflection point. Let us create a future where artificial intelligence serves as a powerful amplifier of human flourishing rather than a force for displacement, concentration, or control—a future worthy of our highest aspirations as a species.

This is our moment. Carpe Diem.